THE BIOLOGICAL BASES OF PERSONALITY AND BEHAVIOR

THE SERIES IN CLINICAL AND COMMUNITY PSYCHOLOGY

CONSULTING EDITORS

Charles D. Spielberger and Irwin G. Sarason

Averill Patterns of Psychological Thought: Readings in Historical and Contemporary Texts

Bermant, Kelman, and Warwick The Ethics of Social Intervention

Brehm The Application of Social Psychology to Clinical Practice

Burchfield Stress: Psychological and Physiological Interactions

Cattell and Dreger Handbook of Modern Personality Theory

Cohen and Ross Handbook of Clinical Psychobiology and Pathology, volume 1

Cohen and Ross Handbook of Clinical Psychobiology and Pathology, volume 2

Friedman and Katz The Psychology of Depression: Contemporary Theory and Research

Froehlich, Smith, Draguns, and Hentschel Psychological Processes in Cognition and Personality

Iscoe, Bloom, and Spielberger Community Psychology in Transition

Janisse Pupillometry: The Psychology of the Pupillary Response

Kissen From Group Dynamics to Group Psychoanalysis: Therapeutic Applications of Group Dynamic Understanding

Krohne and Laux Achievement, Stress, and Anxiety

London The Modes and Morals of Psychotherapy, Second Edition

London Personality: A New Look at Metatheories

Manschreck and Kleinman Renewal in Psychiatry: A Critical Rational Perspective

Morris Extraversion and Introversion: An Interactional Perspective

Olweus Aggression in the Schools: Bullies and Whipping Boys

Reitan and Davison Clinical Neuropsychology: Current Status and Applications

Rickel, Gerrard, and Iscoe Social and Psychological Problems of Women: Prevention and Crisis Intervention

Smoll and Smith Psychological Perspectives in Youth Sports

Spielberger and Diaz-Guerrero Cross-Cultural Anxiety, volume 1

Spielberger and Diaz-Guerrero Cross-Cultural Anxiety, volume 2

Spielberger and Sarason Stress and Anxiety, volume 1

Sarason and Spielberger Stress and Anxiety, volume 2

Sarason and Spielberger Stress and Anxiety, volume 3

Spielberger and Sarason Stress and Anxiety, volume 4

Spielberger and Sarason Stress and Anxiety, volume 5

Sarason and Spielberger Stress and Anxiety, volume 6

Sarason and Spielberger Stress and Anxiety, volume 7

Spielberger, Sarason, and Milgram Stress and Anxiety, volume 8

Spielberger, Sarason, and Defares Stress and Anxiety, volume 9

Spielberger and Sarason Stress and Anxiety: Volume 10, A Sourcebook of Theory and Research

Strelau, Farley, and Gale The Biological Bases of Personality and Behavior, volume 1: Theories, Measurement Techniques, and Development

Strelau, Farley, and Gale The Biological Bases of Personality and Behavior, volume 2: Psychophysiology, Performance, and Applications

Ulmer On the Development of a Token Economy Mental Hospital Treatment Program

IN PREPARATION

Auerbach and Stolberg Crisis Intervention with Children and Families

Diamant Male and Female Homosexuality: Psychological Approaches

Hobfoll Stress, Social Support, and Women

Munoz Depression Prevention Research

Spielberger and Diaz-Guerrero Cross-Cultural Anxiety, volume 3

Spielberger and Vagg The Assessment and Treatment of Text Anxiety

Williams and Westermeyer Refugee Mental Health in Resettlement Countries

THE BIOLOGICAL BASES OF PERSONALITY AND BEHAVIOR

VOLUME 2

Psychophysiology, Performance, and Applications

Edited by

Jan Strelau
University of Warsaw, Poland

Frank H. Farley
University of Wisconsin, Madison

Anthony Gale
University of Southampton, England

HEMISPHERE PUBLISHING CORPORATION

Washington   New York   London

DISTRIBUTION OUTSIDE THE UNITED STATES

McGRAW-HILL INTERNATIONAL BOOK COMPANY

*Auckland   Bogotá   Guatemala   Hamburg   Johannesburg
Lisbon   London   Madrid   Mexico   Montreal   New Delhi
Panama   Paris   San Juan   São Paulo   Singapore   Sydney
Tokyo   Toronto*

THE BIOLOGICAL BASES OF PERSONALITY AND BEHAVIOR, Volume 2:
Psychophysiology, Performance, and Applications

1 2 3 4 5 6 7 8 9 0 BRBR 8 9 8 7 6 5

Library of Congress Cataloging in Publication Data

Main entry under title:

The Biological bases of personality and behavior.

> *(The Series in clinical and community psychology)*
> *Includes bibliographies and indexes.*
> *Contents: v. 1. Theories, measurement techniques and*
> *development — v. 2. Psychophysiology, performance, and*
> *applications.*
> *1. Individuality—Physiological aspects. 2. Personality—*
> *Physiological aspects. 3. Temperament—Physiological*
> *aspects. I. Strelau, Jan. II. Farley, Frank H. III. Gale,*
> *Anthony. IV. Series.*
> *BF697.B48 1985   155.2   84-10802*
> *ISBN 0-89116-380-8 (v. 2)*
> *ISSN 0146-0846*

Contents

Contributors   ix

Preface   xi

Introduction: Overview and Critique
Anthony Gale, Jan Strelau, and Frank H. Farley   1
Chapter Reviews   2
Recurrent Themes   18
Critique: An Attempt at Constructive Criticism   19
Conclusions   21
References   21

I
PERSONALITY AND PSYCHOPHYSIOLOGY

1   **Extraversion-Introversion and Spontaneous Rhythms of the Brain: Retrospect and Prospect**
Anthony Gale   25
Introduction   25
H. J. Eysenck's 1967 Theory   26
The Post Hoc Hypothesis   27
Some Problems of Measurement   32
Sources of Arousal in the Psychological Laboratory   34
Social Psychology and the Psychology Experiment   35
Prospects   36
Conclusion   38
References   38

2   **Typology of Mental Activity as a Temperamental Trait and the Level of Activation of the Nervous System**
M. V. Bodunov   43
Formal-Dynamic Aspect of Activity   44
Factor-Analytic Study of EEG Parameters of Activation   46
Relationships between Factor Structure of Activity and Integral EEG
    Parameters of Activation   47
Conclusions   51
References   54

3   **N_2 Wave of the Evoked Potential: Scalp Reflection of Neuronal Mismatch of Orienting Theory?**
Risto Näätänen   59

Neuronal Model   59
N_2 Wave of the Evoked Potential   61
N_2 —A Tool for Progress in Orienting Research   71
References   72

4   **Contingent Negative Variation: Relation to Personality, and
    Modification by Stimulation and Sedation**
    P. F. Werre   77
    Contingent Negative Variation and Personality   78
    Effect of Stimulation and Sedation on the Contingent Negative
        Variation   81
    Concluding Remarks   84
    References   88

5   **Dynamics of AEP and Heart Rate as Indicators of Individual
    Arousal Level and Learning**
    N. N. Danilova   91
    Method   91
    Results   92
    Discussion   94
    References   96

6   **Personality and Regulatory Functions**
    Anton Uherík   97
    Theoretical Background   97
    Regulatory Functions and Bioelectrical Skin Reactivity   97
    Personality Dimensions and Bioelectrical Skin Reactivity   101
    Discussion and Conclusion   102
    References   104

7   **Dynamics of Psychophysiological Changes under Hypoxia and
    Sensory Deprivation in Subjects with Different Reactivity and
    Anxiety Levels**
    Jan Strelau, Tytus Sosnowski, and Włodzimierz Oniszczenko   107
    Method and Experimental Procedure   107
    Results   109
    Discussion   115
    References   116

II
PERSONALITY AND PERFORMANCE

8   **Reactivity and Performance: The Third Side of the Coin**
    Tatiana Klonowicz   119
    Method   121
    Results   122
    Discussion   125
    References   126

9   Nervous System Properties and Coding Processes
     Olga Halmiová and Elena Šebová   127
     Experiment I   128
     Experiment II   131
     Discussion   133
     References   133

10   Polychronicity and Strength of the Nervous System as
     Predictors of Information Overload
     Richard F. Haase   135
     Method   137
     Results and Discussion   138
     References   142

11   Temperamental and Informational Determinants of Problem Solving in
     Person-Computer Interaction
     Czesław S. Nosal   143
     The Problem and Research Model   143
     Hypothesis, Methods of Measurement, and Analysis Design   144
     Results   145
     Discussion and Conclusion   150
     References   150

12   Self-Exposure to Sensory Stimuli in Rats as Activity Motivated by the
     Sensory Drive
     Jan Matysiak   153
     Stimulation Enhancement versus Reduction   153
     Method   155
     Results and Discussion   156
     Conclusions   160
     References   160

13   Temperament Differences in Vigilance Performance as a Function of
     Variations in the Suitability of Ambient Noise Level
     Robert Hockey   163
     Extraversion-Introversion and Vigilance   163
     Method   165
     Results and Discussion   167
     Discussion   169
     References   170

III
APPLIED IMPLICATIONS

14   Psychopathy, Stimulation Seeking, and Stress
     Robert D. Hare and Jeffrey W. Jutai   175
     Assessment of Psychopathy in Criminal Populations   175
     Psychopathy and Need for Stimulation   177

Psychopathy and Stress   179
References   182

15   Intensity of Interpersonal Aggression in Relation to
      Neuroticism and Psychopathy
      Wanda Ciarkowska and Adam Frączek   185
      Neuroticism in Regulation of Interpersonal Aggression   185
      Psychopathy and Interpersonal Aggression   187
      Conclusions   191
      References   192

16   Reactivity and Empathic Control of Aggression
      Hanna Eliasz and Janusz Reykowski   195
      Empathy and Aggressive Behavior   195
      Reactivity and Capacity for Empathy   196
      Effect of Reactivity on Aggression Formation   198
      Studies on the Relationship between Empathy and Aggression   199
      Conclusions   203
      References   203

17   Hypertension and Response to Stress: Need for Stimulation?
      Tatiana Klonowicz, Hanna Ignatowska-Świtalska, and
      Bożena Wocial   207
      Method   207
      Results   208
      Discussion   211
      References   212

18   Activity and Reactivity: Theoretical Comments and an Experimental
      Approach
      Wolfgang Schönpflug and Hermann Mündelein   213
      Measures of Reactive Behavior   213
      Self-Regulatory Behavior   214
      Method   215
      Results   216
      References   217

19   Activity Structures as Related to Individual Differences in
      Temperament
      Peter Schulz   219
      The Concept of Reactivity   219
      Method   219
      Results   221
      Discussion   225
      References   226

      Index   227

Contributors

M. V. BODUNOV, Academy of Sciences, Moscow, USSR
WANDA CIARKOWSKA, University of Warsaw, Poland
N. N. DANILOVA, Moscow University, USSR
HANNA ELIASZ, University of Warsaw, Poland
FRANK H. FARLEY, University of Wisconsin, Madison, Wisconsin, USA
ADAM FRĄCZEK, University of Warsaw, Poland
ANTHONY GALE, University of Southampton, England
RICHARD F. HAASE, State University of New York at Albany, USA
OLGA HALMIOVÁ, Academy of Sciences, Bratislava, Czechoslovakia
ROBERT D. HARE, University of British Columbia, Vancouver, Canada
ROBERT HOCKEY, University of Durham, England
HANNA IGNATOWSKA-ŚWITALSKA, Academy of Medicine, Warsaw, Poland
JEFFREY W. JUTAI, University of British Columbia, Vancouver, Canada
TATIANA KLONOWICZ, University of Warsaw, Poland
JAN MATYSIAK, University of Warsaw, Poland
HERMANN MUNDELEIN, Free University of Berlin, West Germany
RISTO NÄÄTÄNEN, University of Helsinki, Finland
CZESŁAW S. NOSAL, Technical University of Wrocław, Poland
WŁODZIMIERZ ONISZCZENKO, University of Warsaw, Poland
JANUSZ REYKOWSKI, Polish Academy of Science, Warsaw, Poland
WOLFGANG SCHÖNPFLUG, Free University of Berlin, West Germany
PETER SCHULZ, Free University of Berlin, West Germany
ELENA ŠEBOVÁ, Academy of Sciences, Bratislava, Czechoslovakia
TYTUS SOSNOWSKI, University of Warsaw, Poland
JAN STRELAU, University of Warsaw, Poland
ANTON UHERÍK, Academy of Sciences, Bratislava, Czechoslovakia
P. F. WERRE, Psychiatric Centre Rosenburg, The Hague, The Netherlands
BOŻENA WOCIAL, Academy of Medicine, Warsaw, Poland

Preface

The publication of *Pavlov's Typology* by J. A. Gray in 1964 introduced Western psychologists to the Pavlovian theory of nervous system traits. Particular attention was paid to the modifications proposed by B. M. Teplov and V. D. Nebylitsyn, who, unlike Pavlov, investigated human subjects and were able to enrich the theory with many novel ideas.

Recognizing the theory as an interesting attempt to account for the biological bases of personality, Western psychologists began to search for parallels between the Pavlovian nervous system traits, notably strength of nervous processes, and other dimensions of personality. An overture was Eysenck's address to the International Congress of Psychology in Moscow (1966) in which he drew our attention to certain affinities between his extraversion-introversion dimension and nervous system strength. There followed a series of comparative studies by G. L. Mangan disclosing the common elements in the dimensions of extraversion-introversion and neuroticism, on the one hand, and in the strength and mobility of nervous processes on the other.

Other milestones in the promotion of comparative research in this area, and in the popularization of the theory of nervous system traits in the West, were the volume of studies, *Biological Bases of Individual Behavior*, edited by Nebylitsyn and Gray (1972), and the publication in 1972 in English of Nebylitsyn's 1966 book, *Nervous System Properties in Man*.

The work of the Department of Psychophysiology and Individual Differences at Warsaw University has been closely related to the Pavlovian theory of nervous system traits ever since the laboratory was established in 1966.

Working on problems of nervous system typology since the late 1950s, and collaborating in this respect with Teplov and Nebylitsyn's laboratory (where I had a chance to work for six months in 1966), I focused my attention on the mechanisms underlying partial nervous system traits and on the methods of their investigation.

From this work there emerged a theory to which my collaborators and I have come to refer as the *regulative theory of temperament*. The theory leans heavily on Pavlovian typology, but at the same time it takes note of Western work on the biological determinants of personality dimensions, with special reference to activation theory.

In view of these affinities it was perfectly natural to seek an extended collaboration with investigators concerned with nervous system typology and the personality dimensions related to such a typology, just as much as with researchers interested in those behavioral dimensions that bear some relation to activation theory.

The idea of holding an international conference of psychologists working in this field grew in our laboratory in the early 1970s. Organized under the title *Temperament and Personality*, the conference took place in October 1974 in

Warsaw. The modest number of participants and the absence of both U.S. and Soviet researchers was a source of considerable concern at the time, but today the meeting may be safely assessed as a success: We had the opportunity to take a closer look at the theoretical work of some biologically oriented Western personality psychologists. This led to insights that could not fail to affect our subsequent research; and at the same time Western psychologists took note of our theoretical framework.

As we set out to organize the second international conference five years later, the interest shown by our colleagues abroad exceeded our expectations. In fact, our limited resources forced us to impose restrictions on the number of foreign participants. The meeting in September 1979 (the second Warsaw conference devoted to *Temperament, Need for Stimulation and Activity* and supported by the University of Warsaw and the Polish Academy of Sciences) was attended by 51 psychologists from 12 countries. Among the participants were some leading psychologists in the field.

In view of the role taken by the Department of Psychophysiology and Individual Differences at the University of Warsaw in preparing for and organizing the conference, it is appropriate to give a short account of the Department's work, to which all of our ten faculty members have contributed.

Broadly speaking, our investigations converge upon temperament, but the particular manifestations of temperament are studied from several points of view: in normative and pathological aspects, in developmental and general terms, in the laboratory and in practical school and work conditions, and in psychophysiological, psychomotor, psychometric, and comparative terms. We also conduct experiments on rats.

The following problems are encompassed by our research.

1. The notion of temperament and the structure of temperamental traits. Approaching temperament as a set of relatively stable and formal features of behavior that reveal themselves in the energy level and in the temporal characteristics of behavior, we tend to focus upon energy level, wherein we have come to identify *reactivity* and *activity* of behavior. We are particularly interested in temperament as one of the mechanisms that regulate mankind's relations with the world.

2. The role of reactivity in the regulation of a person's *need for stimulation* and the psychophysiological mechanisms associated with the demand for stimulation constitute another group of problems. Here we study situations of varying stimulation load. In addition to the stimulation load of the environment, where we pay attention to ecological aspects, we are concerned with the stimulation derived from behavior. The psychophysiological mechanisms of the need for stimulation are investigated in the rat.

3. Temperament and its interrelation with personality is studied on the assumption that *temperament is a product of biological evolution,* whereas personality is an outcome of sociohistorical conditions. The interdependence of the two concepts is investigated in a number of theoretical and experimental projects. Further research is in progress on anxiety level, neuroticism, extraversion-introversion, and their interdependence with some of the temperament traits we have identified, with special attention to reactivity and mobility of behavior.

4. Another problem we are interested in is temperament and *cognitive functioning.* This area involves the study of cognitive style, in particular the reflexive-impulsive dimension and its stimulation load, with a developmental orientation.

We are further interested in the relationship between certain abilities (flexibility and fluency of thinking) and temperamental traits, and also in the interaction of temperamental traits and general abilities as affecting creativity.

5. Exploring the effect of temperamental traits on the development of a person's *individual style of action,* we seek to determine the influence on this style of different types of activity, partly from a developmental perspective.

6. Studying the role of temperament traits in performance under difficult situations we expose subjects to extreme conditions that supply them either with exceedingly strong stimulation (resulting from overload, threat, emotional tension, and the like) or with very weak stimulation (sensory deprivation, monotonous work, and similar conditions). We are interested chiefly in the interrelation of temperament traits and *tolerance to stressing conditions as reflected in performance efficiency.*

7. The relation between temperamental traits and *mental disorders,* notably neurosis, neuroticism, and psychopathy, is another line of study. We have demonstrated the nonspecific effect of temperament traits on mental disorders. In psychopathy we are concerned with its physiological mechanisms and its association with the physiological mechanism of reactivity.

8. We are also concerned with techniques for diagnosing temperament and certain dimensions of personality. We have constructed the Strelau Temperament Inventory (TI) and a questionnaire for measuring the temporal characteristics of behavior. Several scales for estimating reactivity at different ages and a method for measuring reactivity in rats have been developed.

A rough picture of our activities emerges from the chapters written by the Warsaw group for inclusion in the present volumes.

Reverting again to the Second Warsaw Conference, we realize that the common desire of all the participants was to become familiar with investigations conducted in other parts of the world and to work out common ground and mutual understanding, in an effort to grasp the essence of the theories, concepts, and methods developed by the "other" side.

The conference contributors focused on such dimensions as nervous system strength, extraversion-introversion, arousability, activation, stimulus modulation intensity, sensation seeking, and reactivity, dealing either with the underlying physiological mechanisms, with the interrelations between the dimensions, or with how the dimensions relate to various aspects of human behavior.

Irrespective of their specific qualities these dimensions have certain elements in common; therefore the participants of the conference could freely communicate with each other. The common features are easy to enumerate:

1. They all conceptualize the relevant behaviors in terms of either dimensions or traits.

2. Among the focal notions employed in the analysis of the dimensions or traits is the notion of individual differences. Hence there is frequent reference to such categories as strong type–weak type, extravert–introvert, sensation seeker–sensation avoider, lower arousable–higher arousable, low activated–high activated, reducer–augmenter, low reactive–high reactive.

3. All contributors share the view that the dimensions under discussion are biologically determined; hence the many references to "biological dimensions of personality."

4. A fair number of people agree that the physiological mechanism of the

identified dimensions must lie in, among others, individual differences in activation and/or arousal.

While assertions about the breadth of the common ground may sound overly optimistic, there is no denying that the common ground is broad enough to ensure free traffic of ideas and mutual understanding.

A large number of the papers presented at the second Warsaw conference are presented in these two volumes. In addition, many papers from the first Warsaw conference were thought to be of considerable theoretical or empirical significance. We decided to include them, in updated form.

These two volumes would never have existed without the selfless devotion of my two colleagues, Anthony Gale and Frank Farley, who not only persuaded me of the practicability of the undertaking but also offered their generous editorial assistance. Their enthusiasm and diligence, as well as each contributor's responsible approach, is greatly appreciated. We are also grateful to Ms. Kerry Thompson for her vigilance and enthusiasm in checking the proofs of both volumes.

It is to be hoped that both volumes will strengthen the links between psychologists in the West and in the Socialist countries and that it will lead to a closer collaboration in the study of the biological bases of personality.

Jan Strelau

THE BIOLOGICAL
BASES
OF PERSONALITY
AND BEHAVIOR

Introduction: Overview and Critique

Anthony Gale, Jan Strelau, and Frank H. Farley

This Introduction provides the reader with a guide to this work, published in
two volumes. Each chapter is reviewed so as to present a critical framework for
the evaluation of work in this field. We hope for another conference in a few
years, when the issues covered in this work will have achieved a greater synthesis. The book provides an unusual opportunity for the reader to sample
theory and research on individual differences -- results of work generated in
laboratories across the northern hemisphere. We have here authors from the following countries: Canada, Czechoslovakia, England, Finland, France, West
Germany, the Netherlands, Norway, Poland, Sweden, the United States, and the
Soviet Union; at the original conferences there were delegates also from East
Germany and Rumania. From the various Reference sections we see that the traffic
of scientific knowledge appears to have been unidirectional; works by East
European authors frequently cite work published by Western authors, but the
reverse is rarely true. The contributors to this book no longer have a valid
excuse for further neglect of their colleagues. Perhaps for the first time the
Western reader may read work hitherto published in journals inaccessible to him.
At a time when the world is in political turmoil, it is encouraging that psychologists, concerned as they are with the eternal qualities of the human spirit, un-
fettered by the vagaries of contemporary history, should see sufficient common
ground in their enterprise to justify a cooperative and potentially collaborative
venture of this nature.

What is remarkable is the communality of themes that runs through all the papers
without exception, be they theoretical or empirical in style. The emphasis is
on the biological determination of key elements that account for individual differences and the functional interaction of these elements with our physical and
social environment, to produce elaborate and adaptive patterns of behavior.
Within this central superordinate theme, the range of topics considered is un-
usually extended. The variables referred to in the papers include the following:
genetic transmission of traits, biochemical correlates of personality, the early
development of social behavior, feedback and mutual regulation, evolution of
individual styles of action, self-stimulation in rats, the factorial structure
of behavior, the factoring of psychometric instruments, interaction of cognitive
and emotional factors in information processing, hemispheral specialization and
other aspects of brain organization, physiological stressors, physiological
indexes, biological energy, analysis of complex actions, anxiety, psychopathy,
empathy and retaliatory aggression, sensory deprivation, hypoxia, subjective
estimates of arousal, sedative drugs, addiction, hypertension, occupational
choice, and environmental stress.

These topics provide a family of sets overlapping constructs, within which there
is a subset of common terms and concepts: personality, biological factors,

1

arousal, the need for stimulation, and the regulation of activity. At another level there is also communality in the use of psychometric instruments, commitment to a transactional approach, and the use of empirical experimental means to test aspects of theory. As one might expect in such a rich field of endeavor, there is also a set of common faults in strategy, methodology, and interpretation. We shall come to these faults at the end of this introduction, where we anticipate future developments. First, however, we provide a brief introduction to each chapter.

CHAPTER REVIEWS

Volume I (Theories, Measurement Techniques, and Development)

Theoretical approaches. Chapter 1, by Strelau, should be read before sampling the contributions of the other East European authors, because he raises a number of major conceptual issues and provides a background to much of the work in his own laboratory and in those laboratories that have inherited the legacy of Pavlovian typology. He draws a fundamental distinction between temperament (basic properties of the nervous system of both animals and man), and personality as a product of external social conditions and thus an essentially human phenomenon; this he suggests is the prevailing Soviet view. However, he points to the difficulties involved in making such distinctions, for temperamental traits must themselves be modulated by experience, and animals do not live in an unresponsive world. Nevertheless, he suggests that many confusions would disappear if "dimensions of behavior, which have a large physiological component and are a result of a biological evolution, were considered an aspect of temperament, whereas all the traits (mechanisms) that are mostly a product of social-historical conditions were included under personality." This does not mean, of course, that temperamental traits are impervious to environmental influence.

Strelau then identifies those traits in Eastern European and Western psychology that can be treated as temperamental traits and shows how such apparently different constructs may be related both theoretically and in terms of existing empirical data. He discusses, in particular, the long line of studies by Mangan and his associates that were designed specifically to build bridges between the two traditions. A correlation matrix is presented summarizing many studies investigating relationships between excitation strength, inhibition strength, mobility, and balance of nervous processes on the one hand, and extraversion-introversion, neuroticism, and anxiety on the other. Excitation strength and extraversion appear to be consistently well correlated in a positive direction, whereas neuroticism correlates inversely with this measure. On the other hand, extraversion-introversion seem to be unrelated to strength of inhibition, which, as might be expected from the previous findings, relates to anxiety. The highest correlation with extraversion holds for mobility, one of the traits that has been neglected both theoretically and empirically. Correlations between mobility and neuroticism or anxiety are low and trivial.

Strelau then turns to his own theoretical viewpoint, in which temperament is seen as a set of relatively stable traits that are revealed in the energy level of behavior and in the temporal characteristics of reaction. An important point is that such traits are seen as formal since they have no content and do not affect behavior directly; rather temperament, as a regulative mechanism, is manifested in behavior, independent of its direction or content. For the Polish group, energy level incorporates all traits that reflect individual differences in the physiological mechanisms involved in the accumulation and release of energy, that is, at endocrinal, autonomic, and brain stem levels, including those corticial mechanisms that are integrated with lower centers in the regulation of excitation. These physiological mechanisms are seen as operating as a system with stable characteristics and in which the contributory elements vary between individuals.

Two basic features of energy level are reactivity and activity. The former relates to a stable pattern of response to stimulus intensity in a person, as compared with others within the population; the latter refers to the intensity and frequency of aspects of performance. These two features, although seen as independent, interact in a complex fashion both as a function of individual development and of situational requirements. Highly reactive people are those who are particularly sensitive to stimulation and have a high stimulation-processing coefficient, which reflects a deficiency within physiological mechanisms that serve to suppress stimulation. Activity is related to the notion of optimal level of arousal in that the person acts to increase or decrease incoming stimulation to achieve the optimum. Thus we see how reactivity characteristics may interact with activity characteristics, such that weakly reactive people will seek additional stimulation, while highly reactive people will act to reduce it.

Strelau then provides a detailed discussion of the possible logical relations between temperament and personality, citing empirical data that support his theoretical position.

As the reader will discover from the remaining chapters written by members of the Warsaw laboratories, the empirical data are unique in their range, for they extend from detailed parametric studies of reactivity and activity in rats, to occupational choice and response to high- and low-stimulating environments in residential accommodation.

The development of the theoretical themes is taken up by Eliasz (Chapter 2), who explores in depth the nature of the functional characteristics of the mechanisms of temperament. Here we have a detailed discussion of the evolution of behavior in the individual and the ways in which the mechanisms described by Strelau, initially devoid of content, become elaborated into characteristic styles of individual behavior. Eliasz emphasizes regulatory activity, the constant interplay of a person with physical and social aspects of his environment, which in turn affects the behavior of other persons toward the individual. This view enables a retreat from deterministic concepts of temperament that predict a precise one-to-one relationship between traits and specific behavior patterns.

Eliasz then takes the concepts of reactivity and activity and shows how they may be used to predict aspects of behavior in natural settings. Thus complex interactions are demonstrated between temperament, occupation, sporting activities, and domestic accommodation, revealing the interplay between the person's actions, stimulation available within the environment, and the regulatory steps taken to ensure an optimal level of arousal. Such a challenging combination of real-life variables is rarely seen in Western personality research. The notion of defining situations by employing concepts and descriptors which are common coin in trait theory, provides a basis for the resolution of controversies relating to Trait × Situational interactions.

Farley (Chapter 3) sketches the outline of a model linking arousal and intellective and cognitive function, in which individual differences in arousability are presumed to have a moderating effect on the interrelatedness of cognitive processes. Thus, persons of low arousability show greater relatedness, in the correlational sense, among cognitive processes, than do persons of high arousability. It is proposed that cognitive processing associated with low arousability, as contrasted with cognitive processing associated with high arousability, would show greater flexibility, stronger functional dependencies among cognitive processes, greater transferability between modes of cognitive representation, or perhaps "swapping" in computer terminology, more emphasis on simultaneous than successive or sequential processing, more emphasis on parallel than serial processing, and a general characteristic that Farley labels <u>transmutative thought</u> -- an ease of transforming one mode of representation into another, as in hypostatizing the abstract into the concrete, or transmuting the concrete into the abstract. The model is extended to a practical problem of immense social importance, but also one with significant theoretical interest, that of human creativity in general, and scientific creativity, discovery, and inventiveness in particular. Farley argues that creativity, particularly scientific creativity, requires to a substantial degree transmutative thought, and that such transmutative processes conducive to discovery and creativity are more characteristic of low-arousable people than of people of higher arousability on a trait dimension of arousability.

Although this arousal and cognition model is but barely outlined in the Farley chapter, its implications for integrating some of the work on arousal with contemporary conceptions of cognitive processes seem substantial. In addition, the implications for creativity and discovery in science, and other domains, extends the reach of the psychobiology of personality to an important but neglected area.

Farley reports a number of studies bearing on some of the foregoing ideas. He uses the moderator design, traditionally applied to the more usual psychometric instruments only, in identifying a <u>biological moderator</u>, that is, individual differences in arousability, with the effects of this biological moderator on the relatedness of the cognitive processes being examined. These studies show that associative and conceptual processes are much more strongly correlated in low- than in high-arousable persons. Similar, although less striking, results were also obtained for verbal versus pictorial processing, and speed versus accuracy in an intellective task. Some studies bearing on creativity are also mentioned, although none directly concerns scientific discovery. The latter aspects of the model await empirical consideration. One fascinating implication of the model is that of a biological basis, at least in part, for creativity.

The chapter providing the most panoramic theoretical view of personality is without doubt that of Royce and Powell (Chapter 4), who present us with a universal factorial structure, or rather a conceptual program for integrating past and future work. Within this complex model it is possible to assign proportional variance to different levels, from sensory and motor systems (heredity dominant) to style and value (environment dominant). Each level within the factor hierarchy is itself multidimensional and hierarchical, and integration occurs both within the six interacting systems and between them. Within the general factorial structure that describes individual differences, integrative principles operate on the basis of concepts derived from general systems theory and information-processing theory . The inevitable complexity of this theoretical approach is well characterized in the figures, which reveal the inadequacy of an Occam's razor approach to individual-differences theory.

What is particularly striking is the constant endeavor to synthesize the two traditions of personality and cognitive psychology. The reader will need to return to the original chapters reviewed here to identify the precise nature of the tests employed and the operationalization of the key constructs. Royce's approach, which has a long and sustained history, is an immediate and pressing challenge to those who would have us discard the psychometric tradition. At the same time, it still raises the problem of how such complex theoretical structures are to be tested empirically within the current framework of experimental procedures, where even a triple interaction between factors stretches the explanatory power of the background theory.

Zuckerman (Chapter 5) reviews the early history of the development of the Sensation Seeking Scale (SSS). In an early formulation of his theory, the optimum level of arousal was a central concept, namely that sensation seekers look for stimulation to sustain the optimum. Thus individual differences in people are influenced by differences in optimum level of arousal. He reviews the evidence that leads him to reject this view, and the burden of his argument is that sensation seekers seek change and detest constancy of arousal level; thus some of the things they seek clearly reduce arousal. This is demonstrated in drug use, where there is little evidence of a preference for stimulants as such. Zuckerman then presents a metadiscussion of the nature of models designed to link psychobiology to behavioral traits, including a critique of sociobiology. Critics who challenge trait theory on the ground that it cannot predict specific behaviors are setting up a man of straw, since the trait represents averaged behaviors sampled across situations and time. Prediction is improved when the trait test refers to specific actions in specific contexts, and if the tasks offered to subjects are designed to reflect the theory in question. The SSS subscales and the empirical tests applied to them satisfy these requirements and yield good correlations. In reviewing the subscales of the SSS, Zuckerman points out that these reflect biological correlates when taken separately, rather than in combination, to yield a total sensation-seeking score. He then reviews the psychophysiological data, gonadal hormone data, and the more recent work on neurotransmitters and endorphins. The evidence here is novel and enticing and reveals potential links between sensation-seeking, activity, depression, and monoamine oxidase (MAO). MAO and its genetic determination play a central role in the most recent version of Zuckerman's theory. Gonadal hormones regulate MAO, which regulates dopamine and norepinephrine, which in turn are involved in approach behavior and reward mechanisms; reward affects the arousal systems and positive emotions. Zuckerman demonstrates how the systematic accumulation of data over a broad range of domains of description, based on a sound theoretical framework, may serve fully to exploit an essentially correlational approach. Nor is Zuckerman afraid to leap beyond the accumulating and coherent body of knowledge to push toward new avenues of enquiry.

Chapter 6, by Thayer, is particularly interesting because he allows us the privilege of looking over his shoulder as he develops new ideas. After reviewing standard criticisms of activation as a unitary dimension, he then proposes that at least two activation dimensions underlie behavior. He focuses in particular on the activating effects of exercise and the demonstration that exercise diminishes the activating effects of anxiety. He points to a number of paradoxes that illustrate the need to have more than one continuum: the tiredness associated with anxiety, the use of arousing drugs with hyperactive children, the presence of anxiety and tiredness after sleep deprivation, and tranquilizers that reduce anxiety yet do not make the patient tired. His two Activation Dimensions, A and B, are positively correlated at moderate levels of energy expenditure and negatively correlated at high levels. The two dimensions bear relationships both to different behavioral processes and to external and internal stimuli. Dimension A is seen as endogenous in nature and related to circadian rhythms in activity, whereas B is seen to be related to emergency reactions and the mobilization of energy. He then reviews studies showing differential effects of the two dimensions on a range of psychological variables. He concludes with a consideration of conscious awareness as "an excellent organismic integrating system." The reader should recall that it was subjective report that yielded the highest correlation with composite physiological scores in Thayer's early work. Apart from the fact that the reader is able to witness the evolution of a new theoretical model, this chapter stands out as one that strongly emphasizes the importance of subjective experience in the measurement of individual differences.   It contrasts with many studies that seem to emphasize physiological and performance measures, adding subjective report almost as an afterthought and at a point in the development of the research design that makes it too late for subjective measurement to determine the key features of the procedure.

Roubertoux (Chapter 7) provides an account of the rationale for behavioral genetics, showing how genetic analysis (a field in which only few personality theorists have been willing to engage) is appropriate to the study of individual differences.   This lucid account will be most valuable for those who are unfamiliar with alternative genetic analyses and inferential procedures.   He provides examples of behavioral and pathological traits whose mode of genetic transmission is known.   In the case of one disorder, a variety of muscular dystrophy, Roubertoux is able to show that differential response in a conditioning procedure yielded a highly significant identification of different groups.

After a brief discussion of difficulties in estimating heritability and the caution required in interpreting heritability studies, Roubertoux then goes on to review twin-study findings.   These have generally yielded higher correlations for personality traits in monozygotic than in dizygotic pairs.   Although electroencephalogram (EEG) and average evoked potential (AEP) studies show evidence for genetic determination, autonomic nervous system measures yield more equivocal data.   He argues that low intercorrelations between autonomic variables need not imply their unsuitability for genetic study but rather their sensitivity to situational variation.   Modality of presentation and time within the epoch appear to be differentially sensitive to genetic variation.   If such variation may be related to behavioral variation, then the dissociation within the physiological indexes may be used to discriminate within behavioral processes.

Although Roubertoux claims his is not an exhaustive review, it provides an excellent and comprehensive introduction to this complex field of enquiry, providing not only a justification for the approach but an account of the key methods employed and some landmark studies.

Measurement aspects.   Two detailed studies of the incorrelation among different scales, by Carlier and by Gilliland, show that comparison between Western and Eastern European scales is not a straightforward matter.

Carlier (Chapter 8) presents a thoroughgoing factor analysis of Strelau's scales, relating them also to the Eysenck Personality Inventory (EPI) and Cattell's Anxiety.   The results of her careful and systematic analysis, like those of Gilliland, cannot be a source of comfort to the Warsaw school.   Strelau's Excitation and Inhibition scales, although they correlate well with extraversion-introversion and neuroticism-stability/anxiety, respectively, may be considered to be poor substitutes for these well-established scales.   For Excitation also loads on both neuroticism and anxiety, as well as Inhibition and Mobility. There is, in addition, little evidence from Carlier's study for the integrity of the Mobility factor.   Given the intercorrelations between Strelau's constructs and the demonstrable orthogonality of Eysenck's constructs, there are surely grounds for suggesting that studies based on the Strelau scales are likely to be less reliable.   If Mobility is a worthwhile theoretical construct, it appears not to be embodied as a separate entity in the Strelau scales. When the theory is subjected by Carlier to empirical test, it appears that threshold for transmarginal inhibition is related to anxiety/inhibition qua Gray (1964), rather than to excitation/extraversion, as claimed by both

Strelau and Eysenck. These data then provide insufficient support for the
Warsaw School and at the same time yield contradictory evidence that is difficult to absorb into Strelau's theoretical framework.

Gilliland (Chapter 9) provides a brief introduction to Pavlovian typology and
points to the paucity of Western studies either using the Pavlovian framework
or exploring relations between it and Western scales. One problem is the complexity not only of the constructs but of the procedures employed to classify
individuals. The Strelau scale presents a straightforward procedure. He
describes the method of extinction with reinforcement as applied to EEG conditioning, which he suggests is one of the best measures of strength of the
nervous system (excitation). He points to the similarity between strength and
extraversion and reviews empirical findings that show parallels between the constructs (perception, reaction time, sustained attention, and drugs).

Gilliland presents data showing intercorrelations between scores on the EPI,
the Eysenck Personality Questionnaire (EPQ), and the Strelau Scales. Like
Carlier, he demonstrates the lack of independence of the Strelau scales, but
in his case, there are more modest correlations between the Strelau and Western
scales. Correlations with the Zuckerman scales are also modest. Finally, he
shows that his EEG procedure fails, as a test of construct validity, to discriminate among the Strelau temperamental types. Gilliland urges caution in
the use of the Strelau scales. The reader should find the comparison of tables
in the Strelau, Carlier, and Gilliland chapters most instructive, since they
do suggest some unity in factor structure albeit not wholly compatible with the
theoretical views of either Strelau or Eysenck.

Barnes (Chapter 10) presents a review of studies using the Vando Reducing-
Augmenting Scale, which he suggests presents the most straightforward technique
available for measuring individual differences in stimulus intensity modulation.
Correlation data from a variety of studies indicate that stimulus reducers in
relation to augmenters are more tolerant to pain, more extraverted, less hypo-
chondriacal, less guilty, and heavier smokers. Reducers are short sleepers;
they are less socialized, more optimistic, and higher on ego strength than are
augmenters. They internalize on locus-of-control measures; they are sensation-
seekers (external) and risk takers. Reducers prefer stimulants (including
marijuana and amphetamines), and they give less socially desirable responses
in a faking test (although Barnes suggests this effect is not powerful enough
to undermine the validity of the earlier findings).

Many of these findings are consistent with predictions from Petrie's original
theory (1967), although some of the predictions concerning drug use are not.
Barnes suggests that in the latter case, the fault may well be in the theory,
since the reliability, construct, and discriminant validity of the Vando scale
seem high. Thus Barnes shows (albeit in the absence of intercorrelations with
many of the scales reported in these volumes) that the sensation-seeking construct
may have useful applications in terms of habitual behaviors, aspects of self-
concept, and modes of construing the world.

Schalling and Åsberg (Chapter 11) commence with an important assertion, that
results relating to extraversion-introversion may be contradictory, and even
self-defeating, if the investigator fails to distinguish impulsivity and sociability components. These not only give different results, but may yield findings
in opposite directions. They cite Guilford's characterization of extraversion
as "a shotgun marriage between impulsivity and sociability." Their own view
is that impulsivity is more consistently associated with biological correlates.
This has important implications for consideration elsewhere in the volume of
the relationship between factors in scales developed in different countries and

different laboratories.   This is, of course, not a purely empirical issue, but
one of theoretical significance.

The main body of the chapter is devoted to a review of their laboratory's work
on impulsivity, based on their newly devised Impulsiveness and Monotony
Avoidance Scales.   It should be noted that the title of the latter scale emphasizes avoidance rather than sensation seeking.   Analyses using other scales,
however, show that it loads on thrill seeking, low conformity, and low anticipatory anxiety.   They report correlations between their scales and biochemical
and psychophysiological indexes in normal and clinical populations.   These correlations are then incorporated into neuropsychological models incorporating
central nervous system (CNS) and arousal constructs.   Thus the high impulsive
is dominated by the immediate environment, while the low impulsive "with his
greater involvement in processing of past events and future projects, is less
easily distracted."   This dependence on immediate stimulation will be associated
with behavior that ensures a varied pattern of incoming stimuli, that is, high
Monotony Avoidance.   They then suggest that such differences in cognitive style
might link up with alleged hemispheral differences in terms of holistic and
serial processing, although their own studies do not appear to employ the tasks
typically used in hemispheral specialization studies.   The second theoretical
notion is that high impulsives are low in arousal.

They then report biochemical studies using the new scales.   Monotony Avoidance
but not Impulsivity correlated with platelet MAO in a sample of depressive
patients .   A larger-scale study with students used several questionnaire
measures.   It will be seen from their Table 4 that although some significant correlations emerge for Monotony Avoidance, the relationship with Impulsivity is
complex and the Zuckerman Scales yield only one modest correlation.   This correlation, however, showing an inverse relation between MAO and Disinhibition
score, corroborates Zuckerman's findings.

Like Zuckerman, Schalling and Åsberg have already invested research effort into
biochemical studies.   The correlations obtained tend to be within the normal
range of magnitude for personality studies and the patterning of correlation
is complex.   The relationship between these neurotransmitter substances and
behavior is yet to be specified within a complex theoretical framework, but
these initial findings are clearly a sound basis for future work; and, as we
have seen, Zuckerman has already attempted an integration.

Feij et al. (Chapter 12) begin with a brief review of Zuckerman's research over
the last 15 years into sensation-seeking characteristics.   Zuckerman's four
scales (Thrill and Adventure Seeking, TAS; Experience Seeking, ES; Disinhibition,
Dis; and Boredom Susceptibility, BS) show some modest common variance, but are
best seen as independent constructs relating to different aspects of behavior.
They review briefly relations between sensation seeking as a construct with various scales, the Minnesota Multiphasic Personality Inventory (MMPI), 16PF, Kipnis,
and EPI; and its independence from anxiety and neuroticism.

In considering biological aspects of sensation seeking, they draw our attention
to certain key problems: (a) there is a need to be specific about the notion
of optimum level of arousal (i.e., is the optimum common for all people or does
it vary?);   (b) arousability is a characteristic of extraverts for Zuckerman,
but of introverts for Eysenck;   (c) similarly, for Zuckerman extraverts are
augmenters, while for Eysenck they are reducers;   (d) researchers need to specify
levels of stimulation used in experiments and to state in precise terms what
individual constructs mean, (as H. J. Eysenck has pointed out elsewhere (1981),
these views are not necessarily contradictory when one considers the curvilinear
relationship between level of stimulation and magnitude of response);   (e) trans-

marginal inhibition may be a crucial characteristic for distinguishing groups and demonstrating parallel relationships between different personality constructs; and, (f) the important distinction drawn by Zuckerman between sensation seeking and arousal seeking, since there is no evidence from his work that prior to stimulation there is a difference between high and low sensation seekers in arousal level.

They then present their own data based on their specially developed questionnaire. This has four traits (extraversion, emotionality, impulsiveness and sensation seeking) and uses Likert response mode rather than forced choice.

On the basis of their own factorial data and related studies, they conclude that "sensation seeking is related to two largely orthogonal dimensions: social extraversion and lack of constraint, that is, rejection of conventional norms and values." This construct is then related to several behavioral measures: more smoking, less sleep, and higher coffee intake. In the case of sleep habits, Feij et al. point to the complexities involved in making predictions and interpreting data, particularly since emotionality is positively associated with sleep need.

The Amsterdam workers report that they obtain a factor structure for dimensions of sensation seeking similar to that of Zuckerman and report one of their psychophysiological studies, focusing on their equivalent of the disinhibition scale, since this, they believe, is most related to biological factors and closest to the notion of strength. Using Galvanic Skin Response (GSR) and heart rate (HR), they predict that high disinhibitors (strong nervous system, stimulus augmenting) will show cardiac deceleration (orienting responses) while low disinhibitors will show acceleration (defensive responses). Both groups will show equal GSR responses; but general sensation seekers will be more responsive to stimuli, yield higher GSRs, and habituate quicker. Generally speaking, their predictions were confirmed.

The papers by Schalling and Åsberg and Feij et al., like that of Zuckerman, review extended programs of work, based on similar conceptual frameworks and thus demonstrate the universality of their key constructs. They also show how specific predictions may be made not only within a correlational model, but within highly controlled laboratory investigations.

Developmental issues. The paper by Thomas and Chess (Chapter 13) is a brief historical account of their work and the thinking that went behind it, including a comment on the resistance of their early contemporaries to the notion of longitudinal studies, designed to be interactional in nature, at a time when (a) cross-sectional data was considered to be supreme, and (b) the heredity/environment controversy and the polarization of viewpoint it fostered was at its peak. This brave strategy, in the face of the prevailing zeitgeist, has clearly paid dividends, as witnessed by the richness of the data produced by the New York study and its clear implications for developmental theory and personality theory. They provide a detailed discussion of the crucial problem of measuring consistency of behavior over time, the need to see every action within its social context, and the constant interplay between people and their social environments. The value of their work is clearly demonstrated in the longitudinal study by Torgersen (Chapter 14), which owes its essential strategy and methodology to the pioneering foresight of Thomas and Chess. The thrust of the argument is reflected in many of the remaining papers.

Torgersen presented a paper at both Warsaw conferences and thus was able to provide a follow-up study of her unique sample of identical and nonidentical twins. It is difficult to overestimate the importance of this study. Using the nine Thomas and Chess behavioral categories, she studied her sample at three time periods: shortly after birth, at 6 months, and at 6 years. A striking feature of this study is not only the range of measures taken, but the care taken to ensure reliability. The reader must go to Chapter 14 for a precise account of all the findings. The study clearly supports a genetic determination of temperamental aspects of behavior, showing the relative importance of genetic factors for different aspects of behavior at different ages. Torgersen provides a subtle discussion of her data in terms of the interaction of genetic and environmental factors in the determination of observed patterns of behavior. This includes consideration of interuterine conditions that may have served to mask characteristics at the time of her earliest observations. She points to the difficulty of teasing out causal sequences from correlational data, a common source of controversy in the heredity/environment debate. One particularly fascinating outcome is that characteristics associated by Thomas and Chess with the "difficult child syndrome" are low on heritability and thus most easily modified by environment. Torgersen's painstaking and extended work reveals the benefits to psychological theory of longitudinal studies carried out within an adequate conceptual framework and reinforces again the benefits of twin study in genetic research.

Friedensberg (Chapter 15) employs a constructional task to study developmental trends in style of action, that is, the proportion of basic and auxiliary actions. High reactives show a greater proportion of auxiliary actions in adult populations. Friedensberg's sample ranges from 6 to 16 years. This age range must necessitate use of tasks of varying levels of complexity, a problem encountered in several developmental studies, so that the data shown for different age groups in her tables are not, strictly speaking, comparable. The most powerful source of variance in her study appears to be intelligence, as measured by the Progressive Matrices. Taking high- and low-reactive groups separately, however, it is in the latter group that intelligence correlates with a variety of performance indexes. She also shows an age trend toward deliberate and controlled operations, rather than corrective actions. This study reveals a number of problems of interpretation in this field and, in particular, difficulties involved in discovering variables that may be confounded. In two of her five age groups, Matrices score and Reactivity are related, high reactives being less intelligent. The task employed resembles the Koh's block task, used in the Wechsler Intelligence Scale for Children (WISC) and the Wechsler Adult Intelligence Scale (WAIS), and the operations involved in solving the Matrices bear some resemblance to the dependent variables studied. At the same time, there must be a confounding between the measures of performance, because a speedy solution reduces the opportunity for occurrence of subsidiary operations. Friedensberg employs a variety of extreme group and correlational statistics, each treated independently; it may be that a multivariate analysis would be more appropriate to the clarification of the complex relationships between age, intelligence, and the development of style of action. Also, generalizability of the findings would be more certain if a variety of tasks were employed; for example, would an analysis of performance of classroom students yield similar findings? The power of developmental studies of this nature is that they enable us to examine basic processes before the person has acquired strategies to compensate for performance discrepancies.

Volume 2 (Psychophysiology, Performance, and Applications)

Psychophysiological studies. Gale (Chapter 1), in reviewing EEG studies of extraversion-introversion, appeals for a change of direction in research. Of the 30 or more studies he identifies in the literature, most are almost theory free, resting quite simply on the hope that there will be a correlation between personality, as measured by questionnaire, and cortical activity, as measured by the EEG. Even so, measurement of personality and EEG in these studies leaves much to be desired. He shows that the discrepant findings in the literature can be reconciled by use of a <u>post hoc</u> hypothesis derived from H. J. Eysenck's (1967) theory, the notion of sensation seeking in extraverts, and the characterization of the testing situation as one of extreme monotony, in which subjects are obliged to devise different strategies to comply with ambiguous experimental instructions. He draws attention to a number of confounding variables and potential sources of measurement error, and claims that the absence of performance data makes interpretation of results difficult. It is clear from other chapters that the means are available for following Gale's advice and that, indeed, many of the Soviet workers appear to have established a long tradition of integrated research in which personality, performance, and electrocortical measurement share common paradigms. One feature of Gale's paper, however, that has general application is his brief analysis of the experimental situation itself as a context in which several sources of arousal may combine to confound personality research. Such confusion exists particularly in those areas that emphasize sensation seeking, the effects of novelty, fear of evaluation or punishment, and personal regulation of stimulus input. Thus notions of <u>regulation</u> and <u>cost</u> emphasized by the Warsaw group -- and, in particular, the strategy of focusing on <u>process</u> as well as <u>outcome</u> -- would be seen by Gale to apply to the experimental situation <u>per se</u> and the coping strategies used by the subject to handle a threatening or ambiguous stimulus field. In general, Gale indicates that little has been achieved in the West in relating EEG characteristics to extraversion-introversion.

Bodunov (Chapter 2) presents a considerable contrast; it is clear from his work that the use of well-structured performance tests and a thoroughgoing analysis of EEG parameters can demonstrate the relationship between brain function and individual differences. Moreover, references cited by both Bodunov and Danilova show that such studies have an established tradition of sustained research behind them. Bodunov focuses on the detailed analysis of the dynamics of <u>activity</u>, which he demonstrates must be explored in a multidimensional fashion, because different indexes of activity do not necessarily intercorrelate. Thus, he devises three groups of tests measuring individual tempo, persistence under pressure, and variety seeking. Principal-components analysis was used to derive factors whose reliability were established on a second sample. He demonstrates that the relationships between the different parameters of activity are complex, for example, yielding a curvilinear function between tempo and variety seeking. This demonstrates the multidimensional but interactive nature of the components of activity. The EEG parameters were also subjected to factor analysis, yielding four factors. In the final stage of the work the activity variables are related to the EEG variables. Many of the loadings obtained in the final-factor table are of considerable magnitude and far exceed those obtained in Western work, even at its very best (see Rösler, 1975). Thus the strategy, supported in Zuckerman's paper, of being specific about the tasks to be correlated with other (psychometric and physiological) measures is clearly vindicated. A point made by Bodunov and by other contributors is that well-designed studies of individual differences provide an adequate data base for the construction of <u>general</u> models in psychology and, in this case, of brain function. It is to be hoped that workers in the West will examine studies of this nature and follow Bodunov's example, not only in terms of methodology but in terms of theoretical orientation; the concept of activity is clearly central to any model of brain function that purports to explain the constant feedback and regulatory actions that occur between the organism and its environment.

Näätänen's contribution (Chapter 3) is important in several respects. Given
the ease with which evoked brain potentials may now be measured and quantified,
there is little excuse for those investigators who persist in focusing on peripheral indexes which, apart from heart rate, are sluggish and nondiscriminating.
He shows that by designing a series of carefully devised and logically rigorous
experiments, one can show which aspects of the evoked potential are sensitive
to which aspects of the task. He concludes by locating the neuronal mismatch
aspect of Sokolovian neural model orienting-response (OR) theory, at the neuronal
mismatch negativity (N2) stage of the evoked potential. Moreover, he suggests
that at this stage of information processing, one is witnessing electrocortical
events at a preconscious level. The basic paradigm involves a sequence of homo-
genous and repetitive stimuli among which occasional stimuli, deviant in physical
characteristics, are interspersed. By taking us through the experimental sequence, he argues as follows.

The repeated stimulus sets up the neuronal model, the N2 component show
a difference in amplitude. Yet in a dichotic listening task, N2 fails to differentiate attended and nonattended stimuli, although they are discriminated
at P300. The first major negative deflection (N1) and N2 are different in
similar style for latency. Thus he claims the N2 mismatch occurs at a preattentive level, whereas stimulus "significance" must wait for a positive deflection of P300 to show effects. He summarizes further evidence to show (a) that
N2 to standards is small (thus is distinguishable from afferent input effects);
(b) N2 is sensitive to stimulus omission (showing the temporal aspect of the
mismatch process); (c) in contrast to N1, which shows strong generalization
of habituation, N2 displays a vigorous response to slight stimulus change and
also responds even when the subject misses the deviant; (d) N2 fails to distinguish misses and hits (thus is preattentive); (e) although N1 covaries with
input (reducing with reduced intensity), N2 increases with any slight change;
(f) N1 shows a decrement after the first stimulus, while N2 is not responsive;
(g) N2 is responsive to the probability and magnitude of stimulus deviance;
(h) the N2 has foci frontally and in specific sensory modality regions (raising
the possibility not only of a locus of neuronal mismatch, but also of multiple-
level vertical representation from hippocampus upward); and, finally, (i) a more
difficult aspect to determine unequivocally, N2 is insensitive to stimulus
evaluation of significance.

Näätänen argues that his techniques and the style of research study he advocates
could serve rapidly to get to the heart of some of the issues that currently
dominate OR research and, in particular, the controversy as to whether the
stimulus has to be appraised as significant before the OR occurs. Given the
temporal characteristics of the evoked potential and its power to discriminate
among task parameters, it is clear that long-latency peripheral measures like
heart rate and skin conductance represent merely a gross amalgamation, which
in principle could never serve to discriminate among the early stages of information processing. Though Näätänen is modest in his evaluation of the evidence, a
clear conclusion must be that future OR studies must include electrocortical
measures as a sine qua non whatever other measures are taken. We have devoted
considerable space to Näätänen's contribution because its importance should not
be underestimated. It has the potential to influence future thinking even more
than did his excellent and much-cited review (1975) of evoked potential studies.
At the same time, the psychophysiologist must surely acknowledge that his linear
model of information processing is conceptually far removed from contemporary
approaches to attention, as exemplified by the Attention and Performance series.

The Näätänen paper is not addressed directly to personality research. However,
as O'Gorman shows (1977), the OR and its habituation has been a popular tool
for personality research, has been limited almost exclusively to noncortical

measures, and has yielded equivocal results. The lesson is surely clear.

Changes in the Contingent Negative Variation (CNV) are studied by Werre (Chapter 4) in a reaction time procedure, in which several subject variables were
controlled for (extraversion, action preparedness, neuroticism, and intelligence)
and the data handled by means of factor analysis. He demonstrates a complex
pattern of relationships that alter as a function of time in task and treatment
conditions. In a second study, stimulants, sedatives and white noise were used.
Both studies demonstrate the sensitivity of the CNV to a variety of conditions.
Its relationships with action preparedness are, of course, of significance in
a work devoted to activity and its part in the regulation of stimulation and
feedback. This study demonstrates a number of fundamental points: (a) the
relation between activation and performance is curvilinear; (b) temporal
analysis is a powerful source of data in psychophysiological studies; (c) slight
variations in procedure can shift relationships, even in an opposite direction;
and, finally, (d) the practiced subject employs different strategies from those
of the naive subject. At the same time, the study shows that multiple determinants of physiological arousal may be combined in one study and interpreted within
a unitary framework. Werre reports that future studies in this newly developing
field will include subjective reports as well.

The study by Danilova (Chapter 5) explores evoked potential and heart rate
changes in subjects with strong and weak nervous systems (Strelau questionnaire)
during the learning of temporal discrimination of light-flash stimuli. Differences are obtained in performance, basal physiological indexes, and in the
interrelationships among the variables for the two groups. She interprets her
findings both in terms of individual differences in the patterning of general
and localized orienting responses, and in the alleged differences between subjects with strong and weak nervous systems in cognitive style (verbal and nonverbal) and arousability. Danilova adopts the strategy of repeated measures
within a small experimental population, representing extreme scores for personality trait. The remarkably high correlations obtained may attest to the wisdom
of this strategy. Again, this study by a Soviet worker reveals how well advanced
are Soviet studies in the integration of personality, performance, and physiological measures.

Uherík (Chapter 6) sees the individual as a complex and open psychophysiological
feedback system, and personality is defined in terms of characteristic modes
of interaction with the environment. Activation and conscious regulation are
seen as crucial and interacting features. Personality integrates these features.
He reviews work at the Bratislava laboratory directed at the comparison of Russian
and Western personality traits. Using skin conductance responses as a dependent
variable, a number of experiments were set up comparing responses in criterion
groups selected on the basis of the EPI, the MAS and other Western instruments.
Experimental variables include performance under stress, stimulus-intensity
judgments, sleep deprivation, transmarginal inhibition, self-stimulation and
relaxation, the Stroop test, autogenic training, and hypnosis. Other studies
involved schizophrenic patients in whom Uherík provided one of the first demonstrations of extreme bilateral asymmetry, foreshadowing the work of Gruzelier
(1976). He summarizes many studies and provides a detailed discussion of error
sources. The chapter includes a valuable bibliography which will enable the
Western reader to seek out detailed procedural aspects from the original papers.

Strelau, Sosnowski and Oniszczenko (Chapter 7) report a detailed study of the
effects of hypoxia and sensory deprivation on psychophysiological indexes and
state anxiety. Scores on the Strelau scale and measures of trait anxiety were
also included. The study demonstrates how a relatively straightforward set of
questions can lead to complex data, particularly when trends over time are

considered. There is no doubt that the key experimental manipulations affected
the dependent measures: one difficulty demonstrated here is that variance attributable to treatments can wash out intersubject effects or, at least, interact
with them in a particularly complex fashion. The authors provide a sensitive
discussion of error sources and the problems associated with designs that call
for partitioning of novelty effects.

Personality and performance. In one of her two contributions to this volume,
Klonowicz (Chapter 8) draws our attention to the notion of psychological and
psychophysiological costs. Following Tomaszewski, she states that performance
depends on "the equilibrium between the acting subject, the task, and the working
environment." These elements have to be balanced; and in successful performance,
one aspect is compensated for by another. That is why we do not often find differences in performance between criterion groups selected for particular traits;
subjects compensate for the mismatch between temperamental characteristics and
task or situational requirements. In her own study, she confirms that subjects
selected on the basis of reactivity perform equally well. When a cost index
is devised, however, it appears that in stressful environments, high-reactive
subjects are required to exercise additional actions to maintain performance.
Thus, though her measure of quality differentiates conditions, but not subjects,
temperament groups are differentiated for a number of operations and plasticity
(corrective operations). This elegant and simple task demonstrates a problem
that runs through many of the experimental studies reported in this volume,
namely, that of selecting the theoretically appropriate variables for examination. Here we see that groups selected for different traits nevertheless
achieve identical outcomes, but by employing different strategies. It is the
notion of cost that Klonowicz refers to when she talks of "the third side of
the coin."

Studies of the relationship between individual differences and memorial processes have been greatly stimulated in the West by the publication of
M. W. Eysenck's volume, Human Memory: Theory, Research and Individual Differences (1977). Such work sets the scene for a rapprochement between traditional
areas of concern in experimental psychology on the one hand and psychophysiology
and individual differences on the other. Thus the chapter by Halmiová and
Šebová (Chapter 9) is likely to be received with considerable interest by
Western workers, because these authors manipulate task difficulty in working
memory in one experiment and word frequency (familiar and rare surnames) in
another, to explore memorial performance in subjects selected for strength and
weakness of the excitatory process (Strelau scales) in the first study, and a
law-of-strength reaction-time procedure in the second. Although the authors
appear to be not wholly satisfied with the outcome, their data are reminiscent
of Western studies manipulating item arousal and individual differences; strong
subjects perform better, particularly under difficult and stressful conditions.
They interpret this as a reflection of a lower working capacity in weak subjects.
Analysis of skin-conductance measures differentiates the groups as a function
of relationships between activation and performance, weak subjects being more
activated at the outset and showing a parallel change in performance and reactivity.
These studies demonstrate again the value of experiments designed to test specific
predictions against a background of established data on performance and a coherent theory.

A brief chapter by Haase (Chapter 10) focuses on the notion of stimulus overload,
providing details of his Polychronicity Scale, which measures subjective report
of experienced disturbance under intense levels of informational input. The
polychronic style is one that fails to structure action in a manner that reduces

perceived stress. He presents a number of intercorrelations between the subtests of his scale and scores on the Strelau questionnaire.

Nosal (Chapter 11) provides an empirical study of strategies used in problem solving, using a naturalistic task. Subjects are studied while they learn elementary aspects of computer programming. Temperament and scores on intelligence scale subtests are among the independent variables; the dependent variables, in relation to program initiation, checking on errors, and time scores, enable him to construct a model of the interaction between temperamental and cognitive variables to produce individual styles of information processing. The data are subjected to a sophisticated multivariate analysis, which enables Nosal to partial out different sources of variance and attribute proportions of overall variance to them. This sort of approach enables a precise measurement of style of action (see Friedensburg, Chapter 15, Volume 1) enabling the investigator to explore the microstructure of problem-solving strategies along the lines of artificial intelligence studies. He identifies three basic styles of cognitive activity, all reflecting an interaction between temperament and intellect: (a) a conservative style, characterized by delays and a concern for long-term consequences of actions; (b) an impulsive style, in which control is imposed after action; and (c) a balanced approach representing a compromise between the processes involved in (a) and (b). A characteristic of this task, which personality researchers would do well to note, is that the task, like those used by the Schönpflug group (Chapter 18), has meaning and ecological validity for the subject; thus opportunities for uncontrolled error variance in the form of subject interpretation of demand characteristics, lack of involvement, or even withdrawal of attention, are minimized. At the same time, the task is not so uncontrolled and free running that it cannot provide a basis for comparison of strategies between subjects, in spite of wide differences in their approach.

An early study of stimulus hunger in humans carried out by one of the present authors revealed how difficult it is to distinguish stimulus intensity, stimulus change, activity, and activity cost effects, without detailed parametric studies (Gale, 1969). Matysiak (Chapter 12), by using rats as subjects, is able to overcome many of the problems raised, in an economic and rigorous fashion. Of course, he cautions us against ready extrapolation to humans. His approach has an additional advantage of allowing the use of populations bred for certain characteristics. Intensity of stimulation, modality of stimulation, sensory deprivation, and sensory overload may all be studied within one design, providing answers to a number of important questions. Thus he enables us to ask (a) whether need for additional stimulation is correlated with scores for reduction of stimulation under overload (a crucial problem for many participants in the volume); (b) whether stimulation from different modality sources has equivalent effects and whether there can be cross-modality additivity; and (c) how intensity of stimulation, change within or between stimulation sources, and amount of activity incurred are interrelated (again a central issue). Because researchers of the Warsaw school, following the Pavlovian tradition, believe that temperamental characteristics are seen in nervous systems as such, the use of nonhuman species to test particular hypotheses and to find complex interrelationships is clearly justified. At the same time, Matysiak's studies provide a model for human studies that personality theorists might do well to imitate. The question must be asked whether the limits to systematic and parametric work in humans are not truly logical, technical, or ethical, but stem rather from a tradition of experimental sloppiness that reflects a zeitgeist in the history of our discipline, rather than a well-thought-out strategy. Many issues raised in this volume call for a careful accumulation of basic data, filling in all the cells logically generated by the implications of theory.

A possible basic paradigm for parametric studies is devised by Hockey (Chapter 13),

who presents an ingenious study in which subjects were tested in threes. One
subject (introvert or extravert) determined the level of noise during a vigilance
task, and the yoked subjects were one introvert and one extravert. Extraverts
chose higher levels of extraneous noise during the task, and both groups increased their call for noise as the task proceeded. Introverts performed better,
and extraverts performed worse, when paired with an introvert noise control.
Introverts were relatively unaffected by task conditions. The power of the results using this paradigm indicates that it might be developed further, for it
allows for parallel measures of performance, sensation seeking, and physiological
response. It also demonstrates nicely the effects of regulatory behavior on
arousal and efficiency and the disruptive influence of stimulus conditions
that are ill-matched to the individual characteristics of the subject. This
theme is also one take up by Klonowicz (Chapter 8).

Applied implications. Hare and Jutai (Chapter 14) preface their discussion on
sensation seeking in psychopaths with a cautionary note on problems of diagnosis
and classificaton, indicating that the then current American Psychiatric Association's Diagnostic Manual was likely to yield a high false-positive rate (more than
doubling the estimate of psychopathy in one sample, compared with the procedures
devised by Hare & Cox, 1978). Their own early procedures, on their own admission,
involve considerable experience and judgment which of course undermines their
psychometric purity. They report preliminary findings on a new 22-item checklist;
even here the reader may observe that many of the characteristics are not defined behaviorally ("glibness", "lack of sincerity"), whereas others would seem
to guarantee the reported overall correlations with global measures they report
(i.e., one item is "previous diagnosis as psychopath (or similar)"; another is
"lack of affect and emotional depth"). Hare and Jutai then review evidence for
high levels of sensation seeking in psychopaths. Again the authors express
caution, because several studies reviewed indicate statistically significant
but small correlations between scores on Sensation Seeking scales and psychopathy in prison populations. They are particularly concerned with response sets
that are adopted by prison populations. In contrast with psychometric studies,
however, experimental studies and case histories do indicate support for a model
proposed by Farley (1973) in which delinquency might result from the combination
of stimulation-seeking behavior and an absence of socially acceptable channels
for the expression of such behavior. Hare and Jutai then report studies of
coping strategies in psychopathic subjects. It is clear that the problem of
psychopathy will continue to challenge the ingenuity of both theoreticians and
experimentalists.

Two empirical studies follow that explore aspects of aggressive behavior in relation to neurotics, psychopaths, and high and low reactives. Ciarkowski and
Fraczek (Chapter 15) explore in a subtle fashion the complex interrelationships
between individual characteristics (neuroticism and psychopathy) and frustration,
exposure to aggressive stimuli, conditioning to stimuli of positive and negative
emotional value, anger, and expressed aggression. There is evidence that both
neuroticism and psychopathy modulate the interpretation of incoming stimuli
associated with aggression. Neuroticism appears to facilitate the release of
anger. Levels of psychopathy seem to interact in a complex fashion with task
conditions, since highly psychopathic subjects appeared to be impervious to
opportunities for increased aggression in the presence of stimuli that evoked
negative emotion. The authors conclude with an appeal to researchers to employ
measures that reveal cognitive mechanisms operating on the structural and dynamic
properties of interpersonal aggression. Such measurement would presumably have
to apply to several data sources: (a) reports from subjects of their response
to life situations; (b) subject responses (including social desirability effects,
as warned by Hare and Jutai) to instruments designed to measure emotional and

and psychopathic traits, and (c) cognitive evaluations of the experimental procedures per se, their demand characteristics, and, in particular, the unusual
context of procedures inviting public expression of anger and retaliatory
aggression. Studies of this nature capture the methodological and interpretative dilemmas faced by those who wish to measure emotion in the laboratory.

H. Eliasz and Reykowski (Chapter 16) provide an interesting analysis of empathy
in terms of Strelau's theory. High reactives are more susceptible to social
influence and adjust their responses to others while showing reduced adjustment
to features of the physical environment; thus their behavior is selectively tuned
to people. Such a sensitivity is presupposed by the expression of empathy toward
others. The empathic response, however, will be regulated by the degree of emotional experience perceived in another, since that determines the level of stimulation provided by another's suffering. Eliasz and Reykowski are able to make
specific predictions concerning retaliatory aggression under conditions in which
empathy is manipulated. At the same time, aggressive acts may be seen as a means
of increasing stimulation and thus provide a means of stimulus regulation for
the low reactive.

Thus, Eliasz and Reykowski predict that low reactives will not respond empathet-
ically to low levels of suffering in others. Even when empathy does occur, it
may serve to increase arousal and thus lead to increased aggression toward the
victim.

The reverse holds for high reactives, who will experience empathy at low levels
of suffering in others, and will reduce aggressive acts as a means of lowering
incoming stimulation.

Thus aggression and empathy are not seen as primary traits but as aspects of
regulation of stimulation that depend on higher-order needs.

Klonowicz, Ignatowska-Świtalska, and Wocial (Chapter 17), as in the earlier
chapter by Klonowicz (Chapter 8) provide a clear demonstration of individual
differences in strategy -- in this case, coping with stress. Hypertensive and
normal subjects are exposed to noise stress, and measures are taken of subjective activation and output of prostaglandin, adrenaline, and noradrenaline.
Again, performance of continuous arithmetic did not vary for the two groups for
correct additions, yet did vary for errors and the dynamics of errors. Hypertensives were less accurate under noise stress, making most errors at the start
of the task. Though normals decreased in perceived activation as time pro-
gressed, the reverse held for hypertensives (Thayer Deactivation Scale) who were
continuously at a higher level. Whereas healthy subjects showed increased
adrenaline, hypertensives started at a higher level and did not increase. We
select only a few of the findings here; the reader must go to the chapter for
the full discussion. A good feature of this paper is its attempt to integrate
performance, biochemical, and experiential data within one theoretical framework.

The chapters by Schönpflug and Mundelein (Chapter 18) and Shulz (Chapter 19)
are considered together here because they come from the same laboratory and are
based on a number of common conceptions and research procedures. Using a computer both to present problems and to store data concerning the subject's pattern of response, they are able to simulate realistic tasks, generate detailed
and continuous records of complex behaviors, and combine these with measures
of subjective report and physiological change. A taxonomy of actions is presented that enables the analysis of regulatory behavior. One study (Schönpflug
and Mundelein) centers on the simulation of an insurance office in which subjects
(unemployed, experienced clerical workers) are required to check insurance

claims against the claimant's file, ascertaining whether premiums have been paid, time since the last claim, and so on. The authors are able to explore the subjects' working strategies, that is, care taken in checking work, need to refer to stored information, rest behaviors, response under work pressure, and fatigue over extended periods of work.

The Shulz study provides the subjects with a number of problems to be solved and a variety of information sources with which to solve them. Again, a detailed analysis is possible of the structuring of the subjects' performance, their responses to the task, and their reactions to stress. In both studies, high and low reactives (measured by Strelau questionnaire) are seen to perform differently. This work clearly has an affinity of objectives with that of Nosal (Chapter 11) and enables a rapprochement between personality theory and artificial intelligence studies, demonstrating yet again that studies of individual differences can themselves provide a base for devising models of performance in general experimental psychology. One aspect of the work is that it generates a tremendous quantity of data. Only a small sample is provided here; nevertheless it is more than sufficient to tantalize the reader into further study of the work of the Free University of Berlin group.

RECURRENT THEMES

A set of recurrent themes runs throughout these theoretical and empirical studies.

1. Individual variation is, in part, attributable to biological factors.
2. Such factors are transmitted through genetic mechanisms.
3. There is a constant interplay between biologically determined dispositions and physical, biochemical, and social events.
4. The individual is seen as regulating crucial aspects of this interplay.
5. The principles of regulation are themselves derivable from the biological dispositions and their interaction with the external world.
6. Factors that play an important role in the regulation of behavior are arousal level, optimal levels of arousal, optimal levels of stimulation, changes in stimulation, and activity. All these constructs are in some sense related to the input and output of energy.
7. The dispositional variables may be tapped by use of psychometric instruments.
8. Because of the range of identified dispositional variables and because each person evolves within a constantly emerging feedback system, it is not expected that there will be a simple one-to-one relation between trait variables and behavior, even where the number of traits specified by the theory is limited.
9. The appropriate description of the individual will encompass behavioral, psychophysiological, and experiential domains of description.
10. The understanding of personality structure is impossible without consideration of dynamics; therefore experimental studies are obliged to focus on process as well as outcome.
11. There are no grounds for sustaining the historical division between the psychology of individual differences and general experimental psychology, nor between physiological, cognitive, and social psychological approaches. Indeed, the psychophysiology of individual differences has the power to integrate these various fields. Data derived from studies of individual differences may provide a base for describing general processes.
12. The examination of individual differences and the patterning of behavior is therefore of heuristic value in all branches of psychology.
13. In examining data derived from experiments, the investigator must be aware that individual differences will determine not only the patterning of

response, but the <u>individual's response to the experimental situation per se.</u>

15. It is the recognition of the biological nature of temperamental character-istics that enables a cross-mapping of constructs devised in both Western and Eastern laboratories, and thus provides for the evolution of a common language for the description of crucial aspects of human behavior.

CRITIQUE: AN ATTEMPT AT CONSTRUCTIVE CRITICISM

It would be an abuse of our twin roles as contributors and co-editors if we were to appear to criticize our colleagues in their absence. All the critical points made here were stated either in individual papers, or in the lengthy discussions (here unpublished) that followed each paper session at the Conferences. We attempt therefore to draw them together in a coherent fashion.

As a preliminary statement of formal requirements for theory in personality re-search, let us return to the criteria set out by Hall and Lindzey in the first edition of their classic text <u>Theories of Personality</u> (1973). (a) The key constructs of the theory should be clearly stated, as must be the domains of behavior they seek to describe and explain. (b) Because most theories have several key constructs, there should be interaction rules for relating the con-structs, so that we might see how they interact, as well as their relative importance in different contexts. (c) Rules are also required for translating the constructs into observable phenomena, either in the natural world or in the experimental context; without such empirical definitions, the theory can have no factual basis. (d) There should be internal consistency, for an internally inconsistent theory may be used to predict any observation. All the issues raised by these simple requirements have been considered in this volume.

Constructs

There is a handful of constructs that clearly are crucial for contributors: excitation, inhibition, strength, mobility, arousal, activation, regulation, reactivity, activity, optimum arousal, anxiety, sensation seeking, dynamism, and energy exchange. It is surely clear that if the works presented here are to progress as an integrated endeavor, then there must first be a thoroughgoing theoretical evaluation of these constructs, their logical limits, and their degree of dependence or independence. Thus we really do need to know whether workers in different laboratories are using common constructs only at the most superficial level, whether there is true cross-mapping of meaning and content, or whether they are talking of different entities. The investigation of this communality of constructs must be conducted at the theoretical level before much more empirical work is done; otherwise, the work will diverge in different direc-tions, and an opportunity for synthesis will be lost.

Such an analysis must presuppose a detailed consideration of the internal struc-ture of the concepts themselves. We have seen, for example, how the notion of optimum level of arousal has been used in several ways. The optimum is viewed as a biologically determined factor common for all individuals, or varying between individuals, or acquired by individuals, or required by particular task demands. At the same time arousal, activation, arousability, arousal threshold, stress-induced arousal, and pathological states of hyperarousal or hypoarousal, are all confounded. Thus a basic concept, which is probably referred to by all our authors, requires urgent elucidation. This must also be true for most of the variables to which arousal is said to relate. The temptation to oversimplify is challenged by several of our authors, who point to the need to be specific in

the use of subscales and in the specification of conditions under which hypotheses are to be tested. Such empirical rigor is incompatible with conceptual
sloppiness.

Mind and Body

A perennial problem, and one that must be tackled by investigators who report
data on biochemistry, electrophysiology, performance, subjective report, and
psychometric scale scores, all within one study, is the challenge of interre-
lating these domains of discourse within a conceptual framework that allows for
cross-mapping or translation across the domains. It is difficult for personality
theorists with both a biological emphasis and an emphasis on information processing
and conscious regulation, to avoid the mind-body problem in its modern manifestation. These problems are hinted at in several chapters; but there is no formal
recognition of the need to tackle the logical problems that psychophysiological
approaches to personality and behavior must raise. In a sense, this may be considered by some to be the central issue in psychology; but to be close to a
central issue does not imply that we should so regulate our thinking as to
devise strategies to avoid it.

Instruments of Measurement

A good proportion of the data reported here is directly related to test scores
and intercorrelations between them, or is based on criterion groups selected
by psychometric instruments. The former are perhaps the most crucial empirical
data in the two volumes, because failure to demonstrate the validity of a scale or
failure to show strong intercorrelations with scales devised to measure allegedly
related constructs must surely cause us to stop and think. Even when intercorrelations hold in the predicted direction, they are often modest in magnitude
and account for only a small proportion of the variance. Moreover, several of
our authors, given the set of looking for corroboratory data, often fail to comment on obtained correlations within their matrixes, which, according to theory,
should not occur. The principle of selectivity applies to all of us, but it
must not be allowed to distort the perceptions of scientists. Despite the
studies reported here, there is still a gap to be filled, within which all the
scales used by our contributors may be cross-related in the style of approach
adopted by Carlier (Chapter 8, Vol. 1). Again the crucial question must be,
Are we examining similar factors? And are the factors we examine themselves
valid? The multivariate, hierarchical factor structure of Royce and Powell
(Chapter 4, Vol. 1) stands in stark contrast to the two- and three-dimensional
models of many of the contributors.

Standardizing Procedures

Just as there is a need to explore systematically the nature of the theoretical
constructs employed, so also should there be an agreed taxonomy of the varying
tasks employed in different laboratories. The temptation to devise a new procedure or experimental paradigm is symptomatic for all branches of psychology;
but it does not aid comparisons between laboratories, particularly when they
are based in different countries where conventions for reporting procedural and
methodological detail seem to vary. An attempt to force all workers into a
common approach would be sterile and would stifle creativity; however, it should
be possible, at least, to provide a classification of tasks and to specify the
parameters that Laboratory A would wish to see included in studies carried out
by Laboratory B. For example, we have not thought it proper to tamper with
terminology employed by contributors; but in psychophysiology, for example, there
appears to be some agreement in the West on terminology to be used and the characteristics of devices employed to measure psychophysiological response. This is

not a tyranny, but merely an attempt to create a language of common discourse. Similarly, Western workers would benefit from a clear explication of procedures employed for measuring the neo-Pavlovian indexes of temperamental traits, so that these may be incorporated in future studies.

Autonomic or Cortical Measures?

Näätänen (Chapter 3, Vol. 2) raises some fundamental issues. He suggests quite baldly that autonomic indexes, which are typically sluggish and gross in nature, are too far removed from central processes in both location and time to be of much use in testing hypotheses about information processing. The cognitive element in the regulation of behavior is mentioned by several authors; thus, there seems to be a prima facie case for focusing on the central nervous system in our exploration of the physiological correlates of regulatory and, specifically, cognitive strategies. Bodunov (Chapter 2, Vol. 2), Danilova (Chapter 5, Vol. 2), Näätänen (Chapter 3, Vol. 2), Werre (Chapter 4, Vol. 2), and Farley (Chapter 3, Vol. 1) all demonstrate how this is possible, and how rich the data may prove to be. It is surely the brain that is the final common path for information within the nervous system.

Appropriate Statistical Models

Nosal (Chapter 11,Vol. 2) reveals how necessary it is when dealing, as experimental personality studies do, with very many variables, to employ a multivariate approach. The repeated use of several t tests and the accumulation of many separate correlations is both wasteful of the parent data and an abuse of the data sampled. In addition, when studies must be correlational, but reasonably well-developed and coherent theory is available, greater use of quantitative techniques of causal modeling is recommended. Use of path analysis, structural equations, maximum likelihood methods, and analysis of covariance structures might well be examined. Given the important role of measurement and psychometric instrument development in this area, such technqieus as latent trait analysis, Rasch scaling, and other important developments should be considered.

CONCLUSIONS

The preparation of this work leaves us with a sense of great optimism. We may look forward to a revival in the fortunes of personality research, at a time when the sense of direction has perhaps been lost for many workers in the West. It is particularly pleasing that a basis for future work should be provided by the meeting of minds from different cultures and the discovery of so many refreshingly original and productive approaches. If we have seemed unduly critical in the foregoing section, it is only because our enthusiasm is accompanied by caution. We believe that the program for future work, if it acknowledges some of the difficulties to which we have referred, will surely thrive.

REFERENCES

Eysenck, H. J. (1981). General features of the model. In H. J. Eysenck (Ed.), A model for personality. Berlin: Springer Verlag.

Eysenck, H. J. (1967). The biological basis of personality. Springfield, IL: Charles C Thomas.

Eysenck, M. W. (1977). Human memory: Theory, research and individual differences. Oxford: Pergamon Press.

Farley, F. (1973, September). A theory of delinquency. Paper presented at the meeting of the American Psychological Association, Montreal, Canada.

Gale, A. (1969). Stimulus hunger: Individual differences in operant strategy in a button-pressing task. Behaviour Research and Therapy, 7, 265-274.

Gray, J. A. (1964). Pavlov's typology. Oxford: Pergamon Press.

Gruzelier, J. (1976). Clinical attributes of schizophrenic skin conductance responders and non-responders. Psychological Medicine, 6, 245-249.

Hall, G. S., and Lindzey, G. (1973). Theories of personality. New York: Wiley.

Hare, R. D., and Cox, D. N. (1978). Clinical and empirical conceptions of psychopathy and the selection of subjects for research. In R. D. Hare and D. Schalling (Eds.), Psychopathic behavior: Approaches to research. Chichester, NY: Wiley.

Näätänen, R. (1975). Selective attention and evoked potentials in humans. A critical review. Biological Psychology, 2, 237-307.

O'Gorman, J. (1977). Individual differences in habituation of human physio-logical responses: A review of theory, method and findings in the study of personality correlates in non-clinical populations. Biological Psychology, 5, 257-318.

Petrie, A. (1967). Individuality in pain and suffering. Chicago: University of Chicago Press.

Rösler, F. (1975). Die abhangigkeit des electroenzephalogramms von den persön lichkeitsdimentionen E und N sensu Eysenck und unterscheidlich aktivierenden situationen. Zeitschrift für Experimentelle und Angewandte Psychologie, 12, 630-667.

I

PERSONALITY
AND PSYCHOPHYSIOLOGY

1

Extraversion-Introversion and Spontaneous Rhythms of the Brain: Retrospect and Prospect

Anthony Gale

INTRODUCTION

We administer a questionnaire consisting of two or more scales. Each scale has 24 items. The items ask respondents questions about how they feel, react, and respond in different situations. They are not allowed to make subtle responses, to make guarded answers; they must say yes or no. On the basis of their answers to such questions, reflections on their own behavior, we then predict voltage and frequency characteristics of electrical activity recorded from the scalp. How is such a leap possible, from the domain of subjective report to the domain of biological function, the electrical activity of the brain? We can under-estimate the drama of this translation from one level of description to the other, from the behavior of the living organism, to the exploration in vivo of the physiological mechanisms that underlie it. Some 30 studies have been set up to determine the relationship between these two rather simple -- yet, on the face of it, unreliable -- measures of the person. The notion of accounting for individual differences between people in terms of physiological mechanisms is as old as formalized knowledge itself, yet we are not so near to discovering the answers. Some studies relating extraversion-introversion to the electro-encephalogram (EEG) owe a great deal to theory; but many others smack of blind empiricism, a sort of "let's see what happens if" type of approach to science. Thus the studies vary in intention and quality, and we require a formal model or structure within which to evaluate them. In the present evaluation of the work, I shall consider the research carried out on several different levels: the theory, hypothesis construction, methods of measurement, experimental procedures and contexts employed, and the treatment and interpretation of data. My evaluation is not original; it draws upon several other publications, in which I have attempted, over the last 15 years, to review this field (Gale, 1973, 1981, 1983; Gale, Coles & Blaydon, 1969). Unfortunately, the quality of research in this field has hardly altered in that time. Some studies (e.g. Rösler, 1975; O'Gorman & Mallise, 1984) are a notable improvement upon earlier practice, whereas others (e.g. Travis, Kondo & Knott, 1974) represent a regression.

Why should there be more than 30 studies? Why is it necessary, given the simple assumption that brain waves and personality are related, to repeat the same

---

This chapter is a combination of two papers, presented at the first and second Warsaw Conferences. More extended discussions of the issues raised are to be found in Gale (1973; 1981; 1983) and Gale & Edwards (1983a, 1983b, 1984). The interpretation of existing research findings presented here has been challenged by O'Gorman (1984) and O'Gorman & Mallise (1984).

experiment more than two dozen times? The truth is that the outcome of these
studies has been rather disappointing, yielding, in fact, all three logically
possible results, as follows: if the EEG is taken to measure the level of
arousal within the brain, then extraverts have been found to be (a) more
aroused, (b) less aroused, or (c) no different from, introverts. Even so, few
of the findings have reached a high level of statistical significance, and the
correlations obtained leave much of the variance unaccounted for. In this
chapter I attempt to explain why this should be. Unfortunately, the explanation
of these failures and discrepancies must be post hoc, for the appropriate experiment, derived formally from theory and conducted with due care, has yet to be
carried out; the nearest approximation to an adequate study is that of O'Gorman
and Mallise (1984). Workers in the field seem condemned to repeat the same mis-
takes and increase the credibility gap between mainstream psychology and the
examination of spontaneous rhythms of the brain. After more than 40
years of research, we still do not understand what the rhythms of the brain
mean. Personality studies have added to the confusion, and the major thrust of
contemporary interest in the electrical activity of the brain revolves around
event-related potentials and not the background rhythms. Yet in the case of
personality, a systematic testing of theory is possible; even though I paint a
gloomy picture of the past, there are grounds for optimism for the future. To
see how proper experiments may be carried out, we need to explore the literature
at three levels; the conceptual issues bound within the theory, the empirical
definiton of the theoretical constructs, and the microstructure of the individual
experiment. In certain experiments in psychology, factors extraneous to the variables manipulated or measured may have a profound influence on outcome. The
study of personality, within the psychosocial context of the psychophysiology
experiment, is a good candidate (Gale and Baker, 1981; Rosenthal & Rubin, 1978;
Rumenick, Capasso & Hendrick, 1977). Thus apart from the explicit hypotheses
explored within these experiments, we must examine also potential sources of
error, hidden within the procedures adopted.

A good proportion of contemporary studies derive from theory. But a good way to
illustrate the research is to start at the beginning, with a theory-free yet
methodologically sensitive study, that of Lemere (1936). He worked with 26
young adults and made between three and five recordings over a month. If the
EEG is a measure of some fundamental aspect of the person, then, he argued, it
should remain stable over time. He observed such stability, yet noted the ex-
ceptions. First, between-subject differences were maintained even in noisy
environments. Yet the quality of the alpha rhythm deteriorated over sessions,
and in two cases was particularly affected by external life events. One subject
had an important rugby football match that day, and another had a secret assig-
nation with a lover. Lemere considered what factors might cause stability and
ruled out simple possibilities, such as head size and skull thickness. The EEG
correlated with no general trait; sex, personality, memory, and extraversion
were all mentioned, but it is not clear how they were estimated. All students
of this subject should read Lemere's paper, for it is written with an intellectual
discipline and sensitivity to possible sources of artifact that are absent in much
contemporary work. Lemere was a pioneer who had a firm grip on the issues to be
resolved. We will return to these later.

H. J. EYSENCK'S 1967 THEORY

H. J. Eysenck claimed that certain personality factors are ubiquitous in their
appearance. Emotional stability-lability and introversion-extraversion have
their counterparts in many psychometric scales and emerge as factors from the
statistical analysis of questionnaire item protocols. This view has been challenged by a number of authorities, including contributors to the present volume.
A particular concern is whether a single instrument, with forced choice response

mode, can satisfy the requirement of generalizability, so often ignored by personality theorists, and provide an adequate basis for factorial analysis. (For
a discussion of this and related issues, see Jackson & Paunonen, 1980). Nevertheless, Eysenck claimed that neuroticism-stability and introversion-extraversion
are human universals and that they represent the external manifestation of basic
biological factors. Thus neuroticism-stability is a reflection of the potential
for activation within the nervous system, attributable to the "emotional" circuits
to be found in the limbic system, whereas introversion-extraversion reflects the
threshold for arousal determined by the characteristics of the reticular-cortical
network. The present chapter is concerned with the latter, although research
that in its design ignores the former is likely to encounter difficulty. For
both activation and arousal will influence the electrical activity of the neocortex and the voltage and frequency characteristics of the EEG. Three research
strategies have been employed to overcome this problem: subjects with high
neuroticism scores have been eliminated from samples; a quadrant analysis has
been used in treating neuroticism and extraversion as two factors with two levels
within an analysis of variance; and, on occasion, correlational analysis is
employed, partialing out either factor. Unfortunately, there is a fourth
strategy, which involves ignoring this fundamental issue (e.g. Montgomery, 1975).
Eysenck claimed that extraverts are born with an inherently high threshold for
reticular arousal, whereas introverts are born with a low threshold. In addition,
there is said to be an optimum level for arousal, such that extraverts require
additional stimulation for achieving a state of hedonic satisfaction (e.g. Gale,
1969), and introverts need to shun additional stimulation in order to allow their
inherently high level of arousal to subside. Additional stimulation arrives at
the reticular system via the collateral paths from the classical pathways (see
Figure 1). These embellishments to the theory are important for our present
purposes. We argue that the experimental conditions under which hypotheses concerning the relationship between EEG and introversion-extraversion have been
tested, may themselves be scaled along a continuum for their arousing-dearousing
properties. These characteristics of the testing environment may be seen to
interact with the characteristics of the subjects to produce a variety of outcomes. Thus the discrepancies among the research findings may be accounted for
post hoc in a systematic manner, which itself should lead to ante hoc predictions
for future research.

THE POST HOC HYPOTHESIS

If we examine the procedures employed, we see that, roughly speaking, there are
three categories. At one extreme, subjects lie supine in a soundproof room and
are instructed to do nothing but not to fall asleep. There may be a simple
stimulus schedule, for example, a habituation procedure to repetitive visual
or auditory stimuli, or there may be no stimulation at all, the subject being
left to his own devices. This procedure is almost unique in experimental psychology because it makes virtually no explicit demand upon the subject; I argue
later that it creates conflict for extraverted subjects but not for introverted
subjects. It is clearly a low-arousing treatment. At the next level are studies
in which subjects are given simple tasks to perform, or are tested in groups or
in the same room as the experimenter; such tasks include opening and shutting
the eyes upon instruction, responding to a biofeedback signal, or performing
simple reaction time tasks. This is an intermediate arousal condition. Third
are high-arousing and more stressful conditions, including rapid arithmetic calculations and explicit competition. Let us see how extraverted and introverted
subjects might respond to these three treatments in the light of theory.

Our account here follows very closely that given by Gale (1981). Under low-
arousing conditions, the introvert, normally highly arousable and, in addition,
having to cope with the stimulation provided by laboratory testing per se,

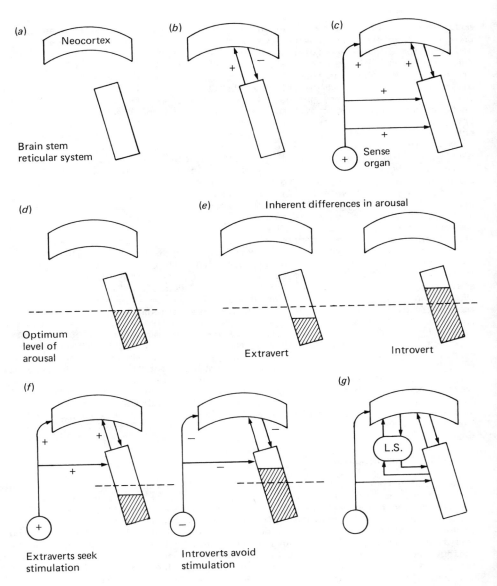

FIGURE 1. A schematic version of Eysenck's 1967 theory of the neurophysiological basis of extraversion-introversion and neuroticism-stability. (a) and (b) there are reciprocal relationships between neocortex and ascending reticular activating system (ARAS); (c) the ARAS receives collateral inputs from sensory organs as sensory information travels to the cortical reception areas; (d) there is an optimal level of arousal; (e) extraverts are born with an inherent level of arousal below the optimum and introverts vice versa; (f) extraverts seek additional sensory stimulation to elevate arousal, while introverts avoid additional stimulation; (g) the threshold of activation of the limbic system determines neuroticism-stability, thus both extraversion-introversion and neuroticism-stability have influences on cortical activity levels.

finds himself able to relax. He has been told he need do nothing and that no
demands will be imposed on him; once adapted to the laboratory, he is free of
additional stimulation, indeed is cut off from the extraneous stimulation that
is part of everyday life. Thus conditions are ideal for relaxation. The extravert, in contrast, once he has adapted to the laboratory, finds the lack of
stimulation disconcerting. He is placed in conflict, for the monotony of the
laboratory drives him to sleep, whereas the need to obey instructions calls for
wakefulness. There is some evidence that extraverts report greater vividness
of imagery than do introverts, and it is possible that internal self-stimulation
is employed as a substitute for stimulation within the external environment
(Morris & Gale, 1974). Thus the extravert may stimulate himself in order to keep
awake. Under low-arousing conditions, therefore, we see that it is possible to
obtain results contrary to those predicted; relaxation will be low-arousing to
introverts, and self-stimulation will be high-arousing to extraverts, yielding
either a null difference between the criterion groups or even showing extraverts
to be more aroused. So far as theory is concerned, only under intermediate or
moderate arousal conditions will the basic assumption that extraverts are less
aroused than introverts be shown to hold. Such conditions are sufficient to
keep extraverts in a state of relaxed wakefulness, yet combine with the stimulation provided by laboratory testing, to be too arousing (compared with low-
arousing conditions) for introverts. To interpret the effects on subjects of
highly arousing conditions (e.g., rapid arithmetic calculations), we need to
propose an additional construct analogous to Pavlov's notion of transmarginal
inhibition. Eysenck's theory accounts for the strategies used by extraverts
and introverts in everyday life to cope with the combination of inherent biological characteristics relating to arousal and the potential for stimulation
within the environment. Thus extraverts go to parties and seek variety and
intensity of stimulation in interpersonal, working, and consummatory activities.
Introverts, in contrast, stick to well-worn and predictable paths in work,
hobbies, and interpersonal relations. How does the introvert react when, despite
precautions, incoming stimulation becomes too high to be tolerable? In such circumstances, it is essential that a state of internal inhibition be induced, to
divert attention away from sensory input and inducing a state of calm. Such a
view implies that under intensely stimulating laboratory task conditions, introverts may remove attention and "switch off." Though extraverts might find the
challenge of rapid work welcome, introverts might find it intolerable; thus
under highly arousing laboratory conditions, extraverts may be found to be more
highly aroused, which again is contrary to prediction.

Thus an adequate experimental investigation of H. J. Eysenck's theory of the neurophysiological basis of introversion-extraversion must include the classification
of experimental treatments along some continuum of arousal and must employ these
treatments systematically within one design. Only two studies (Rösler, 1975;
O'Gorman & Mallise, 1984) come near to satisfying this requirement. We argue
later that the experimental treatments employed should themselves be derived from
paradigms that yield differences in performance between introverts and extraverts
and that the inclusion of such behavioral and performance measures enables, first,
a more confident interpretation of the EEG data and, second, a rapprochement between the EEG studies and the body of empirical work on performance. There is a
long history of performance studies in sustained attention, sensation seeking, memory, and circadian effects (Eysenck, H. J., 1971). So far, unfortunately, virtually
all the EEG studies have eschewed performance measures or have failed to report them.

How successful is our post hoc analysis in accounting for discrepancies in outcome? Our evaluation must, of course, be hedged with caution, for rarely do we
have sufficient information to be confident about the precise nature of the procedures employed. Table 1 lists all available studies, subclassified for low,
intermediate, and high arousal conditions. Asterisks indicate those we know
to have yielded statistically significant findings.

TABLE 1. Studies of introversion–extraversion and the EEG classified in accordance with Gale's (1973) Post Hoc Analysis

Arousal Level	Outcome
Low Arousal	
Lamere (1936)	No difference
Gottlober (1938)*	Extraverts less aroused
Henry & Knott (1941)	No difference
McAdam & Orme (1954)*	Extraverts more aroused
Mundy-Castle (1955)*	Extraverts more aroused
Savage (1964)*	Extraverts less aroused
Pawlik & Cattell (1965)*	Extraverts less aroused
Fenton & Scotton (1967)	No difference
Gale, Coles, Kline, & Penfold (1971)	No difference
Gale, Harpham, & Lucas (1972)*	Extraverts more variable
Gale (1973)*	Extraverts less aroused
Travis, Kondo, & Knott (1974)	No difference
Strelau & Terelak (1974)	No difference
Montgomery (1975)*	Extraverts less aroused
Kondo, Bean, Travis, & Knott (1978*)	Extraverts more aroused
Venturini, de Pascalis, Imperiali, & San Martini (1981)*	Extraverts less arousable
Gilliland, Andress, & Bracy (1981)*	Extraverts less aroused
Intermediate Arousal	
Claridge & Herrington (1963)	No difference
Nebylitsyn (1963)	Extraverts less aroused
Marton & Urban (1966)*	Extraverts less aroused
Hume (1968)	Extraverts less aroused
Gale, Coles, & Blaydon (1969)*	Extraverts less aroused
Young, Lader, & Fenton (1971)	No difference
Morris & Gale (1974)*	Extraverts less aroused
Deakin & Exley (1979)*	Extraverts less aroused
Irmis (1979)*	Extraverts less aroused
Gale, Kingsley, Edwards, Porter, & Smith (in preparation)*	Extraverts less aroused
High Arousal	
Shagass & Kerenyi (1958)*	Extraverts less aroused
Glass & Broadhurst (1966)*	Extraverts more aroused
Broadhurst & Glass (1969)*	Extraverts more aroused
Winter, Broadhurst, & Glass (1972)*	Stable extraverts less aroused
Baker (1978)*	Extraverts less aroused
Intermediate and High Arousal	
Becker-Carus (1971)	No difference
Low, Intermediate, and High Arousal	
Rösler (1975)*	Extraverts less aroused
O'Gorman & Mallise (1984)*	Extraverts more aroused

Note: Full details of samples, procedures and outcomes are provided by Gale (1983).
(*) indicates studies in which the effects obtained are statistically significant.

Table 1 indicates that of the 35 studies available, some 19 show extraverts to
be less aroused, some 7 show them to be more aroused, while the remaining studies
yield null effects. There is a tendency for the intermediate-arousal conditions
(based on the present author's post hoc evaluation) to yield results directly
compatible with the basic and unelaborated theory, whereas the low and high
arousal conditions give more variable results. The reader should, of course,
be skeptical of this analysis, because the author may be justly accused of
attempting to fit facts to theory; however, it does provide a modicum of confidence for future studies. Table 1 neither indicates the quality of individual
studies, nor shows where results are inferred from data derived either for completely different purposes or based on personality scales devised independently
of those of Eysenck. A detailed analysis of each study is given in Gale (1973,
1981). O'Gorman (1984) claims that my analysis is quite misleading. He suggests
that I have misinterpreted Eysenck's theory and the conditions under which it
can be confirmed or denied, have been biased in the selection of research studies,
and have misclassified them in terms of their arousing qualities. O'Gorman supports his arguments with a systematic meta-analysis of the research, using judges
of high inter-judge reliability to rate both the arousing properties of individual
studies and their quality. He concludes that the arousing properties of the testing conditions play a very minor role in determining outcome. Gale (1984)
attempts a rebuttal of O'Gorman's powerful challenge to my interpretation.

As an indication of the range of quality available in this research, we present
here a detailed report of three studies. Rösler (1975) presents the most sophisticated study to date. After reviewing the literature in some detail, he set
out predictions relating the EEG to both introversion-extraversion and neuroticism-
stability, in accordance with H. J. Eysenck's (1967) theory. Seven different task
conditions were used to vary subject involvement and stress; these included rest,
attentive listening, and mental calculations with and without stress. It is unfortunate that the tasks employed owe little to the theory except insofar as they
seem more appropriate to the testing of predictions concerning neuroticism-
stability rather than introversion-extraversion. Thirty-two university students
were used, and all completed several personality tests, amounting to 16 different
scales, including the Eysenck Personality Inventory, the Cattell 16PF, and several
scales of European origin. The use of multiple scales is unusual, and only
Pawlik and Cattell (1965) and Strelau and Terelak (1974) appear to have used
either multiple questionnaire measures or questionnaire measures combined with
objective tests. Most authors have been content with the single administration
of one questionnaire. Gale (1973) showed that after two administrations of the
Eysenck Personality Inventory, some subjects shifted criterion groups, changing
from introverts to extraverts in a matter of weeks. Rösler factor analyzed the
item scores to yield four factors, which he labeled emotional lability, extraversion, cyclothymia, and sociability; and he suggested that the second factor
reflects brainstem activating system activity. Eysenck's neuroticism-stability
loaded highly on the first factor (0.91) and introversion-extraversion on the
second factor (0.70), and there was a loading of -0.34 of introversion-extraversion
on factor 4. The EEG was recorded from a single-channel, digitized, subjected to
fast fourier transformation, and the frequency components which emerged then subjected to varimax rotation yielding four factors which accounted for almost 80%
of the variance. Rösler's treatment of the EEG data is the most elaborate available, although Gale, Coles, and Blaydon (1969) and Gale, Coles, Kline, and Penfold
(1971) presented findings for the traditionally measured range, broken down into
different bandwidths. Such an analysis allows for differentiation, in functional
terms, of the different frequency bands, although as yet it is not clear whether
the traditional frequency groupings have a meaning in psychological terms within
the waking state (Gale & Edwards, 1983; Schacter, 1977). Rösler computed analyses
of variance for each of the four frequency bands, varying extraversion, emotional
lability, and experimental treatments. The treatments yielded very high F ratios
in all cases, demonstrating that the EEG was sensitive to variation in psychological

conditions. Extraversion emerged as a main effect for 20-40 Herz (p < .05), gave modest interactions with experimental treatments for theta and alpha, and was significantly involved in a triple interaction with lability and situations for theta, showing that the difference between extraverts and introverts held only among the high lability (neurotic) group under the more stressful conditions of mental calculations with and without stress (p < .01). This latter finding is consistent with that of Savage (1964), where extraversion and neuroticism combined to give the highest alpha amplitudes. Rösler's study is rigorous and well planned and it must be disappointing that, given the power of the analysis employed, the findings in favor of Eysenck's theory and indeed in favor of our post hoc analysis are so modest. One of the difficulties with Rösler's design is the possibility of transfer effects between conditions, since subjects were tested on only one occasion. There is also a possibility of interaction between laboratory adaptation and task adaptation effects (discussed in a later section).

In contrast to the work of Rösler are the studies by Travis and his associates. Travis, Kondi, and Knott (1974) began with a highly selective review of the literature and then proceeded to measure alpha feedback trials and during the intertrial rests. Subjects with low neuroticism scores showed less alpha during feedback than did those with high scores. The EEG readings and introversion-extraversion were unrelated. What is remarkable about this study is that it ignored Eysenck's theory; gave no reason for believing that personality will relate to biofeedback or to the EEG, provided no evidence that changes in alpha amplitude over trials were in any way contingent on feedback, and attempted no explanation, even post hoc, either for the findings relating to neuroticism-stability or the null findings for introversion-extraversion. This, we would submit, is a good example of blind empiricism, and the authors' view that their technique "provides a new approach to the examination of relationships between EEG and personality traits" is surely no source of comfort. The study by Kondo, Bean, Travis, and Knott (1978) followed earlier studies in obtaining a resting sample of 5-minutes' duration from 60 subjects, sitting in a soundproofed cubicle, with eyes closed. Here the EEG related to introversion - extraversion (introverts being less aroused), but not to neuroticism-stability. The t tests for the two personality factors were computed separately rather than by a 2×2 design (qua Savage, 1964), and thus no attempt was made to partial out the effects of one scale score on the other. The authors made no attempt to relate their 1978 findings to their 1974 findings, which is, of course, puzzling in view of the discrepancies between them; one can be as selective about one's own work as one can be about the work of others. One consolation perhaps about this work is that the lack of theory guarantees that the results are authentic and unlikely to have been influenced by experimenter expectancy effects.

The recent study of O'Gorman and Mallise (1984) is of good quality, including retest reliability coefficients for EEG and personality scores, state scales to test for the arousing properties of different testing conditions, a large sample, and the use of correlational as well as extreme group statistical analysis. Unfortunately, although the study is entitled "a test of Gale's hypothesis," the conditions of testing employed owe little to Eysenck's theory nor to Gale's hypothesis; nevertheless, in one condition where Gale (1973) would predict an effect consistent with theory (an eyes open condition), O'Gorman and Mallise (1984) find extraverts to be more aroused! A detailed critique of the study is provided by Gale (1984).

SOME PROBLEMS OF MEASUREMENT

It has been suggested that samples employed in psychological research are not representative of the general population (Silverman, 1977). In some branches of research, this may not matter; however, in the case of personality studies, there are grounds for believing that the use of highly intelligent undergraduate populations might lead to undetected systematic interactions and other forms of confounding results. For example, to win a place in a British university, a student must overcome a number of hurdles; high attainment is achieved only by the development of systematic work habits, freedom from distraction and anxiety, and a high level of motivation. If extraversion and neuroticism are at their extremes deleterious for sustained and continuous study, then students who pass the examinations have acquired the skills necessary to counterbalance the influence of extreme personality tendencies. Students with high scores on these scales have made high achievements despite biological predispositions; thus they might not be ideal candidates for studies designed to demonstrate the effects of such traits. Some 80% of psychological research is conducted on about 3% of the population. In the United States, samples appear to be highly intelligent, middle-class, sophomore undergraduates who are enrolled in courses in psychology and participate in experiments as course requirements. Thus the student, apart from being a member of a special subsample, has a personal investment in the outcome of the experiment. Whether such factors account for much of the overall variance is difficult to demonstrate. However, in studies that involve so small a degree of stimulus control over the subject, as in the studies reviewed here, it seems likely that there is considerable opportunity for subject-borne error variance. Gale (1973) speculated about what goes on in the subject's mind in psychophysiological experiments and the possible consequences for outcome. We have already considered possible strategies employed by extraverted and introverted subjects in coping with the absence or excess of laboratory-based stimulation. We would urge experimenters in this field to draw on a wider subject base.

In our discussion of Rösler's study we pointed out that few experimenters have considered it worthwhile to administer a variety of questionnaire scales, or to combine these with objective or performance tests in order to assign subjects to criterion groups. It appears that even a minor adjustment to the response mode of tests like the Eysenck Personality Questionnaire can have effects on the factor structure that is subsequently derived. Carlier's chapter in Volume 1 of this work demonstrates the absolute necessity to use well-constructed and cross-validated tests. Retest reliability estimates for the questionnaire in use for the sample in question are essential; the EEG seems to be highly reliable (e.g., Gale, Harpham, & Lucas, 1972; Strelau & Terelak, 1974), and retest correlations often exceed 0.8. The chance of obtaining a reliable correlation with a personality measure, however, will clearly be diminished if that measure is not in itself particularly reliable. The partialling of extraversion scores on the basis of impulsivity and sociability items (as argued by Schalling and Åsberg in Volume 1 of this work) has proved of value on several occasions but, so far as we are aware, has never been performed in EEG studies. A discriminant analysis based on EEG, scale scores, performance scores, and subscales would certainly be worthwhile. It is clear that there is much room for improvement so far as the measurement of personality is concerned.

The measurement of EEGs in these studies begs a number of assumptions. First, EEG characteristics vary across the scalp and in their degree of correlation with personality factors (see Pawlik & Cattell, 1965), but most studies report data from only one channel of recording, even when more are used (e.g., Deakin & Exley, 1979). Even so, several different measures of the EEG are employed, including amplitude, frequency, percent time, index, rate of change of potential, mean dominant frequency, abundance, full fourier transform, delta, theta, alpha (sometimes divided into subfrequencies), beta, and very fast activity. There is no parametric study exploring the relationships between these different measures of cortical activity. Even where measures appear to be quite similar, there is no guarantee that different researchers are measuring the same thing. More recently, the burgeoning of EEG studies in relation to differential hemispheral

function makes simple measures of the EEG more questionable. One reason it is
important to include measures of task performance in these studies is that this
will enable the construction of systematic sets of data, plotting the relationships between the EEG, performance and personality, thus benefiting both EEG and
personality research.

In addition, a number of procedural problems must be tackled. The ideal experiment should be run blind, such that the experimenter does not know the subject's
personality score during recording or indeed during data analysis. If analysis
is done by hand, there is a particular opportunity for experimenters to be biased
in interpreting and selecting data. While automated analysis is always to be
preferred, it is possible, by a careful design and the use of scorer reliability
coefficients, to produce scrupulously objective data (e.g., Deakin & Exley, 1979).
It is likely that the experimenter who knows the personality score of the subject
and who understands H. J. Eysenck's theory is likely to behave differently with
different subjects. As Gale and Baker (1981) pointed out, the psychophysiological
experiment is a very special sort of social-psychological situation in which the
experimenter intrudes on the personal space of the subject, engages in touching,
frequently requests the removal of clothing, and requires passive compliance from
the subject. They suggest that the experimenter is likely to act in a more solic-
itous manner to subjects who are believed to have high-neuroticism or low-extra-
version scores. Such differential treatment may perhaps be a means of mediating
experimenter expectancy effects.

In his original discussion of this source of error, Rosenthal (1967) referred not
only to experimenter behavior but to experimenter attributes. Rumenik, Capasso,
and Hendrick (1977) reviewed studies of experimenter sex effects and concluded
that in certain areas of research there is powerful evidence for their influence.
In our own recent studies (Gale, Kingsley, Edwards, Porter & Smith, in preparation) we have found experimenter and subject effects to be more powerful than
personality in their influence on the EEG. Thus female subjects and female experimenters were found to be associated with higher EEG amplitudes; but there
were no interactions between sex and personality. We have evidence of experimenter sex effects on the EEG in only one experiment, whereas the subject sex
effect has appeared on more than half a dozen occasions. The ideal experiment
will employ several experimenters of each sex (to control for individual experimenter effects) and subjects of both sexes within a balanced design. Baker (1978)
obtained very persistent sex effects for both EEG and performance measures.

SOURCES OF AROUSAL IN THE PSYCHOLOGICAL LABORATORY

Arousal is a much abused and overused construct, and its explanatory power has
undergone inflationary trends over the years. Moreover, its logical status varies
from context to context. We have seen earlier, in considering H. J. Eysenck's
theory of the neurophysiological basis of personality, that arousal may be treated
as a trait; such use is also to be seen in psychopathology, in which arousal is
employed to account for aspects of schizophrenia, autism, psychopathy, and hyper-
activity. The term is also used to describe stimulus characteristics, as a correlate of circadian variation, as a state variable, as response to stimulation,
as a correlate or consequence of action, as a measure of intensity of action, or
as a drive or motivator of action. Does such ubiquitous use reflect the power
of the construct as a unifying principle, ranging from endogenous rhythms of the
body to aspects of social and group behavior, or does it merely reflect the tendency of psychologists to cling to simple-minded concepts?

So far as the present context is concerned, we believe that a model of sources
of arousal within the laboratory context is essential in the design of psychophysiological research. Gale (1977) set out a framework that enables us to plot

the course of arousal from the beginning to the end of the experiment. There are certain common features in the experimental procedures: the subject is recruited, makes his appointment, appears for the first time in the laboratory, is prepared for experimentation, receives instruction and explanation, undergoes the formal and explicit experimental procedures (which often involves learning), experiences some form of feedback on performance, finishes the experiment, and leaves. We wish to suggest that each stage within the sequential model may be associated with variations in the general level of subject arousal, apart from any trait-based arousal the subject brings to the laboratory. Thus we identify nine components for our laboratory arousal model: stable characteristics of the subject (the focus of the present review), cyclic rhythms, manner of recruitment, laboratory encounter, task acquisition, task mastery, task specific arousal, situational arousal, and feedback. Each of these elements is seen as a separate and identifiable source of subject arousal.

Now it is easy to see that these sources will be overlapping and interactive; as a consequence, the time at which physiological measurement is taken will influence the obtained result. Thus, for example, subjects with high trait arousal may take longer to overcome the effects of laboratory encounter. Spratt and Gale (1979) showed how schizophrenic subjects exhibited a significant change in EEG activity as a function of visits to the laboratory, whereas nonclinical controls showed no such effects. Thus sampling on only the first visit would have indicated massive trait differences between schizophrenics and normals, whereas the true picture was a significant interaction between trait and laboratory adaptation. To take another example, task specific arousal for vigilance tasks involves a decline in arousal with time, whereas listening to a funny story with a punch-line involves a monotonic increase. We suspect that in studies of introversion-extraversion and the EEG, subjects have indeed been sampled at different points in the sequence, particularly when records showing scoreable amounts of alpha activity are selected either for measurement and/or for the presentation of stimuli. These are possibly times when subjects are moving into a light sleep or at least becoming drowsy. Thus in low-arousing conditions, when the subject has nothing to do, and when extraverts become dearoused earlier in time by virtue of the interaction between trait arousal and situational arousal (the soundproof cubicle), even a strict sampling schedule could lead to misleading results. In the case of habituation studies, it has been demonstrated that stimulation after an initial habituation stage leads to dishabituation, as well as an increase in alpha abundance following the stimulus. Issues of this nature are part of what we call the microstructure of the experiment. If we believe that brain and behavior are intimately related, and if factors such as these are known to influence behavior, then if the EEG is a worthwhile measure of brain activity it should also be sensitive to the same sources of variation. We believe, therefore, that to conduct research in this field, the experimenter must have a much more explicit model of sources of arousal within the laboratory than is apparent from a scrutiny of existing studies.

SOCIAL PSYCHOLOGY AND THE PSYCHOLOGY EXPERIMENT

We have already made it clear that we believe the laboratory to be a rich source of stimulation and that such stimulation is appraised by the subject in terms of its arousing or dearousing properties. We have seen that the soundproof room may be a source of comfort to the introvert but a source of irritation to the extravert. We considered very briefly some of the theoretical viewpoints which have a bearing on the laboratory situation and in some cases were explicitly concerned with notions of arousal, activation, or anxiety.

Zajonc's (1965) theory of social facilitation theory is of particular relevance because it accounted for differences in behavior when the individual is alone

or in the presence of others. Other persons are said to be arousing, and the
arousal which another person induces in the individual acts on that individual's
behavior in the manner of a Hull-Spence-type drive. Thus simple and well-
established tasks are facilitated by the increased arousal the presence of
others induces, while complex and novel tasks are disrupted, because they are
themselves arousing and the additional increment in arousal pushes the individual's
level beyond the optimum. Clearly the laboratory presents a novel and challenging
environment, and the presence of the experimenter adds to the subject's arousal.
Thus the laboratory situation is potentially both disruptive and deleterious for
the performance of complex tasks; arousal under such conditions will elicit
higher probability responses, and these are those associated with old learning
rather than new learning. Over and above such allegedly biological effects are
responses related to the subject's cognitive appraisal of the laboratory. Thus
Rosenberg (1969) used the term "evaluation apprehension" to describe the person's
anxiety about what others might think of him or her. Combined with such anxiety
is the subject's concern over the true purpose of the experiment. Orne (1962)
argued that the subject searches to find meaning in the laboratory and is strongly
motivated to determine why the experimenter has brought him there. The subject
creates a hypothesis on the basis of what he perceives to be the "demand characteristics" of the situation and then sets out to validate that hypothesis.
Similarly, it is suggested by attribution theorists that we seek to explain the
other person's behavior.

Notions of this sort help us to illuminate studies of introversion-extraversion
and the EEG, for the psychophysiological laboratory is in many aspects threatening
and ambiguous at one and the same time, and the instructions given to subjects in
these studies are conducive to a variety of interpretations on the subject's
part, because rarely do they call for specific behaviors. From this it follows
that the experimental paradigms employed should have face validity for the subject. We have suggested elsewhere that subjects in these experiments are often
treated as stimulus-response lumps; but such a notion conflicts with contemporary
views of perception and cognition, which see the individual as constantly interpreting and acting on his environment.

Thus we see that there are several theories available to assist us in the characterization of the psychology experiment. The good experimenter will apply
psychological knowledge to the devising and interpretation of his own experiments.

PROSPECTS

In this brief review of studies designed to measure the relationship between
introversion-extraversion and the spontaneous rhythms of the brain, we see that
a number of errors have been committed. Studies are conducted in ignorance of
theory; even when theory is used, its full implications are not realized; subjects
are selected from a narrow range of the population; allocation to criterion groups
is based on limited information about personality; the EEG is measured in a variety of unrelated ways; subject performance is rarely measured or reported, and
the procedures used leave much to chance. Several studies are also subject to
criticism on grounds of abuse of statistical treatments and faulty interpretation
of outcome; see Henry and Knott (1941) for a reworking of the Gottlober (1938)
data. Results have been misinterpreted either by authors themselves (Savage,
1964) or by other authorities; see Eysenck's reversal of Mundy-Castle's (1955)
data, Eysenck (1953).

Nevertheless, when all is said and done, and in spite of all these deficiencies,
there appears to be some ground for optimism. Several studies of good quality
have demonstrated relations between alpha amplitude and extraversion in the direction predicted by theory. The problem now is whether there should be a change

of direction in the work, for yet more studies of the same variety are unlikely to take us nearer to the truth.

H. J. Eysenck's theory was designed to explain differences in behavior between extraverts and introverts; it is, therefore, rather perverse of researchers to deny the subject the opportunity to behave. We suggest that, in future studies, the EEG of subjects be monitored while they perform tasks. The tasks selected should be those that are already associated with a systematic body of data and that have been shown to yield differences in performance for extraverts and introverts. We have devised in our laboratory a number of variants on such tasks in a form that allows for EEG monitoring of the subject and the plotting of EEG relations with performance.

One of the potentially richest seams for research along these lines is the study of memorial processes, since this allows for a rapprochement between studies of individual differences and a vital area of experimental psychology. Michael Eysenck (1977) reviewed such studies, within the framework of contemporary theorizing about memory. Earlier, Howarth and Eysenck (1968) had demonstrated that extraversion has beneficial effects for short-term recall and deleterious effects for recall in the longer term, compared with introversion. The rationale for this is Walker's theory of consolidation of the memory trace (Walker, 1968). Just after learning, the trace is protected as it is laid down. High arousal protects the trace from interference, while low arousal allows access to it. Thus extraverts may gain access in the short term, whereas in introverts the trace is protected and therefore available, undisturbed, for subsequent recall. In our own studies (Gale, Jones, & Smallbone, 1974) we have shown how the EEG is affected systematically as material is presented for immediate recall. In our first experiment, low arousal (as measured by EEG abundance) was negatively correlated with error prior to the experiment, during the presentation of material, and during early trials when general error rate was higher. In view of performance studies demonstrating differences in memory for extraverts and introverts, we consider the paradigm used by Gale, Jones, and Smallbone to be appropriate for exploring the relationship between personality and the EEG, although our more recent studies (Jones, Gale, & Smallbone, 1979) indicate that one needs to take into account the interactive effects of personality, experimental instruction, and learning.

Another field of research in which concepts of arousal have been operationalized by measurement of peripheral autonomic and cortical functions, and where performance differences have been found in relation to introversion-extraversion, is sustained attention or vigilance. Here the EEG studies present a varied picture, and findings are not altogether robust, although this is in part due to an over-inclusion of too many different tasks under the notion of vigilance. In these tasks, monotony is said to induce a state of drowsiness, which is deleterious for performance, and which occurs earlier in extraverts, given their initially low level of arousal. Factors that increase arousal, such as the presence of others, performance at later times in the day, and the availability of additional stimulation, are all seen to improve the performance of the extraverted subject. A volume drawing together much of the theory and empirical work on vigilance is presented by Mackie (1977). Our own studies, reported in that volume (Gale, 1977), show changes in the EEG as a function of time, the rate of signal presentation, and fluctuations in the cue value of individual stimuli. There are indeed many EEG studies and, more recently, event-related potential studies of sustained performance (Parasuraman, 1983).

Some of our earlier studies explored the relationship between stimulus complexity and EEG responses, following the pioneering work of Berlyne (1960). In a number of studies, EEG amplitude was shown to vary as a function of the number and variety of elements in a visual display; moreover, such fluctuation relates to a signal detection measure of stimulus recognition in a posttest. This paradigm has been used with some success in the comparison of schizophrenic and control groups and their EEG responses to stimuli of varying complexity (Spratt & Gale, 1979). Given the evidence that extraverts, when in a state of mild sensory deprivation, will take the opportunity to seek additional stimulation (Gale, 1969), it would be worth studying EEG changes during deprivation and during access to stimulation, varying the arousal potential of the stimulation systematically. One may predict differences in the cumulative record of sensation-seeking responses between introverts and extraverts, paralleled by EEG changes in arousal and dearousal.

Finally, we have recently explored EEG correlates of social interaction, varying factors like prior acquaintance of subjects, interpersonal distance, competition, and eye contact. The two theoretical frameworks used are the social facilitation theory of Zajonc (1965) and the social intimacy theory of Argyle and Dean (1965). Such studies are appropriate in the present context, both because extraversion is in so many senses defined in terms of social behavior, and because there have been demonstrations of the effects of presence of others on task performance (Colquhoun & Corcoran, 1964). Such studies also provide a context for exploring the differential effects of sociability and impulsivity on the EEG and social behavior.

Clearly, in all these studies there are complex problems of design and interpretation; however, such factors are determined ante hoc by virtue of the theoretical and empirical underpinnings of the paradigms employed, rather than the ill-considered procedures that characterize the existing studies of introversion-extraversion and the EEG.

CONCLUSION

Our firm recommendation to those who wish to study the relationship between extraversion-introversion and the EEG is to cast aside the practices employed in the past. In particular, we recommend that personality be measured in a variety of ways and in a fashion that guarantees reliability of personality score; the EEG should not be treated as some gross measure of cortical arousal, detectable from a brief sample, derived from a single channel of recording. Testing situations should reflect the full implications of the theory and draw on contemporary research into performance differences in relation to personality.

The brain is complex. Behavior is complex. Personality is complex. Simple-minded experiments are unlikely to reveal the rich web of relationships between the brain, behavior, and personality.

REFERENCES

Argyle, M., & Dean, J. (1965). Eye contact, distance and affiliation. Sociometry, 28, 289-304.

Baker, S. M. (1978). Social facilitation, coaction and performance. Doctoral thesis, University of Wales.

Becker-Carus, C. H. (1971). Relationships between EEG, personality and vigilance. Electroencephalography and Clinical Neurophysiology, 30, 519-526.

Berlyne, D. E. (1960). Conflict, arousal and curiosity. New York: McGraw-Hill.

Broadhurst, A., & Glass, A. (1969). Relationship of personality measures to the Alpha rhythm of the electroencephalogram. British Journal of Psychiatry, 115, 199–204.

Claridge, G. S., & Herrington, R. N. (1963). An EEG correlate of the Archimedes spiral after-effect and its relationship with personality. Behavior Research and Therapy, 1, 217–219.

Colquhoun, W. P., & Corcoran, D. W. J. (1964). The effects of time of day and social isolation on the relationship between temperament and performance. British Journal of Social and Clinical Psychology, 3, 226–231.

Deakin, J. F. W., & Exley, K. A. (1979). Personality and male–female influences on the EEG alpha rhythm. Biological Psychology, 8, 285–290.

Eysenck, H. J. (1953). The structure of human personality. London: Methuen.

Eysenck, H. J. (1967). The biological basis of personality. Springfield: Charles C Thomas.

Eysenck, H. J. (1971). (Ed.). Readings in extraversion–introversion. Vol. 3. Bearings on basic psychological processes. London: Staples.

Eysenck, M. W. (1977). Human memory: Theory, research, and individual differences. Oxford: Pergamon.

Fenton, G. W., and Scotton, L. (1967). Personality and the alpha rhythm. British Journal of Psychiatry, 113, 1283–1289.

Gale, A. (1969). "Stimulus hunger": Individual differences in operant strategy in a button pressing task. Behaviour Research and Therapy, 7, 265–174.

Gale, A. (1973). The psychophysiology of individual differences: Studies of extraversion and the EEG. In P. Kline (Ed.), New approaches in psychological measurement. London: Wiley.

Gale, A. (1977). Some EEG correlates of sustained attention. In R. R. Mackie (Ed.), Vigilance: Theory, operational performance and physiological correlates. New York: Plenum.

Gale, A. (1981). EEG studies of extraversion–introversion: What's the next step? In R. Lynn (Ed.), Dimensions of personality: Essays in honour of H. J. Eysenck. Oxford: Pergamon.

Gale, A. (1983). Electroencephalographic studies of extraversion–introversion: A case study in the psychophysiology of individual differences. Personality and Individual Differences, 4, 371–380.

Gale, A. (1984). O'Gorman versus Gale: A reply. Biological Psychology (in press).

Gale, A., & Baker, S. (1981). In vivo or in vitro? Some effects of laboratory environments, with particular reference to the psychophysiology experiment. In M. J. Christie & P. Mellett (Eds.), Foundations of psychosomatics. London: Wiley.

Gale, A., Coles, M. G. H., & Blaydon, J. (1969). Extraversion–introversion and the EEG. British Journal of Psychology, 60, 209–223.

Gale, A., Coles, M. G. H., Kline, P., & Penfold, V. (1971). Extraversion-
   introversion, neuroticism and the EEG: Basal and response measures during
   habituation of the orienting response. British Journal of Psychology, 62,
   533-548.

Gale, A., & Edwards, J. A. (1983a). The EEG and human behavior. In A. Gale and
   J. A. Edwards (Eds.), Physiological correlates of human behaviour. Volume II.
   Attention and performance. London: Academic Press.

Gale, A., & Edwards, J. A. (1983b). Psychophysiology and individual differences:
   Theory, research procedures, and the interpretation of data. Australian
   Journal of Psychology, 35, 361-379.

Gale, A., & Edwards, J. A. (1984). Individual differences. In M. G. H. Coles,
   E. Donchin, & D. W. Porges (Eds.), Psychophysiology: Systems, processes, and
   applications. New York: Guilford.

Gale, A., Harpham, B., & Lucas, B. (1972). Time of day and the EEG: Some negative
   results. Psychonomic Science, 28, 269-271.

Gale, A., Jones, D. M., & Smallbone, A. (1974). Short term memory and the EEG.
   Nature, 248, 439.

Gale, A., Kingsley, E., Edwards, J. A., Porter, J., & Smith, D. Sex of subject
   and sex of experimenter effects upon the EEG. (Manuscript).

Gilliland, K., Andress, D., & Bracy, S. Differences in EEG alpha index between
   extraverts and introverts. (Unpublished manuscript, 1981).

Glass, A., & Broadhurst, A. (1966). Relationship between EEG as a measure of
   cortical activity and personality measures. Electroencephalography and
   Clinical Neurophysiology, 21, 309.

Gottlober, A. (1938). The relationship between brain potentials and personality.
   Journal of Experimental Psychology, 22, 67-74.

Henry, L. E., & Knott, J. R. (1941). A note on the relationship between "personality" and the alpha rhythm of the electroencephalogram. Journal of Experimental Psychology, 28, 362-366.

Howarth, E., & Eysenck, H. J. (1968). Extraversion, arousal, and paired associate
   recall. Journal of Experimental Research in Personality, 3, 114-116.

Hume, W. I. (1968). The dimensions of central nervous arousal. Bulletin of the
   British Psychological Society, 21, 111.

Irmis, F. (1979). EEG correlates of vigility and dimensions of neuroticism and
   extraversion. Activ. Nerv. Sup. (Praha), 21, 56-57.

Jackson, D. N., & Paunonen, S. V. (1980). Personality structure and assessment.
   Annual Review of Psychology, 31, 503-552.

Jones, D., Gale, A., & Smallbone, A. (1979). Short term recall of nine-digit
   strings and the EEG. British Journal of Psychology, 70, 97-119.

Kondo, C. Y., Bean, J. A., Travis, T. A., & Knott, J. R. (1978). Resting levels
   of alpha and the Eysenck Personality Inventory. British Journal of Psychiatry,
   132, 378-380.

Lemere, F. (1936). The significance of individual differences in the Berger rhythm. Brain, 59, 366–375.

McAdam, W., & Orme, J. E. (1954). Personality traits and the normal electro-encephalogram. Journal of Mental Science, 100, 913–921.

Mackie, R. R. (1977). (Ed.). Vigilance: Theory, operational performance, and physiological correlates. New York: Plenum.

Marton, M., & Urban, I. (1966). An electroencephalographic investigation of individual differences in the processes of conditioning. Proceedings of the 18th International Congress of Psychology, Moscow, 9, 106–109.

Montgomery, P. S. (1975). EEG alpha as an index of hysteroid and obsessoid personalities. Psychological Reports, 36, 431–436.

Morris, P. E., & Gale, A. (1974). A correlational study of variables related to imagery. Perceptual and Motor Skills, 38, 659–665.

Mundy-Castle, A. C. (1955). The relationship between primary-secondary function and the alpha rhythm of the electroencephalogram. Journal of the National Institute of Personnel Research, 6, 95–102.

Nebylitsyn, V. D. (1963). An electro-encephalographic investigation of the properties of strength of the nervous system and equilibrium of the nervous processes in man using factor analysis. In B. M. Teplov (Ed.), Typological features of higher nervous activity in man. Moscow: Acad. Pedagog. Nauk. R.S.F. R.S.F.S.R., 3, 47–80.

O'Gorman, J. G. (1984). Extraversion and the EEG. I. An evaluation of Gale's hypothesis. Biological Psychology (in press).

O'Gorman, J. G., & Mallise, L. R. (1984). Extraversion and the EEG. II. A test of Gale's hypothesis. Biological Psychology (in press).

Orne, M. T. (1962). On the social psychology of the psychology experiment: With particular reference to demand characteristics and their implications. American Psychologist, 17, 776–783.

Parasuraman, R. (1983). Vigilance, arousal, and the brain. In A. Gale & J. A. Edwards (Eds.), Physiological correlates of human behaviour. Volume II. Attention and performance. London: Academic Press.

Pawlik, K., & Cattell, R. B. (1965). The relationship between certain personality factors and measures of cortical arousal. Neuropsychologia, 3, 129–151.

Rosenberg, M. L. (1969). The conditions and consequences of evaluation apprehension. In R. Rosenthal & R. Rosnow (Eds.), Artifact in psychological research. New York: Academic Press.

Rosenthal, R. (1967). Covert communication in the psychological experiment. Psychological Bulletin, 67, 357–367.

Rosenthal, R., & Rubin, D. B. (1978). Interpersonal expectancy effects: The first 345 studies. Behavioural and Brain Sciences, 3, 377–415.

Rösler, F. (1975). Die abhangigkeit des elektroenzephalogramms von den personlich-keitdimensionen E und N sensu Eysenck und unterschiedlich aktivierenden situationen. Zeitschrift fur Experimentelle und Angewandte Psychologie, 12, 630–667.

Rumenik, D. K., Capasso, D. R., & Hendrick, C. (1977). Experimenter sex effects in behavioral research. Psychological Bulletin, 84, 852-877.

Savage, R. D. (1964). Electro-cerebral activity, extraversion and neuroticism. British Journal of Psychiatry, 110, 98-100.

Schacter, D. (1977). EEG theta waves and psychological phenomena: A review and analysis. Biological Psychology, 5, 47-82.

Shagass, C., & Kerenyi, A. B. (1958). Neurophysiological studies of personality. Journal of Nervous and Mental Diseases, 126, 141-147.

Silverman, I. (1977). The human subject in the psychological laboratory. New York: Pergamon.

Spratt, G. S., & Gale, A. (1979). An EEG study of visual attention in schizophrenic patients and normal controls. Biological Psychology, 9, 249-269.

Strelau, J., & Terelak, J. (1974). The alpha-index in relation to temperamental traits. Studia Psychologica, 16, 40-50.

Travis, T. A., Kondo, C. Y., & Knott, J. R. (1974). Personality variables and alpha enhancement. British Journal of Psychiatry, 124, 542-544.

Venturini, R., de Pascalis, U., Imperiali, M. G., & San Martini, P. (1981). EEG alpha reactivity and extraversion-introversion. Personality and Individual Differences, 2, 215-220.

Walker, E. L. (1968). Action decrement and its relation to learning. Psychological Review, 65, 129-142.

Winter, K., Broadhurst, A., & Glass, A. (1972). Neuroticism, extraversion, and EEG amplitude. Journal of Experimental Research in Personality, 6, 44-51.

Young, J. P. R., Lader, M. H., & Fenton, G. W. (1971). The relationship of extraversion and neuroticism to the EEG. British Journal of Psychiatry, 119, 667-670.

Zajonc, R. B. (1965). Social facilitation. Science, 149, 269-274.

2

Typology of Mental Activity as a Temperamental Trait and the Level of Activation of the Nervous System

M. V. Bodunov

The nature of human activity is one of the most important problems in contemporary psychology. In a general methodological sense, the notion of activity is intimately related to such psychological concepts as need, cognition, and action, which constitute a system permitting explicit determination of the real meaning of active, creative human existence. In many concrete psychological investigations, activity is considered as a substantial characteristic of individuality; in this aspect, it is a cardinal component of temperament and abilities (Leytes, 1971; Nebylitsyn, 1976).

The notion of activity as a temperamental trait plays an important role in differential psychophysiology at its current state of development. This role is determined by evolution of notions about general properties of the nervous system as integral characteristics of its functioning and about temperament and general intelligence, in the works of Nebylitsyn (1976) and Leytes (1971, 1972). According to Nebylitsyn, the study of neurophysiological determinants of integral individual characteristics (among them activity) is the most efficient approach to the solution of the problem of integrative parameters of brain functioning as a whole.

It is generally acknowledged that activity is a characteristic of individuality that appears as an inner condition of interaction between subject and environment and, at the same time, as a qualitative and quantitative measure of this interaction from the point of view of its dynamic tension. It is this conception of activity that was accepted in differential psychophysiology and elaborated in the work of Leytes (1972), Nebylitsyn (1976), Nebylitsyn and Krupnov (1972), Nebylitsyn and Mozgovoy (1972), Kadyrov (1976), as well as in the investigations of a number of other authors (Eliasz, 1974; Heymans & Wiersma, 1909; Guilford, 1959; Strelau, 1974).

Within this context, general activity as one of the internal conditions of performance reflects the subject's tendency "towards efficient assimilation of external reality, towards self-expression with respect to the external world" (Nebylitsyn, 1976, p. 251).

Nebylitsyn identified three levels in this individual dimension of "activity": mental, motor, and social -- the difference between them being determined by the aspect of realization of the given tendency. General activity, for Nebylitsyn, comprises those individual qualities that correspond to the concept of "dynamic" features of personality, constituting a continuum "from inertness and passive meditation ... to higher levels of energy manifestation" (Nebylitsyn, 1976, p. 178).

43

In concrete differential psychophysiological research, activity is defined as a general personality characteristic expressing a person's natural striving for increased and diversified load in mental and psychomotor spheres.

As an integral parameter of individuality, activity has two closely related aspects: the content aspect and the dynamic aspect. The content aspect is determined by a complex of operating motives, sets, interests, and intentions underlying performance of some or other actions. The dynamic aspect is characterized by such formal parameters as tempo, tension, and the distribution of actions in time.

The object of differential psychophysiological research into activity is its formal-dynamic aspect only because, according to one of the founders of Soviet differential psychophysiology (Teplov, 1961), the basic properties of the nervous system mostly affect the dynamic characteristics of activity.

Activity is one of the mediating links due to which the naturally determined properties of the nervous system find their expression at the psychodynamic level, particularly in temperament and general intelligence. Activity serves as a common component by which the interaction is brought about between temperament and abilities (Teplov, 1961).

There is a good reason to consider activity as one of the intermediate variables involved in mutual regulation of behavioral dynamics and the level of activation of the nervous system; moreover, activity mediates the dependence of the processing aspect of a person's behavior on the optimum characteristic level of activation (Strelau, 1974).

The main task in the present study of differential psychophysiology is the analysis of relationships between a person's stable properties of the formal-dynamic aspect of activity and integral EEG characteristics reflecting different parameters of nervous system activation. A comparison of these two sets of data permits us not only to determine the place of systemic parameters of brain functioning in the structure of factors that affect interindividual differences in activity, but also to define more accurately our notions about the neurophysiological nature of general properties of the nervous system.

This chapter discusses such matters as the component structure of the formal-dynamic characteristics of activity, factor composition of integral EEG indicators of activation, and the relationship between the main aspects of processing characteristics of activity and integral activation factors.

FORMAL-DYNAMIC ASPECT OF ACTIVITY

The study of the neurophysiological basis of activity is at its initial stage. At present, only a few investigations have been devoted to an analysis of relationships between indexes of activity and EEG parameters reflecting peculiarities of nervous system activation (Kadyrov, 1976; Krupnov, 1970; Mozgovoy, 1973). Previous work conducted in this field is, however, characterized by a number of serious shortcomings. First, different levels of activity were analyzed in isolation. Second, activity was viewed in a simplified manner as a syndrome of a number of indexes and evaluated summarily by the characteristics of speed, tendency to tensed actions, and variety seeking.

This type of evaluation of activity was perhaps justified at the earliest stages of research; at present, however, the further study of the psychological content of activity requires a more detailed consideration.

Data accumulated recently show rather complicated relationships between such aspects of activity as individual tempo, inclination for tensed actions, and variety seeking. For example, Alexander (1935), Furneaux (1960), Ryans (1938), and Payne (1960) found no significant relationships between indexes of persistence and the speed characteristics of mental operations. These as well as other findings enable one to make an assumption about the relative independence of the main dynamic aspects of activity, thus testifying to the multidimensional nature of this individual parameter.

The elaboration of the problem of relationships between different aspects of activity with the purpose of specifying notions about its structure is one of the main tasks of the present work. With this aim in view, we have used procedures permitting us to characterize and quantitatively evaluate individual stable peculiarities of three main aspects of activity: individual tempo, inclination for tensed actions, and variety seeking.

Individual tempo of mental actions was evaluated by speed characteristics in the solving of nonverbal Cattell tasks and some manipulatory tasks from the Marburg game. The subject's inclination for prolonged mental tension was assessed by the following indexes: time of searching for the solution of an unsolvable task from the Marburg game, time of searching for the goal in an unsolvable version of the "confused lines" maze, the number of refusals to continue to solve Marburg tasks, and the average time preceding the refusal to continue the solution of tasks.

The tendency to diversity and novelty (variety seeking) was evaluated with the following indexes: variability of ways of moving through the maze and the number of refusals to attempt to solve the task from the Marburg game by the second way.

Individual tempo of psychomotor actions was characterized by the indexes of tapping frequency, simple motor reaction time, and handwriting speed. To evaluate the inclination for psychomotor tension, we used indexes of stability of maximum tapping frequency under continuous tapping conditions, as well as the number of responses to a stimulus the response to which was not obligatory by instruction.

Fifty subjects were employed in our experiments. The sample was divided into two groups to check the stability of the factor structure of the dynamic aspects of activity.

The results of investigations of relationships among indexes of activity with the aid of factor analysis (principal components, varimax rotation) using the first group of subjects showed a relative independence of main aspects of activity. The following aspects of dynamic characteristics of activity were identified: speed underlying the individual tempo of mental tempo; ergonic (from Greek "ergon," work), characterizing the inclination for tension in performance; and variety seeking, manifesting itself in the tendency to diversity and novelty. In psychomotor activity two aspects -- speed and ergonic -- were identified.

To verify the interindividual stability of the obtained structure of activity, a factor analysis of intercorrelations between the same indexes obtained in the second group of subjects was carried out. The structure of the factor matrix in this second group of subjects coincided to a considerable extent with that of the first group. Thus the findings show that identified aspects of activity are in reality linearly independent and stable subdimensions.

Bearing in mind that nonlinear relationships are possible between these subdimensions of activity, we have selected from each aspect of activity one index;

for all the pairs of the parameters, we made up contingency tables (3×3). The estimation of dependence of subjects' classification by the selected indexes was carried out by χ^2 test. A tendency to a U-shaped relationship between individual tempo of mental activity and variety seeking was found $(\chi^2 = 11.12 > \chi^2_{0.05} = 9.49)$. In this case, the individuals with average usual speed of mental actions were characterized by a well-pronounced tendency to variety seeking as compared with those with low and high speed. The application of χ^2 tests for evaluation of dependence of classifications of subjects by other pairs of indexes belonging to different aspects of activity did not reveal significant correlations between them.

The data obtained herein are in good agreement with quite a number of findings about the relative independence of similar aspects of psychodynamics (Eysenck, 1963; Furneaux, 1960; MacArthur, 1955; Rimoldi, 1951) and permit us to conclude that the component of temperament in question -- activity -- is a complex multidimensional parameter, the structure of which is formed by a number of relatively independent but interacting aspects or subdimensions.

The research into physiological bases of interindividual variability of activity requires the solution of two main tasks; the first is connected with the search for physiological factors affecting each aspect in particular and determining their relative independence, and the second task consists of identifying those peculiarities of nervous system functioning that underlie the establishment of certain types of interactions between different aspects of activity. To solve these tasks, we have compared the indexes of identified aspects of activity with the wide range of background EEG characteristics reflecting different aspects of nervous system activation and peculiarities of spatio-temporal synchronization of EEG processes from different regions of the brain. According to Russalov (1979) these characteristics of brainwide integration of nervous processes can be considered as indicators of general properties of the nervous system.

FACTOR-ANALYTIC STUDY OF EEG PARAMETERS OF ACTIVATION

The EEG parameters reflecting the peculiarities of activation of the brain were factor analyzed as a necessary intermediate stage of our work, with the purpose of identifying general brain neurodynamic factors.

We have applied modern techniques of spectrum analysis of background EEG processes, permitting an objective quantitative estimation of frequency and energy characteristics of EEG rhythms as well as the level of phase coherence of bioelectrical processes from different regions of the brain. Biopotentials were recorded monopolarly in frontal and occipital regions of the right hemisphere (F_4 and O_2).

In our investigation, we used the values of peak frequencies in autospectral and cross-spectral power density as well as the corresponding values of spectral densities and functions of coherence in standard EEG bands. We analyzed 36 EEG parameters: by five values of peak frequencies for autospectra from frontal and occipital derivations and of the module of cross-spectrum in standard bands, as well as by five values of spectral densities corresponding to these selected peak frequencies and also the level of overall synchronization with five values of coherence function in delta-, theta-, alpha-, beta-1, and beta-2 bands.

As a result of factor analysis (principal components) of these 36 parameters, four main factors were identified. The first factor (F-1) included, with statistically significant loadings, indexes of delta-rhythm energy in both derivations, delta- and theta-rhythm energy in cross-spectral density, as well

as, with the reversed sign, the indexes of alpha-rhythm energy in occipital
derivation and in the cross-spectrum. The second (F-2) consisted of the indexes
of delta-rhythm peak frequencies in both derivations and delta- and theta-rhythm
peak frequencies in the cross-spectrum, as well as the value of coherence function
in beta-2 band. The third factor (F-3) combined frequency and energy indexes of
beta-2 rhythm in both derivations as well as the value of dominant alpha-rhythm
frequency corresponding to the maximum cross-spectral density in alpha-rhythm
band. Finally, a fourth factor (F-4) comprised the indexes of synchronization
and coherence in delta-, theta-, alpha-, and beta-1 bands.

Thus, in the present work, as a result of the factor analysis of intercorrelations
between EEG parameters of two main functional blocks of the brain (regulation and
information processing), the following general brain EEG factors were identified:
slow-wave rhythm energy, slow-wave rhythm frequency, fast-wave (beta-2) rhythm
energy, and frequency and spatio-temporal concordance of bioelectrical activity.

These general brain EEG parameters characterize, on the one hand, peculiarities
of intercentral relations in the cortex (Aslanov, Gavrilova, Monakhov, Solugub,
& Krizman, 1973; Livanov, 1972; Russinov, Grindel, & Boldyveva, 1975) and, on
the other, different aspects of activation of the nervous system as a whole
(Golubyeva, Izyumova, Trubníkova, & Pechenkov, 1974; Kogan, 1962; Livanov, Thrush,
Efremova, & Potulova, 1974; Roytbek, 1975; Yanson, 1973). At the same time, the
combination of EEG slow-wave high energy, with a decreased level of spatio-
temporal concordance, may refer to a low level of nervous system activation.
The absence of slow waves in EEG spectrum, the presence of alpha-rhythm together
with fast rhythms, and the high level of spatio-temporal EEG synchronization
may in totality characterize a high level of brain activation. Other combinations of the identified factors may describe intermediate levels of activation.

Taking into consideration the general brain character of the four factors, we
can assume that these factors reflect essential features of the process of
interaction of different regions of the brain and, therefore, in Russalov's view
(1979), are indicators of some hypothetical general properties of the nervous
system as a whole. Identified integral EEG factors, given their close connection
with processing aspects of behavior (for example, with such components of temperament as activity), are likely to be regarded as electrophysiological indicators
of general properties of the nervous system.

With the purpose of specifying our notions about the nature of classical (partial)
properties of the nervous system, we have conducted a comparison of the identified
EEG factors with the strength and lability of the auditory and visual analyzers.
Data obtained strongly suggest that the indicators of strength (the slope of line
reflecting the dependence of motor reaction time on stimulus intensity -- the
indicator of strength suggested by Nebylitsyn) do not constitute a single characteristic of the nervous system and reflect only partial aspects of brain functioning. On the other hand, the indexes of lability, which demonstrated a close
interrelationship and entered the factor of spatio-temporal concordance of EEG
processes, are likely to be essential indicators of individual stable peculiarities of brain integrative activity determining, in Livanov's (1973) view,
the level of functional lability of the nervous system as a whole.

RELATIONSHIPS BETWEEN FACTOR STRUCTURE OF ACTIVITY
AND INTEGRAL EEG PARAMETERS OF ACTIVATION

At the third, conclusive stage of our work, we have analyzed relationships
between indexes of the formal-dynamic aspects of activity and the identified
EEG factors that reflect peculiarities of functioning of the whole nervous
system. The central task of our investigation was a more detailed identification

of complexes and combinations of integral features of nervous organization that have effects on interindividual variability of formal-dynamic aspects of activity and favor the formation of individual styles of activity. An analysis was undertaken of relationships between the four factors of the EEG parameters and the indexes of activity.

We have selected for comparisons with indexes of activity 20 EEG parameters that had the greatest loadings and therefore best represented the four factors of the EEG indexes. This reduction in the number of bioelectrical indexes permitted us to shorten the amount of calculations to a considerable extent without distorting significantly the information about the factor composition of EEG parameters. For comparison with EEG parameters, we have also chosen a portion of psycho-dynamic indexes representing the factor structure of activity. The investigation of relationships between physiological and psychological indexes was carried out with the aid of correlation and factor analysis.

The results of our investigation not only confirmed the data on the relative independence of the main aspects of activity, but also revealed the functional meaning of the EEG factors in their possible determination of different aspects of activity. It was found that the speed aspect of intellectual activity (as well as some complex psychomotor indexes, e.g., handwriting speed) was positively related to spatio-temporal concordance of bioelectrical processes of different regions of the brain. The ergonic aspect of intellectual and psychomotor activity correlated negatively with slow-wave EEG-rhythm energy. The speed aspect of psychomotor activity was negatively related to slow-wave EEG-rhythm frequency. Finally, the variety-seeking aspect of activity showed a positive correlation with frequency of slow-wave EEG rhythm. The results of factor analysis of the indexes of activity and bioelectrical parameters are given in Tables 1 and 2.

The striking fact of our investigation was that some EEG factors demonstrated relationships simultaneously with several aspects of activity, sometimes belonging to its different domains. This seems to testify to the fact that physiological factors underlying the identified constellations of EEG parameters not only determine a relative independence of main aspects of activity, but also form a basis of relationships between them.

Our findings showed that parameters of spatio-temporal concordance of EEG processes are positively related to the speed aspect of intellectual activity (and some complex psychomotor indexes) and negatively related (data from correlation analysis) to the tendency to diversity. One may assume that the highest level of interaction between main blocks of brain-system organization determining functional lability of the nervous system exerts a positive influence on the speed aspect of activity and apparently hampers manifestation of the tendency to diversity and novelty. Thus the quickness of actualization of formed mental skills underlying the speed aspect of intellectual activity is ensured through close linkage of different regions of the brain. On the other hand, the ease of change of stereotypes determining the extent of the variability aspect of activity is most likely related to such an interaction of the brain functionally specific formations that is characterized by a certain degree of flexibility. Data obtained show that one of the factors causing reciprocal relations between the speed and variability aspects of activity is their reverse dependence on the peculiarities of leveling off functional states of different regions of the human cortex.

As distinct from the speed and variability aspects of activity, its third relatively independent aspect -- ergonic -- showed a negative relationship with the other EEG factor that combined indexes of slow-wave EEG rhythms. The existence

TABLE 1. Factor structure of EEG parameters and indexes of mental activity (after rotation)

Index	Factors				h^2
	F-3	F-4	F-1	F-2	
1	2	3	4	5	6
Speed of solving Cattell's tasks	0.106	0.537*	-0.243	-0.315	0.462
Speed of solving Marburg tasks	0.147	0.715*	-0.002	-0.002	0.535
Duration of solving unsolvable tasks	0.250	-0.126	0.550*	-0.108	0.391
Number of refusals from solving	-0.286	0.153	-0.671*	-0.021	0.562
Number of tactics of solving the maze	0.339	-0.153	-0.153	-0.667*	0.617
Number of refusals from solving tasks by the second way	0.036	-0.285	-0.196	-0.731*	0.654
Delta-rhythm energy, F_4	-0.056	-0.035	-0.715*	0.134	0.533
Delta-rhythm energy, O_2	0.148	-0.107	-0.907*	-0.035	0.869
Theta-rhythm energy in cross-spectrum	0.085	0.013	-0.594*	-0.222	0.411
Alpha-rhythm energy, O_2	-0.167	-0.214	0.661*	-0.265	0.581
Alpha-rhythm frequency, O_2	-0.234	-0.185	-0.539*	-0.105	0.392
Delta-rhythm frequency, F_4	0.002	0.228	-0.147	-0.553*	0.381
Delta-rhythm frequency, O_2	-0.121	0.202	0.166	-0.629*	0.482
Theta-rhythm frequency in cross-spectrum	-0.293	0.146	0.389	-0.597*	0.610
Alpha-rhythm energy, F_4	-0.087	-0.195	0.253	-0.845*	0.821
Beta-2-rhythm coherence	-0.261	0.074	0.011	-0.765*	0.667
Alpha-rhythm frequency, F_4	-0.812*	0.055	-0.051	0.021	0.663
Beta-2-rhythm frequency, F_4	-0.682*	-0.281	-0.106	-0.023	0.553
Beta-2-rhythm frequency, O_2	-0.621*	-0.392	-0.233	-0.171	0.624
Beta-2-rhythm energy, O_2	-0.808*	-0.096	0.100	0.030	0.675
Alpha-rhythm frequency in cross-spectrum	-0.767*	-0.040	-0.075	-0.140	0.617
Synchronization R_0	0.034	0.772*	-0.134	-0.061	0.628
Delta-rhythm coherence	-0.152	0.760*	0.399	0.234	0.821
Theta-rhythm coherence	0.023	0.885*	0.020	0.224	0.784
Alpha-rhythm coherence	0.248	0.587*	-0.051	-0.193	0.444
Beta-1-rhythm coherence	-0.666*	0.540*	0.016	-0.231	0.795

* p < .05

TABLE 2.   Factor structure of EEG parameters and indexes of psychomotor activity (after rotation)

Index	Factors				h^2
	F-2	F-4	F-1	F-3	
1	2	3	4	5	6
Optimum handwriting speed	-0.046	-0.544*	0.126	-0.050	0.322
Maximum handwriting speed	-0.123	-0.791*	-0.111	-0.131	0.675
Optimum tapping frequency	-0.480	0.095	0.208	0.488	0.527
Optimum reaction time	0.727*	0.122	-0.105	-0.117	0.578
Minimum reaction time	0.503*	-0.394	-0.060	0.139	0.431
Maximum tapping frequency	-0.224	-0.347	0.528*	0.053	0.451
Tapping frequency stability	0.111	0.230	0.854*	0.193	0.839
Number of nonobligatory responses	0.043	-0.315	0.486	-0.017	0.340
Delta-rhythm energy, F_4	-0.223	0.053	-0.547*	0.122	0.378
Delta-rhythm energy, O_2	-0.123	0.019	-0.661*	-0.069	0.469
Theta-rhythm energy in cross-spectrum	0.235	-0.112	-0.619*	-0.092	0.460
Alpha-rhythm energy, O_2	0.305	0.107	0.757*	0.080	0.687
Alpha-rhythm frequency, O_2	0.092	0.243	-0.644*	0.310	0.584
Delta-rhythm frequency, F_4	0.497	-0.286	-0.008	-0.048	0.338
Delta-rhythm frequency, O_2	0.823*	-0.014	0.059	-0.071	0.695
Theta-rhythm frequency in cross-spectrum	0.684*	0.105	0.350	0.177	0.632
Alpha-rhythm energy, F_4	0.742*	0.336*	0.197	0.098	0.710
Beta-2-rhythm coherence	0.695*	0.081	0.131	0.304	0.601
Alpha-rhythm frequency, F_4	-0.072	-0.165	0.041	0.882*	0.814
Beta-2-rhythm frequency, F_4	-0.126	0.317	0.135	0.710*	0.643
Beta-2-rhythm frequency, O_2	0.023	0.436	-0.377	0.573*	0.712
Beta-2-rhythm energy, O_2	0.073	-0.036	0.020	0.780*	0.611
Alpha-rhythm frequency in cross-spectrum	0.119	0.062	-0.061	0.802*	0.665
Synchronization R_0	0.178	-0.697*	-0.264	0.083	0.594
Delta-rhythm coherence	-0.044	-0.730*	0.409	0.106	0.714
Theta-rhythm coherence	-0.082	-0.908*	0.034	-0.007	0.831
Alpha-rhythm coherence	0.026	0.549*	0.047	-0.075	0.312
Beta-1-rhythm coherence	0.375	-0.475	0.046	0.627*	0.760

*$p < .05$

of a similar EEG factor has been shown in a number of reports (En Hsi Hsü & Sherman, 1946; Golubyeva et al., 1974). To date a number of investigations have revealed the functional significance of low-frequency components of EEG spectrum (Kogan, 1962; Golubyeva & Pozhdestvenskaya, 1969). These studies showed the existence of a positive relationship between the incidence of slow-wave EEG rhythms with unconditioned protective inhibition.

Our data indicating a negative correlation of the ergonic aspect of activity with the slow-wave EEG-rhythm energy factor indirectly confirm the results about the functional meaning of slow rhythms as well as permit us to make an assumption about protective inhibition (which develops more easily in people with predominant EEG slow activity) as one of the factors underlying individual differences in the ergonic aspect of activity. The constellation of parameters of spectral density of slow-wave EEG components also showed a significant correlation with indexes of inclination for tensed psychomotor activity. This points to the existence of the single common factor of activity -- ergonic -- closely related to the mechanism of regulation of activation level in that zone of its continuum that belongs to lower functional states.

Thus, our data show that the identified independent brainwide peculiarities of nervous system functioning underlie independent manifestations of different aspects of activity as well as their interaction.

In our view, the individual peculiarity of activity manifestation (and at the same time its general level) is determined by a quantitative combination of the relatively independent but interacting aspects. The results of analysis of interrelationships between general brain constellations of EEG parameters and subdimensions of activity indicate that the combination of EEG parameters characteristic of each subject is likely to be determined to a considerable extent by a certain combination of those neurodynamic factors that affect interindividual variability of different aspects of activity.

The presence of certain regular physiologically conditioned relationships between different aspects of activity can determine the existence of their typical combinations, that is, typical styles of activity. Evidently, further research in this field should be directed first at identifying the main types of activity -- the most characteristic combinations of the main aspects of this temperamental dimension.

Preliminary analysis of the structure of interrelationships between main aspects of activity permits us to identify three hypothetical types or variants of individuality. The first, low-activity type, includes subjects with weak expression of all the factors of activity. The second, variety-seeking and high-activity type, consists of people with a middle tempo of mental activity and a strong tendency to the diversity of actions. The third, high-speed and high-activity type includes persons with a fast tempo of mental activity and a middle tendency to novelty seeking.

CONCLUSIONS

Contemporary studies in the field of typology of temperament are aimed not so much at the analysis of its separate components and their structures as at the study of the interaction between its main subdimensions that underlie the individual peculiarity of adaptation to environment, pattern of behavior, and actions. Each orthogonal component of temperament is regarded as a unitary, one-dimensional characteristic of the dynamic aspect of human behavior. However, as is shown in the present work, main dimensions of temperament in each individual may be characterized by a qualitative peculiarity of manifestation, which is

apparently conditioned by a complex multidimensional structure of these
properties, in the context of which the dynamics of mental activity is described.
It was shown in our investigation that activity as a temperamental trait is a
multicomponent parameter of individuality, the structure of which is formed by
a number of relatively independent but interacting aspects called speed, ergonic,
and variety seeking. Concrete combinations of the identified aspects of activity
with their different expression can characterize the formal aspect of individual
and possibly age-specific peculiarity of manifestation of activity. Our results
indicate that possible combinations of aspects of activity are determined to a
considerable extent by constellations of the identified general neurodynamic
factors.

Let us consider the described relationships in terms of the conception of nervous
system activation. The speed aspect of activity proved to be related to indexes
of the level of spatial synchronization of bioelectrical activity of the brain.
It is well known that it is ascending activating influences of the reticular
formation of the brainstem that play an important role in the regulation of
spatio-temporal concordance of functioning of different brain regions (Livanov
et al., 1974; Yanson, 1973). The direction of the given relationship indicates
that a high level of nervous system activation exerting a positive influence on
spatial EEG synchronization is a factor that favors manifestation of the speed
factor of activity. The negative relationship between the variety seeking aspect
of activity and the factor of spatio-temporal synchronization of EEG processes,
as well as the positive relationship between this aspect of activity and alpha-
rhythm energy, which is one of the EEG indexes of quiet wakefulness, suggest that
the middle level of activation of the nervous system is optimal for the manifestation of increased tendency to diversity and novelty.

The reverse dependence of variety seeking and speed aspects on the peculiarities
of leveling-off functional states of different regions of the cortex is very
likely to be one of the factors underlying reciprocal relations between these
aspects of activity. These findings indicate that people with high activation
of the nervous system are characterized by an intermediate striving for diversity
and fast tempo of intellectual activity, whereas people with the middle level
of activation are characterized by a pronounced tendency to diversity and intermediate tempo of intellectual operations.

The third aspect of activity -- ergonic -- turned out to be related to the factor
of slow-wave EEG-rhythm energy, which included also, with reverse sign, the index
of spectral density of alpha rhythm. The given EEG factor can be considered as
evidence of the existence of a single regulatory system of activation level cover-
ing a portion of the continuum of activation from lowered, inhibitory to optimal
state (Golubyeva et al., 1974; Golubyeva & Rozhdestvenskaya, 1969; Kogan, 1962;
Roytbak, 1975). The negative relationship between this EEG factor and the
ergonic aspect of activity shows that the low level of activation manifesting
itself in a considerable power of EEG slow rhythms is one of the basic factors
that run counter to the tendency to mental tension.

On the basis of the data obtained, one can believe that low activation of the
brain as a whole corresponds to a type of low mental activity with weak expression
of all its aspects. The EEG of people with low levels of activity is characterized by asynchrony of all the basic EEG rhythms and by a considerable power
of slow-wave EEG processes. The variety-seeking and high-activity type of person
is related to the middle level of activation of the nervous system. The main EEG
feature of the given type is the absence of slow-wave rhythms, the presence of well-
pronounced alpha-rhythm, and the middle level of spatial synchronization of brain
biopotentials. Finally, the high-speed and high-activity type can be identified
with a high level of activation of the brain, which is characterized by the absence
of the EEG slow-wave rhythms and the high spatial synchronization of EEG processes.

Thus, the results of analysis of relations between types of activity and general brain neurodynamic parameters indicate that the combination of aspects of activity characteristic of each individual (i.e., his or her type) and, at the same time, general level of activity are to a considerable extent determined by a certain combination of neurodynamic factors, which affect the interindividual variability of aspects of activity. The existence of regular physiologically determined relationships between different factors of activity underlies their typical combinations. The decisive factor determining a low-activity type is a low level of activation of the nervous system, because the optimal spatio-temporal concordance of different regions of the brain (the main neurodynamic condition for speed and variety-seeking aspects) is ensured only with a sufficiently high tone of the cortex. That is why people belonging to the low-mental-activity type form a rather homogeneous group in terms of the diversity of manifestation of dynamic aspects of activity. In contrast, the high-mental-activity type consists of at least two categories of people: persons in the variety-seeking subtype are characterized by a middle level of activation and middle level of spatio-temporal synchronization of different parts of the brain, and those in the speed subtype are noted for a high level of activation and a pronounced spatio-temporal concordance of functioning of different regions of the brain.

The suggested notions about the typology of activity are in good agreement with the data on EEG ontogenesis and on the age-specific dynamics of mental activity. Leytes (1971, 1972) showed that each period of age development is characterized by a qualitative peculiarity of activity manifestation. For example, activity of junior schoolchildren manifests itself mainly in open curiosity. In middle-school age, activity is expressed in a diversity of interests. Finally, the mental activity of senior schoolchildren is mostly goal-directed.

We assume that concrete combinations of speed, ergonic, and variety seeking, along with different levels of their expression, can characterize a formal aspect of qualitative peculiarity of manifestation of the given temperamental trait at different stages of ontogenesis.

The peculiarity of activity manifestation at each age period may be caused by heterochroneous actualization of its different aspects. It is evident that the activity of junior schoolchildren is notable for the dominance in its structure of the variety-seeking aspect, whereas there occurs a transformation of relations between aspects of activity, and the ergonic aspect begins to dominate in children of senior school age. A certain tendency to enhancement of the ergonic aspect with age in schoolchildren has been shown in the work of Konoreva (1975). There are also data about the acceleration of individual tempo of mental activity in the course of human ontogenesis (Connolly, Brown, & Basset, 1968).

The age-specific dynamics of the manifestation of aspects of activity correlate with the process of EEG ontogenetic formation. In many studies devoted to the analysis of age-specific changes of EEG spectral composition it has been shown that the summary brain biopotentials at early stages of human development are characterized by predominance of slow waves in the EEG (Lindsey, 1936; Smith, 1937). This predominance is one manifestation of functional immaturity of the mechanisms of regulation of optimal activation level in children. The given functional feature of the child's nervous system, which was conceived as evidence of age-specific weakness of nervous processes manifesting itself in pronounced energy of slow-wave EEG rhythms (Golubyeva et al., 1974), is likely to be an unfavorable condition for manifestation of the ergonic activity aspect in children of early school age.

As is known, the frequency-amplitude EEG pattern characteristic of mature adults is formed approximately by 14-15 years of age (Ravich-Shcherbo & Shibarovskaya,

1972). By this age, the dynamics of behavior begin to a considerable extent
to be determined by the ergonic aspect of activity.

We can make the following assumption concerning age-specific EEG-pattern changes
related to other activity aspects (speed and variety seeking). In a series of
studies (Aslanov et al., 1973; Livanov, 1972) it was shown that the formation
of EEG rhythms in ontogenesis occurs parallel to the enhancement of spatio-
temporal synchronization of brain biopotentials. This enhancement reflects the
process of development of intracortical linkages determining functional maturity
of the brain. In our study it was found that spatio-temporal EEG synchronization
correlated positively with the speed aspect and negatively with the variety-
seeking aspect of mental activity. Therefore, we can claim that an increase in
functional lability of the nervous system related to the process of maturation
of intercentral neuronal connections in ontogenesis is accompanied by an increase
in the speed of mental actions and a certain weakening of the tendency to diversity and novelty.

In conclusion, the EEG parameters reflect essential attributes of integrative
brain functioning that exert an influence on individual and age-specific types
of activity. On the premise that interindividual variability of temperamental
dimensions (including activity) is mainly determined by fundamental characteristics of brain functioning, we may consider the four EEG factors as indicators
of general properties of the nervous system as a whole.

REFERENCES

Alexander, W. P. (1935). Intelligence, concrete and abstract. British Journal
   of Psychology. Monograph Supplement, 19, 3-10.

Aslanov, A. S., Gavrilova, N. A., Monakhov, K. K., Sologub, E. B., & Khrizman,
   T. P. (1973). Prostranstvennaya sinkhronizatsiya elektricheskoy aktivnosti
   mozga cheloveka v norme i patologii (Spatial synchronization of the human
   brain electrical activity in norm and pathology). In Prostranstvennaya
   sinkhronizatsiya biopotentsialov golovnogo mozga (pp. 128-167). Moscow:
   Nauka.

Connolly, K., Brown, K., & Bassett, E. (1968). Developmental changes in some
   components of a motor skill. British Journal of Psychology, 59, 305-314.

Eliasz, A. (1974). Temperament a osobowość (Temperament and personality).
   Wrocław: Ossolineum.

En Hsi Hsü & Sherman, M. (1946). The factorial analysis of the electroencephalogram. Journal of Psychology, 21, 189-196.

Eysenck, H. J. (1953). The structure of human personality. London: Methuen.

Furneaux, W. D. (1960). Intellectual abilities and problem-solving behavior.
   In H. J. Eysenck (Ed.), Handbook of abnormal psychology (pp. 167-192).
   New York: Wiley.

Golubyeva, E. A., Izyumova, S. A., Trubnikova, R. S., & Pechenkov, V. V. (1974).
   Svyas' ritmov elektroentsefalogrammy s osnovnymi svoystvami nervnoy sistemy
   (The relationship between electroencephalographic rhythms and basic properties
   of the nervous system). In Problemy differentsial'noy psykhofiziologii (Vol. 8,
   pp. 160-174). Moscow: Nauka.

Golubyeva, E. A., & Rozhdestvenskaya, V. I. (1969). Izmeneniye biotokov mozga v khode umstvennoy deyatel'nosti i tipologicheskiye razlichiya po labil'nosti i dinamichnosti nervnoy sistemy (Changes in the brain biopotentials during mental activity and typological differences in lability and dynamicity of the nervous system). In Problemy differentsial'noy psykhofisiologii (Vol. 6, pp. 49-73). Moscow: Prosveshcheniye.

Guilford, J. P. (1959). Personality. New York: McGraw-Hill.

Heymans, G., & Wiersma, E. (1909). Beiträge zur speziellen Psychologie auf Grund einer Massenuntersuchung. Zeitschrift für psychologische Physiologie, 51, 1-72.

Kadyrov, B. R. (1976). Uroven' aktivatsii i nekotorye dinamicheskiye kharakter-istiki psikhicheskoy aktivnosti (The level of activation and some dynamic characteristics of mental activity). Voprosy psikhologii, No. 4, 133-138.

Kogan, A. B. (1962). Vyrazheniye protsessov vysshey nervnoy deyatel'nosti v elektricheskikh potentsialakh kory mozga pri evobodnom povedenii zhivotnogo (The expression of processes of higher nervous activity in electrical potentials of the cortex under non-restricted animal behavior). In Elektroentsefalografich-eskoye issledovanie vysshey nervnoy deyatel'nosti (pp. 42-53). Moscow: Nauka.

Konoreva, T. S. (1975). Vozrastnye izmeneniya dinamicheskikh kharakteristik nastoychivosti v mladshemshkol'nom vozraste (Ontogenetic changes of dynamic characteristics of persistence in primary school age). In Voprosy psikhofisi-ologii aktivnosti i samoregulyatsii lichnosti (pp. 71-77). Sverdlovsk: Izdatel'stvo Sverdlovskogo pedinstituta.

Krupnov, A. I. (1970). Issledovaniye sootnosheniya mezhdu fonovymi electro-entsefalograficheskimi pokazatelyami i dinamicheskimi priznakami aktivnosti prvedeniya (The investigation of the relationship between background electro-encephalographic characteristics and dynamic indexes of behavioral activity). Voprosy psikhologii, No. 6, 47-59.

Leytes, N. S. (1971). Umstvennye sposobnosti i vozrast (Intellectual abilities and age). Moscow: Pedagogika.

Leytes, N. S. (1972). Na puti k izucheniyu samykh obshchikh predposylok sposob-nostey (Toward a study of the most fundamental prerequisites of abilities). In Problemy differentsial'noy psikhofiziologii (Vol. 7, pp. 223-232). Moscow: Pedagogika.

Lindsley, D. B. (1936). Brain potentials in children and adults. Science, 84, 354.

Livanov, M. N. (1972). Prostranstvennaya organizatsiya protsessov golovnogo mozga (Spatial organization of the brain processes). Moscow: Nauka.

Livanov, M. N. (1973). K voprosu o pamyati (Concerning the nature of memory). Uspekhi fiziologicheskikh nauk, 4(1), 19-30.

Livanov, M. N., Trush, V. D., Efremova, T. M., & Potulova, L. A. (1974). Svyas' spektral'no-korrelyatsiommykh parametrov EEG s protsessami realizatsii vremennoy svyazi i nekotorykh vidov tormozheniya (The relationship between EEG spectral-correlational parameters and the processes of realization of temporary connection and some kinds of inhibition). In Osnovnye problemy elektrofiziologii golovnogo mozga (pp. 50-64). Moscow: Nauka.

MacArthur, R. S. (1955). An experimental investigation of persistence in secondary school boys. Canadian Journal of Psychology, 9, 42-47.

Mozgovoy, V. D. (1973). Issledovaniye faktorov bioelektricheskoy deyatel'nosti nekotorykh otdelov mozga i ikh otnosheniya k umstvennoy aktivnosti (An investigation of bioelectrical factors of some regions of the brain and their relation to intellectual activity). Unpublished doctoral dissertation, Institute of General and Pedagogical Psychology PAS USSR, Moscow.

Nebylitsyn, V. D. (1976). Psikhofiziologicheskiye issledovaniya individual'nykh razlichiy (Psychophysiological investigations of individual differences). Moscow: Nauka.

Nebylitsyn, V. D., & Krupnov, A. I. (1972). Bioelectrical correlates of motor activity as a temperamental trait. Neuropsychologia, 10, 419-427.

Nebylitsyn, V. D., & Mozgovoy, V. D. (1972). Elektrofiziologicheskiye korrelyaty umstvennoy aktivnosti (Electrophysiological correlates of intellectual activity). Zhurnal vysshey nervnoy deyatel'nosti, 22, 899-906.

Payne, R. W. (1960). Cognitive abnormalities. In H. J. Eysenck (Ed.), Handbook of abnormal psychology (pp. 193-261). New York: Wiley.

Ravich-Shcherbo, I. V., & Shibarovskaya, G. A. (1972). Struktura dinamichnosti nervnykh protsessov u detey shkol'nogo vozrasta (The structure of dynamicity of the nervous processes in schoolchildren). In Problemy differentsial'noy psikhofiziologii (Vol. 7, pp. 95-126). Moscow: Pedagogika.

Rimoldi, H. J. A. (1951). Personal tempo. Journal of Abnormal and Social Psychology, 46, 283-303.

Roytbak, A. I. (1975). K voprosu o prirode korkovogo tormozheniya (Concerning the nature of cortical inhibition). In Mekhanizmy deyatel'nosti golovnogo mozga (pp. 348-364). Tbilissi: Metsniereba.

Russalov, V. M. (1979). Biologicheskiye osnovy individual'-no-psikhologicheskikh razlichiy (Biological bases of individual psychological differences). Moscow: Nauka.

Russinov, V. S., Grindel, O. M., & Boldyreva, G. H. (1975). Issledovaniye dinamiki mezhtsentral'nykh otnosheniy v kore bol'shikh polushariy cheloveka metodom spektral'nogo analiza EEG (An investigation of dynamics of intercentral relations in the human brain cortex with the help of spectral analysis of EEG). In Mekhanizmy deyatel'nosti golovnogo mozga (pp. 365-374). Tbilissi: Metsniyereba.

Ryans, D. G. (1938). The meaning of persistence. Journal of General Psychology, 19, 79-96.

Smith, J. P. (1937). The EEG during infancy and childhood. Proceedings of the Society of Experimental Biology and Medicine, 36, 384-386.

Strelau, J. (1974). Koncepcja temperamentu jako poziomu energetycznego i charakterystyki czasowej zachowania (The conception of temperament as an energetic and temporal characteristic of behavior). In J. Strelau (Ed.), Rola cech temperamentalnych w działaniu (pp. 9-26). Wrocław: Ossolineum.

Teplov, B. M. (1961). Problemy individual'nykh razlichiy (Problems of individual differences). Moscow: Prosveshcheniye.

Yanson, Z. A. (1973). Vliyaniye mezentsefalicheskoy retikulyarnoy formatsii na prostranstvennuyu sinkhronizatsiyu biopotentsialov golovnogo mozga (The effects of mesencephalic reticular formation on spatial synchronization of biopotentials of the brain). Zhurnal vysshey nervnoy deyatel'nosti, 23, 159–165.

3

N₂ Wave of the Evoked Potential:
Scalp Reflection of Neuronal Mismatch
of Orienting Theory?

Risto Näätänen

Being able to detect even slight environmental changes and contrasts is of vital importance to the survival of the organism. This is taken care of in many ways at different levels of the structural and functional sensory systems of different organisms at various phylogenetic levels, including the sensory system of humans. For instance, even at peripheral levels, cells can be observed with a function evidently to "detect" and amplify any contrasts that may prevail in the proximal stimulus pattern. This leads to peripheral patterns of sensory excitation in which nonredundant features of stimulation are emphasized. Such contrast-seeking or creating functions also exist at more central levels of sensory-perceptual systems of organisms. One of the best known of such central sensory phenomena is the neuronal mismatch process of the orienting theory (Sokolov, 1960, 1963). This theory suggests a mechanism by which the probability of detection of even slight changes in the stimulus stream is increased (automatically followed by a complicated pattern of facilitatory and preparatory physiological changes called the orienting response, OR).

NEURONAL MODEL

The delivery of a stimulus leads to the development of a neuronal model[1] of this stimulus; the model is strengthened by further presentations of this stimulus. The more the neuronal model develops, the weaker the response elicited by the repetitive stimulus. This kind of response decrement might be regarded as

---

This paper was prepared while the author held a Humboldt fellowship in the Department of Physiology, University of Marburg (FRG), associated with Professor H. Fruhstorfer. The previous, experimental work of the author and his colleagues dealt with in this review has been carried out in the Institute for Perception TNO, Soesterberg, The Netherlands: in the Department of Psychology, University of Helsinki (supported by the Finnish Academy); in the Department of Psychology, University of Dundee, Scotland (supported by a Carnegie fellowship and by the Medical Research Council). The author is particularly indebted to collaboration and conversations with Drs. N. E. Loveless (University of Dundee) and M. Simpson (now at the University of Aberdeen, Scotland) and to various sorts of help from Professor Fruhstorfer.

[1]The neuronal-model concept is in the present treatment exclusively used in the sense of short-term effects of stimuli on the central nervous system, lasting only a few seconds (equaling the span of echoic memory). Neuronal models based on long-term memory and imagination are hence excluded.

involving the essentials of the phenomenon called habituation (see Fruhstorfer,
1971; Fruhstorfer, Soveri, & Järvilehto, 1970; Megela & Teyler, 1979). Such a
response decrement due to stimulus repetition is plastic and immediately reversible (provided a suitable stimulus), which is not characteristic to the response
decrement caused by factors such as sensory adaptation, neural fatigue, or refractoriness. The less vigorous, habituated response is likely to reflect the
diminished difference between some properties of the incoming sensory input and
the prevailing state of the sensory system. However, when a different stimulus
is presented, a neuronal mismatch process is said to take place between the
sensory input and the neuronal model, "a disconcordance response" (Sokolov,
1975). It is as if the organism were scanning the incoming stimulus stream with
this neuronal model as a "working hypothesis" or tool for internal comparison of
the incoming sensory input with inputs of the immediate past. (This is a physiological process that does not necessarily have conscious or psychological correlates, discussed later in the chapter). One important biological function of
the neuronal model is, presumably, to increase sensitivity of the organism to
environmental changes. The stronger the model, the better the chances of the
organism to detect a deviant stimulus probably are. This is likely to be due
to the highly differentiated physiological state (see Näätänen, 1973) of the
brain superimposed on which any deviant excitation pattern produces a distinct
change. Chances of the organism's detecting an environmental change are probably
directly proportional to the change in the sensory excitation pattern of the
brain (per time unit) caused by the stimulus.

Neuronal mismatch, hence, is regarded as one of the ingenious arrangements by
which Nature amplifies neurophysiological responses to stimulus changes, increasing the representation of the nonredundant (potential) information at the
expense of the redundant. Soviet investigators have held the view that a neuronal
mismatch invariably leads to the OR. On the other hand, some other workers maintain that a mismatch should be experienced as somehow significant by the organism
before the OR is elicited. (For a recent debate on this issue, see Bernstein, 1979;
Maltzman, 1979; O'Gorman, 1979; Siddle, 1979.)

The OR is not only elicited by a deviant stimulus but also by somehow significant
stimuli (task relevant, biologically significant, etc.) even without any neuronal
mismatch (Lynn, 1966). However, the real relationship of the OR to stimulus mismatch and to stimulus significance can be questioned. The dominant use of long-
latency physiological measures in OR research -- electrodermal, vascular, and
cardiac -- has not permitted a phase-by-phase analytic mapping of orienting
processes. In contrast to the speed with which different post-stimulus phases
of information processing follow each other, these measures are indeed slow,
yielding a delayed sum response of the physiological effects associated with
separate information-processing stages. Another serious problem lies in the
nonspecificity of the measures used. Therefore, for instance, the central controversy around the question involving the sufficiency of the neuronal mismatch
alone to elicit an OR is still unsettled. By using these measures exclusively,
there is often no means of deciding which aspect or aspects of the situation and
information processing have elicited the observed physiological changes. (This
has also promoted a confounding, unanalytical use of the OR concept.) Therefore,
short-latency and more specific measures such as cerebral evoked potentials (EP)
should also be used, depending on the questions asked, which might to a crucial
extent supplement the information yielded by the more classical measures of
orienting. By using EP techniques, it might be possible more accurately to map
the relationships between OR-related physiological changes and the situational
aspects or information-processing phases eliciting them. This would lead to
obtaining a much more detailed picture of the temporal and spatial pattern of
the orienting kinds of processes taking place in the brain in different post-
stimulus phases than is possible by using longer-latency and nonspecific physiological measures.

In the following, we examine what progress, if any, the application of the EP techniques in orienting situations has brought into the study of the earliest phase of orienting, neuronal mismatch process, in a stimulus-mismatch situation. This is a process inaccessible without contamination by subsequent processes when the longer-latency and more nonspecific measures of OR are used. [2]

N2 WAVE OF THE EVOKED POTENTIAL

The formation of the neuronal model and its mismatch process are key processes postulated by the orienting theory; but their characteristics (such as locus) are still largely unknown, despite intensive research efforts (e.g., Sokolov & Vinogradova, 1975). However, quite recently EP research conducted with humans has brought up a finding with good promise to provide a measure for the neuronal mismatch process per se. One of the recent studies (Näätänen, Gaillard, & Mäntysalo, 1980a) might illustrate the point particularly well. The subject was performing a dichotic-listening task, instructed to detect and count silently occasional slight pitch changes ("deviant stimuli") in one ear and to ignore the input to the other ear. With constant interstimulus intervals (ISI) of 800 ms, a stimulus was delivered through earphones either to his left or right ear in random order. The left-ear "standard" and deviant stimuli were of 1000 Hz and 1150 Hz, respectively, and the respective values for the right ear were 500 Hz and 575 Hz. The probability of a deviant stimulus varied from 0% to 9% (both for the attended and unattended input) in different stimulus blocks. Evoked potentials were recorded from vertex (Cz), left-temporal (T3) and right-temporal (T4) electrodes, the latter two being located in the vicinity of the two auditory cortexes.

The results are presented in Figure 1. The standards and deviants elicited quite a similar N1 deflection (peak latency approximately 100-120 ms), those elicited by the deviants being somewhat larger, however (measured in reference to the baseline at stimulus onset). However, there was a considerable difference in the N2 deflection [3] (peak latency 250-300 ms), which was not seen at all in the traces for standards. Interestingly, N2 to deviants in the attended and un-attended input was of the same amplitude, demonstrating, therefore, no significance or target effect. On the other hand, the large late positive deflection P3 or P300 (Sutton, Braren, Zubin, & John, 1965) was much larger to the target than nontarget deviants, disclosing, hence, a target or significance effect.

In Figure 2, (mean) subtraction curves in which the same-latency data points of the EP to standards were subtracted from those of the EP to deviants (after super-imposing the corresponding traces at the level of the mean EEG during the last 50 ms before stimulus onset). (This subtraction was carried out separately for

---

[2] The author is aware of the mismatch between this article and the others in this volume, which are dealing with interindividual differences rather than such basic phenomena of the organismic functioning that are, presumably, common to all "normal" human beings. The weak apology of the author is, however, that as long as the basic nature and determinants of the brain potentials dealt with are only poorly understood, their use in the study of interindividual differences cannot be fruitful; consequently, research efforts in the field at this stage should be mainly directed to the "basic" phenomena.

[3] The present N2 should not be confused with the "drowsiness N2" or "sleep N2," a negative deflection at this latency range emerging, and growing very large, as the state of drowsiness of the subject progresses.

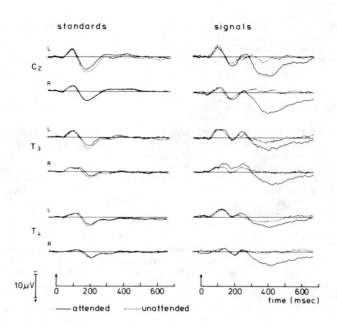

FIGURE 1. Vertex (Cz) and temporal (T3, T4) evoked potentials (EPs) (averaged
across subjects) to standard (left panel) and deviant (right panel) stimuli when
attended and when unattended. From "Brain-potential correlates of voluntary and
involuntary attention" by R. Näätänen, A. Gaillard, and S. Mäntysalo, 1980a. In
Motivation, motor and sensory processes of the brain: Electrical potentials,
behavior and clinical use. Progress in brain research, edited by H. H. Kornhuber
and L. Deeke. Copyright 1980 by Elsevier/North Holland Biomedical Press. Reprinted by permission.

each subject and session.) Figure 2 discloses a large N2 difference wave both
for the attended and unattended input: in reference to the EPs to standards,
those elicited by the deviants disclose a systematic negative shift, with an
onset latency approximately equaling the N1 peak latency and with a duration
of some 200 ms. This negativity indeed is very similar for the attended and
unattended input, followed by a large positive shift only to deviants in the
attended input (target effect).

Similar results were obtained in a previous study (Näätänen, Gaillard, &
Mäntysalo, 1978), with two experimental situations with no difference between
the standards to the two ears within a situation: (a) deviants differed from
standards only in intensity, deviants being of 80 dB (SL) and standards of
70 dB (SL); (b) deviants differed from standards only in frequency, deviants
being of 1140 Hz and standards of 1000 Hz. Further supplementary studies
produced corroboratory results (Näätänen & Michie, 1979, pp. 113-117).

The term mismatch negativity, as they called it, was suggested to reflect
the neuronal mismatch process of the orienting theory. Particular emphasis
was given to the observation involving attentional insensitivity of the mismatch

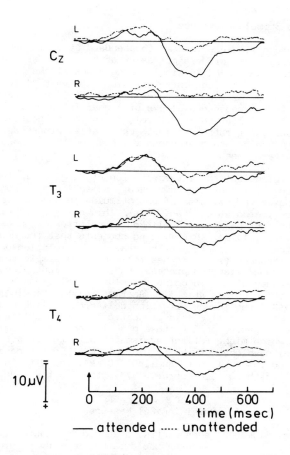

FIGURE 2. The differences between evoked potentials (EPs) to deviant and
standard stimuli, averaged across subjects (EPs to standards subtracted from
EPs to deviants) for vertex (Cz) and temporal (T3, T4) data. Same data as in
Figure 1. From "Brain-potential correlates of voluntary and involuntary
attention" by R. Näätänen, A. Gaillard, and S. Mäntysalo, 1980a. In Motivation,
motor and sensory processes of the brain: Electrical potentials, behavior and
clinical use. Progress in brain research, edited by H. H. Kornhuber and L. Deeke.
Copyright 1980 by Elsevier/North Holland Biomedical Press. Reprinted by
permission.

negativity. The authors suggested that the physiological mismatch process reflected by it is an automatic, basic, sensory process, taking place irrespective
of, perhaps even unmodified by, the task and subjective factors (such as the
direction of attention). Hence, here we might have the possibility of measuring
the neuronal mismatch process as such, without contamination from the stimulus-
evaluation factors and accompanying physiological processes.

However, much more evidence is needed to ensure that N2 reflects some properties
of the neuronal mismatch. This converging evidence is now reviewed.

Specificity of N2 to Stimulus Deviance

There have been numerous findings that N2 to standard stimuli (matches with the neuronal model) is very small or does not exist at all. Snyder and Hillyard (1976) even failed to elicit an N2 to single homogeneous clicks (of quite a strong intensity) delivered at long inter-stimulus intervals (ISIs), but they were able to elicit an N2 even to weaker-intensity clicks interspersed in a sequence of repetitive homogeneous clicks of higher intensity. Such results indeed suggest that N2 elicitation is not related to the properties of the afferent inflow as such, but rather reflects comparative processes, mismatch processes occurring when a disconcordant sensory input "meets" the neuronal model built by the repetitive homogeneous stimulus.

Another set of data ruling out the interpretation of N2 given in terms of the afferent inflow as such (without any comparatory aspect) comes from the omitted-stimulus studies (unexpected omission of one stimulus in a sequence of homogeneous repetitive stimuli delivered at constant ISIs). This omission elicits an N2 kind of potential followed by a P3 positivity (Klinke, Fruhstorfer, & Finkenzeller, 1968; Simson, Vaughan, & Ritter, 1976). This finding suggests that the neuronal model can also incorporate a temporal aspect when the previous stimulation has been homogeneous even in this respect (i.e., it has followed some simple temporal pattern or regularity). A neuronal mismatch process, therefore, might also be caused by a temporal disconcordance of the incoming stimulus in relation to the temporal pattern followed by the previous stimuli. Another related finding was provided by Klinke et al. (1968), who in one situation delivered a click unexpectedly early in a sequence of identical clicks presented at constant ISIs of 860 ms. They observed a large negative peak (with a peak latency of 140 ms) in response to this early click which might reflect a mismatch with the temporal properties on the neuronal model developed by the regular clicks. In the case of this early click (preceding interval only equaling 290 ms), the afferent inflow was probably smaller, if anything (see Butler, 1973), than to the regular stimulus at 860 ms.

Contrast-enhancing Nature of a Physiological Measure

To reflect a neuronal mismatch, such contrasts should be ensured (see Introduction). This means that the measure should rather show no generalization of habituation. For instance, when a subject is habituated to a tone of 1000 Hz, a tone of, say, 1030 Hz should be able to elicit a vigorous response. This is the case with the N2 wave, which is hardly observed in response to the first stimulus in a sequence (Snyder & Hillyard, 1976), but is considerable when even a slight change in any parameter of the stimulus is introduced. Figure 3 represents data from an experiment (Näätänen, Simpson, & Loveless, 1982) in which a tone of 1004 Hz (line SD in Figure 3) is repeating at intervals of 768 ms for 25 min. Two percent of these stimuli are of slightly lower (978 Hz; line DL) and 2% of slightly higher (1034 Hz; line DH) frequency, whereas the remaining 1% are of considerably higher frequency (1404 Hz; line DEx in Figure 3). The subject performed under four different instructions (in different stimulus blocks): "detect slightly lower," "detect slightly higher," "detect all deviants," and "read" (a magazine of interest). Even the slightly deviants (frequency change of only 3%-4%) elicited a remarkable N2. On the other hand, N2 did not reflect which deviant at a time was the target, consistently with the studies of Näätänen et al. (1978; 1980a). Even the reading N2 was approximately of the same amplitude as N2 in detection tasks (however, see later discussion). Interestingly, even P3 failed to reflect target but was rather elicited by the deviants in accordance to their magnitude of deviance (or probability).

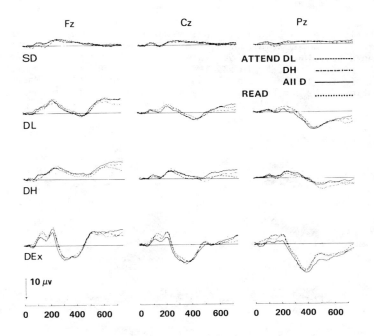

FIGURE 3. Frontal (Fz), vertex (Cz) and parietal (Pz) evoked potentials (EPs) to standard stimuli (1004 Hz, top line), slightly lower (978 Hz) deviant stimuli (2nd line from top), slightly higher (1034 Hz) deviant stimuli (3rd line from top), and widely (1404 Hz) deviant stimuli (bottom line) under 4 task instructions: "detect slightly higher," "detect slightly lower," "detect all deviants," "read." From Stimulus deviance vs. significance and event-related potentials by R. Näätänen, M.Simpson, and N. E. Loveless, 1982. Copyright 1982 by North Holland Publishing Company. Reprinted by permission.

Yet more convincing evidence of the contrast-enhancing character of N2 was the observation that even missed slightly deviants elicited a notable N2 (Figure 6 in Näätänen, Simpson, et al., 1982). This question was further explored by these authors in a study (in preparation) in which the standard was of 1000 Hz and the deviant to be detected usually of 1010 Hz. All subjects produced a notable N2, even to misses, which in most cases was of the same order of magnitude as N2 associated with (correct) detections and "nonsure" responses to deviants. This supports the suggestion of the automatic, psychologically silent nature of the cerebral processes reflected by N2, which then is a necessary, but not sufficient, condition of conscious perception of stimulus deviance. As an interesting contrast, P3 was only elicited by the detected deviants and "nonsures."

The contrast-enhancing nature of N2 is of special theoretical interest in comparison with N1, the first major negative deflection. N1 demonstrates a strong generalization of habituation (e.g., Butler, 1968; Fruhstorfer, 1971; Megela & Teyler, 1979). Even a stimulus of another modality interspersed in a stimulus sequence fails to elicit an N1 of the same size as that elicited by the first stimulus in a sequence (Fruhstorfer, 1971). With small stimulus changes, N1 remains practically unchanged (in Figure 3, compare DL and DH to SD for

electrodes Cz and Pz, which allow a separate observation of N1 and N2 due to no
temporal overlap; see also Butler, 1968; Näätänen, Hukkanen, & Järvilehto, 1980b;
figure 4 here; Näätänen, Sams, Järvilehto, & Soininen, 1983; figures 5 and 6
here). When a stimulus change involves a reduced intensity, the N1 amplitude
is reduced.   In contrast, N2 is elicited even by an intensity reduction
(Näätänen & Michie, 1979, Figure 13; Snyder & Hillyard, 1976). Moreover, as
already mentioned, N2 can be elicited by subliminal stimulus changes, a fact

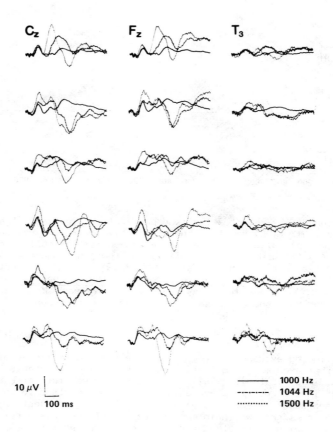

FIGURE 4.   Vertex (Cz) (left panel), frontal (Fz) (center panel), and temporal
(T3) (right panel) evoked potentials (EPs) averaged separately for each subject
(Subject 1, top line; Subject 2, 2nd line from top, etc.) and for each of the
three stimuli (standard stimulus of 1000 Hz, deviant stimuli of 1044 Hz and
1500 Hz). Negativity upwards. Stimulus onset at the beginning of the traces.
Trace length 600 ms. From "Magnitude of stimulus deviance and brain potentials"
by R. Näätänen, S. Hukkanen, and T. Järvilehto, 1980b. In Motivation, motor
and sensory processes of the brain: Electrical potentials, behavior and clinical
use. Progress in brain research, edited by H. H. Kornhuber and L. Deeke. Copyright 1980 by Elsevier/North Holland Biomedical Press. Reprinted by permission.

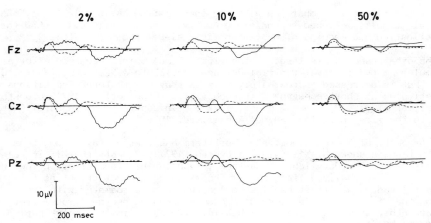

FIGURE 5. Frontal (Fz), vertex (Cz) and parietal (Pz) evoked potentials (EPs)
(averaged across subjects) elicited by the deviant (solid line) and standard
(broken line) stimuli for deviant-stimulus probabilities of 2%, 10%, and 50%.
Trace length 600 ms, stimulus onset at 30 ms, at which points the traces superimposed. The horizontal baseline drawn along this level. Negativity upwards.
Counting condition. From "Probability of deviant stimulus and event-related
brain potentials" by R. Näätänen, M. Sams, T. Järvilehto, & K. Soininen, 1983.
In Psychophysiology: Memory, motivation and event-related potentials in mental
operations, edited by R. Sinz and M. R. Rosenzweig. Copyright 1983 by Elsevier
Biomedical Press. Reprinted by permission.

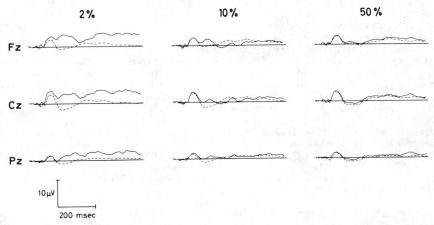

FIGURE 6. Frontal (Fz), vertex (Cz) and parietal (Pz) evoked potentials (EPs)
(averaged across subjects) elicited by the deviant (solid line) and standard
(broken line) stimuli for deviant-stimulus probabilities of 2%, 10%, and 50%.
Trace length 600 ms, stimulus onset at 30 ms, at which points the traces superimposed. The horizontal baseline drawn along this level. Negativity upwards.
Reading condition. From "Probability of deviant stimulus and event-related
brain potentials" by R. Näätänen, M. Sams, T. Järvilehto, & K. Soininen, 1983.
In Psychophysiology: Memory, motivation and event-related potentials in mental
operations, edited by R. Sinz and M. R. Rosenzweig. Copyright 1983 by Elsevier
Biomedical Press. Reprinted by permission.

of great interest in comparison with the fact that no N1 is elicited by subliminal stimuli. (Evoked-response audiometry, a common clinical method for
investigation and mapping of hearing deficiencies, is based on this.)

On the other hand, N1 is large to the first stimulus in a sequence after a
"stimulus empty" interval (initial OR; see Järvilehto & Näätänen, 1980; O'Gorman,
1979) but is decreased approximately by a half by one to three repetitions of
the stimulus at short constant ISIs such as 1 s (Fruhstorfer, 1971; Fruhstorfer,
Soveri, et al., 1970; Öhman & Lader, 1977). (In contrast, N2 is hardly noticeable to the first stimulus; Snyder & Hillyard, 1976.)

This property of N1 to demonstrate short-term habituation (also long-term
habituation is shown by N1; Salamy & McKean, 1977) suggests that it is related
to orienting, too (Järvilehto & Näätänen, 1980). This form of orienting, however, is situationally different from the mismatch-type of orienting to which
N2 is related. The effect on N1 is suggested to be associated with such orienting that is caused by a stimulus presented when no neuronal model (for this
or some other stimulus) prevails; that is, after a "stimulus-empty" period.
(In fact, N1 seems to be composed of two or three overlapping components of
which one, nonspecific vertex component is mainly responsible for the "first-
stimulus effect" and hence associated with orienting.) The relationship of N1
with some form of orienting is lent credence by findings demonstrating transient
increase of motor and sensory sensitivity during N1 (Fruhstorfer, Järvilehto,
Lumio, & Soveri, 1970; Rossignol & Jones, 1976; Semjen, Bonnet, & Requin, 1973).

N2 and Magnitude of Stimulus Deviance

One of the basic assumptions of the orienting theory is that the larger the disconcordance between the neuronal model and the incoming sensory inflow, the
larger the OR (Sokolov, 1975). Consequently, if N2 were a reflector of this
mismatch process, its amplitude should be the larger, the greater the magnitude
of stimulus deviance. This effect is evident in Figure 3 (compare N2 to the
DEx with that elicited by DL and DH). However, some of the difference might be
due to the smaller probability of the widely deviant stimulus. In another related study (Näätänen, et al., 1980b), standard stimuli of 1000 Hz were presented
at the 90% probability and two deviant stimuli (1044 and 1500 Hz), each at 5%
probability, all stimuli in a random order. The task was to count all deviant
stimuli (into one count). The more deviant stimulus elicited a larger and earlier
N2 than did the less deviant stimulus (Figure 4), which elicited an N2 often com-
mencing at the downward limb of the N1 deflection, filling up the P2 trough. For
the larger magnitude of stimulus deviance, N2 onset took place already before the
N1 peak, artificially enhancing the N1 amplitude. (In a previous, similar study,
Ford, Roth, and Kopell, 1976, did not get a significant effect of deviation magnitude on N2 (although the results showed this tendency) which might be due to the
early P3 onset with large magnitudes of deviation canceling some of the N2
negativity in these cases.)

N2 and Probability of Stimulus Deviance

The neuronal mismatch process should be the more vigorous, the smaller the
probability of a deviant stimulus is in a stimulus sequence. Therefore, if N2
were reflecting such a neuronal process, it should be the larger, the smaller
the probability of the deviant stimulus. There is such evidence, too. This
question was studied by Näätänen, Sams, et al. (1983) by using deviant-stimulus
(a tone of 1044 Hz) probabilities of 2%, 10%, and 50% (in different stimulus
blocks). Standard stimuli of 1000 Hz were presented at the complementary probability. (In the 50% condition, no stimulus is a deviant, of course.) The
results from the counting and reading conditions are presented in Figures 5

and 6, suggesting an inverse effect on probability of N2, as predicted. (For compatible results, see Squires, N. K., Donchin, Squires, K. C., & Grossberg, 1977.) In the 2% and 10% counting conditions (Figure 5), note the frontally nega- tive, parietally positive late slow-wave complex (Squires, N. K., Squires, K. C., and Hillyard, 1975) and in the 2% reading condition (Figure 6), the slow negative shift (with no positive counterpart) with an onset probably as early as in the N1 latency range. The frontally negative, parietally positive slow-wave complex is probably associated with some later phases of OR or with its more global aspects than neuronal mismatch process as such and is likely to parallel changes in classical indicators of orienting. On the other hand, the slow negative shift of the 2% reading conditions, extending also to posterior areas, might be triggered by the neuronal mismatch per se if its onset latency indeed was of the order of 100 ms.

Scalp Distribution of N2

Perhaps the scalp distribution of N2 could also be used in assessing its chances of reflecting the neuronal mismatch. Several studies have disclosed a frontal focus (see Näätänen & Michie, 1979; see also Figure 3) which is in line with findings stressing the importance of the frontal areas to orienting (Luria, 1973). Another N2 focus probably exists in the sensory-specific areas, which supports the suggestion of the neuronal-model development and mismatch as taking place in the sensory-specific regions of the brain (Näätänen, Gaillard, & Mäntysalo, 1978, 1980a). Simson et al. (1976, 1977) observed an occipital distribution of N2 to deviant visual stimuli as well as to omissions in a regular visual stimulus sequence, whereas in the parallel auditory tasks the focus was observed in the vicinity of the vertex. However, this potential was explained by the authors as being generated in the sensory-specific areas of audition, reflected to the scalp in this manner. (For compatible results, see Renault, Ragot, & Lesevre, 1980.) Näätänen, Gaillard, et al. (1978, 1980a) observed large N2s in T3 and T4 data (i.e., recorded over the cortical auditory areas) in a dichotic-listening situation, equally large or even larger than the N2 recorded simultaneously from the vertex (see Figure 2). [4]

Also, this modality specificity fits well to the mismatch interpretation of N2, because a natural locus of the neuronal model appears to be the sensory-specific areas of the modality involved. (Sokolov, 1963, 1975, suggests the hippocampus as a locus of the neuronal model; but even if this is the case, a multiple representation of the neuronal model at different levels of the central nervous system appears a reasonable possibility. Such a representation in any case in the sensory-specific areas is likely in view of the high degree of sensory dis- crimination acuity reflected in the formation of the neuronal model and its mis- match as suggested, e.g., by the data reviewed in the present chapter.)

N2 and Stimulus Significance

Finally, if N2 were a reflector of pure neuronal-mismatch processes, it must not reflect stimulus-evaluation factors such as experienced stimulus significance. If N2 also reflected such factors, then it would be another combined measure of mismatch and its experienced significance. In the foregoing, some data have already been reviewed suggesting independence of N2 of stimulus-significance

---

[4]However, in further studies using "uni-channel" listening situations, N2 re- corded from the temporal electrodes was considerably smaller than the N2 recorded from the vertex electrode (e.g., Näätänen, et al., 1980b; see Figure 4 of the present chapter).

factors, etc. In the dichotic-listening situation (Näätänen, Gaillard, et al.,
1978, 1980a), N2 to deviants within the input to be ignored was of the same
amplitude as N2 to deviants within the input to be attended to (stimuli
delivered to a designated ear, Figures 1 and 2). In a similar vein, in a one-
channel listening situation (Näätänen, Simpson, et al., 1982), N2 to target
deviants and nontarget deviants was of the same size (probability and magnitude
being matched, Figure 3). Moreover, it has been observed in several studies
that N2 to deviants in a stimulus sequence presented to a reading subject was
of the same amplitude as when the subject's task was to detect them (Ford et al.,
1976; Squires, K. C., Donchin, Herning, & McCarthy, 1977; Vaughan et al., 1980).

However, here the situation is not that clear. At least in two studies comparing
attending (detect deviants) and ignoring (read) auditory stimuli, some differences between the "detect N2" and "read N2" have been observed (Näätänen, Sams,
et al., 1982, 1983). In the former study (Figure 3), the widely deviant stimuli
in the "detect" conditions also elicited a sharp frontal negative peak in the
data of several subjects, "active N2," appearing to be separable from the
"passive N2" or mismatch negativity: There seemed often to exist two negative
waves in the N2 latency range. The slower, "passive" N2 (which alone was
present in the reading condition) was overlapped by the sharp negative peak,
which might be closely associated with the subsequent large positive process.
In Näätänen, Sams, et al. (1983), a somewhat similar effect (but with a more
posterior distribution) could be observed in the 10% counting condition. (Some
of this effect was also seen in the 2% counting condition, Figure 5.) Moreover,
it is possible that another type of negative shift, "processing negativity"
(Näätänen, Gaillard, 1978; for a review, see Näätänen & Michie, 1979), was also
elicited by deviants in the 10% counting condition of this study, producing the
early, anterior difference between the counting and reading N2 (compare the 10%
conditions in Figures 5 and 6).

Even if there were a genuine difference in the mismatch negativity type of N2
between the active and passive conditions, this would be no strong evidence for
significance effects on N2, because basic state differences, e.g., in general
physiological responsiveness or excitability, might account for N2 differences
(for review, see Karlin, 1970; Näätänen, 1967, 1975; Tecce, 1970).

The N2 observed in the elegant study of Ritter, Simson, Vaughan, and Friedman
(1979), whose latency correlated with reaction time to deviants and with P3
latency in a reaction-time experiment, might well be of the active-discrimination
type of N2 as suggested by the authors. Later these authors have also observed
a "passive" type of N2 (Vaughan et al., 1980).

Perhaps the most unequivocal evidence for the independence of N2 of significance
factors is N2 waves elicited by undetected stimulus deviances mentioned previously.

We conclude that N2 can be used as an indicator of the neuronal mismatch process
as such. In detection conditions, some other negative waves, probably reflecting
discrimination process ("processing negativity") or its outcome ("active N2") might
sometimes overlap the (mismatch type of) N2 but appear to be separable from it
at least by differences in distribution, latency, or wave form. Here the
principal-components analysis (PCA) is likely to be of great help (see Squires,
K. C., Donchin, et al., 1977b).

In sum, evidence for N2's providing a pure measure of the neuronal mismatch
processes per se appears quite convincing though, still, some sort of converging
evidence might be assuring. For instance, it has not been shown that N2 to a
second consecutive deviant is smaller than to the first deviant in a sequence of
homogeneous repetitive stimuli. Another demonstration for which evidence is
awaited is the co-existence and correlation of N2 with some other physiological

measures already well established as measures of orienting processes, such as spinal-excitability changes. (Comparable evidence for N1 already exists for its being associated with orienting in some other kinds of situations, as mentioned earlier in the present chapter.)

N2 -- A TOOL FOR PROGRESS IN ORIENTING RESEARCH

In the foregoing we have, hopefully, provided evidence for the possibility suggested that N2 of the EP could be used as a pure (noninvasive) measure of the neuronal mismatch process itself. This could pave a way for new progress in OR research which seems at present to be preoccupied with controversies concerning basic issues that are insoluble by using the commonly employed recording methods. These do not provide an unconfounded measure of the various individual stages of the OR. If N2 could be used as a measure of the neuronal mismatch process, that would make it possible to clarify problems such as those involving the relationship between this process and the OR. Moreover, it would also shed more light on events that occur at the initial stages of orienting. Similarly, the neuronal mismatch process itself, for example, its location and situational and state determinants, could be better studied. N2 might also provide an indirect measure for studying the development and decay of the neuronal model and their determinants (through its mismatch process).

One of the most controversial of the current issues is that involving the neuronal mismatch per se as a sufficient eliciting agent for the OR. In measuring the neuronal mismatch process by means of N2 and simultaneously recording those physiological functions usually considered as reliable indicators of the occurrence and magnitude of the OR, it might be possible to resolve this basic problem. The present suggestion is that neuronal mismatch as such is sufficient to elicit an OR. This OR, however, might be somewhat different from ORs elicited by other agents, such as experienced stimulus significance, which can elicit an OR with no neuronal mismatch and strengthen an OR elicited by a neuronal mismatch. Another OR-eliciting agent seems to be the firstness of (any kind of) a stimulus after a stimulus-empty interval, in which case an OR cannot be based on a neuronal mismatch (unless there also exists a neuronal model for stimulus silence or steadiness of stimulus background).

Although experienced stimulus significance certainly is an important factor in eliciting and strengthening orienting kinds of reactions, neuronal mismatch as such is suggested to be sufficient for the elicitation of an OR. It is biologically meaningful that there would be an automatically onsetting series of facilitatory and preparatory organismic processes triggered already at that stage (neuronal mismatch process) of response to a deviant stimulus at which stimulus evaluation has not yet started, or at least not finished. If OR were only triggered by subjective results of stimulus evaluation, then the favorable effects of the OR might often be fatally late. Moreover, a mismatch-triggered OR probably facilitates the further perceptual and cognitive analysis of the stimulus leading to experienced stimulus significance, helping the organism in the accurate determination of, for example, the message contained in the stimulus, its predictive value to the immediate future, and demands for responses and actions.

Significance evaluation of the mismatch can take place only after the neuronal mismatch process (some outcome of it), which is the first selective response of the brain to stimulus deviation. There is no way that the organism can know of the stimulus deviation before some stage of that process, which, in fact, provides a central stimulus to the higher-order, evaluative processes. An early significant response to a stimulus is possible only when for some reason the onset of the stimulus, or its mere existence without any further processing requirements, is known beforehand to be somehow significant (e.g., the subject knows that if a stimulus will be presented within 3 s from his response to a discrimination-task stimulus, the response was wrong; whereas if no stimulus will be delivered, the performance was correct). For a discussion of the preevaluation and postevaluation of stimulus significance and their effects on EEG measures such as EPs, see Näätänen (1975).

Hence, it is suggested that any neuronal mismatch leads to automatic orienting kinds of changes such as transient increase in spinal excitability and reticular and thalamic (nonspecific nuclei) arousal with their typical widely spread reflections in different functional systems of the organism. However, these changes might be quite short lived if the mismatching stimulus is experienced as insignificant. If it is experienced as significant, further orienting kinds of physiological events follow (which might already show some patterning in line with the kind of experienced significance, forthcoming behavioral response, etc.). The P3 component of the EP might be of great import here. In the foregoing, studies have been reviewed showing that stimulus deviance elicits an N2 independently of stimulus significance, but P3 is only elicited when a stimulus deviance has some sort of significance. Consequently, an N2 without a subsequent P3 might signify an OR based solely on neuronal mismatch; whereas when P3 is elicited, too, evaluative processes also play a role. In this latter case, several slower brain potentials are also elicited that are small or nonexistent to the same stimulus deviance with no task relevance (Rohrbaugh, Syndulko, & Lindsley, 1978).

In some situations, however, a P3 is elicited by deviant stimuli with no task relevance, such as deviant tones in tone sequence presented to a reading subject (for a review, see Donchin, Ritter, & McCallum, 1978). This P3 seems to be smaller and later than in "active" conditions and is only elicited by widely deviant stimuli such as to be noticed by the reading subject (Näätänen, Simpson, et al., 1982). Strong neuronal-mismatch process appears to reach consciousness -- a stimulus mismatch is perceived -- irrespective of whether what the subject is engaged in is also biologically meaningful.

REFERENCES

Bernstein, A. S. (1979). The orienting response as novelty and significance detector: Reply to O'Gorman. Psychophysiology, 16, 263-273.

Butler, R. A. (1968). Effect of changes in stimulus frequency and intensity on habituation of the human vertex potential. The Journal of the Acoustical Society of America, 44, 945-950.

Butler, R. A. (1973). The cumulative effects of different stimulus repetition rates on the auditory evoked response in man. Electroencephalography and Clinical Neurophysiology, 35, 337-345.

Donchin, E., Ritter, W., & McCallum, W. C. (1978). Cognitive psychophysiology: The endogenous components of the ERP. In E. Callaway, P. Tueting, & S. H. Koslow (Eds.), Event-related brain potentials in man (pp. 349-411). New York: Academic Press.

Ford, J. M., Roth, W. T., & Kopell, B. S. (1976). Auditory evoked potentials to unpredictable shifts in pitch. Psychophysiology, 13, 32-39.

Fruhstorfer, H. (1971). Habituation and dishabituation of the human vertex response. Electroencephalography and Clinical Neurophysiology, 30, 306-312.

Fruhstorfer, H., Järvilehto, T., Lumio, J., & Soveri, P. (1970). Changes in spinal excitability during an auditory vertex response in man. Acta Physiologica Scandinavica, 80, 42.

Fruhstorfer, H., Soveri, P., & Järvilehto, T. (1970). Short-term habituation of the auditory evoked response in man. Electroencephalography and Clinical Neurophysiology, 30, 306-312.

Järvilehto, T., & Näätänen, R. (1980). Ereignisbezogene Potentiale des menschlichen Gehirns und der Orientierungsreflex. In W. Hacker & H. Raum (Eds.), Optimierung von kognitiven Arbeitsanforderungen (pp. 215-219). Berlin: VEB Deutscher Verlag der Wissenschaften.

Karlin, L. (1970). Cognition, preparation and sensory-evoked potentials. Psychological Bulletin, 73, 122-136.

Klinke, R., Fruhstorfer, H., & Finkenzeller, P. (1968). Evoked responses as a function of external and stored information. Electroencephalography and Clinical Neurophysiology, 25, 119-122.

Loveless, N. E., Simpson, M., & Näätänen, R. Manuscript in preparation.

Luria, A. R. (1973). The working brain. New York: Basic Books.

Lynn, R. (1966). Attention, arousal and the orientation reaction. Oxford: Pergamon Press.

Maltzman, I. (1979). Orienting reflexes and significance: A reply to O'Gorman. Psychophysiology, 16, 274-282.

Megela, A. L., & Teyler, T. J. (1979). Habituation and the human evoked potential. Journal of Comparative and Physiological Psychology, 93, 1154-1170.

Näätänen, R. (1967). Selective attention and evoked potentials. Annales Academiae Scientiarum Fennicae B, 151, 1-226.

Näätänen, R. (1973). The inverted-U relationship between activation and performance: A critical review. In S. Kornblum (Ed.), Attention and performance IV (pp. 155-174). New York: Academic Press.

Näätänen, R. (1975). Selective attention and evoked potentials in humans: A critical review. Biological Psychology, 2, 237-307.

Näätänen, R., Gaillard, A., & Mäntysalo, S. (1978). The N1 effect of selective attention reinterpreted. Acta Psychologica, 42, 313-329.

Näätänen, R., Gaillard, A., & Mäntysalo, S. (1980a). Brain-potential correlates of voluntary and involuntary attention. In H. Kornhuber & L. Deecke (Eds.), Motivation, motor and sensory processes of the brain: Electrical potentials, behavior and clinical use. Progress in brain research, 54, 343-348.

Näätänen, R., Hukkanen, S., & Järvilehto, T. (1980b). Magnitude of stimulus deviance and brain potentials. In H. H. Kornhuber and L. Deecke (Eds.), Motivation, motor and sensory processes of the brain: Electrical potentials, behavior and clinical use. Progress in brain research, 54, 337-342.

Näätänen, R., & Michie, P. T. (1979). Early selective-attention effects on the evoked potential: A critical review and reinterpretation. Biological Psychology, 8, 81-136.

Näätänen, R., Sams, M., Järvilehto, T., & Soininen, K. (1983). Probability of
    deviant stimulus and event-related brain potentials. In R. Sinz & M. Rosenzweig
    (Eds.), Psychophysiology: Memory, motivation, and event-related potentials
    in mental operations.(pp. 397-405). Jena: VEB Gustav Fischer Verlag.

Näätänen, R., Simpson, M., & Loveless, N. E. (1982). Stimulus deviance and
    evoked potentials. Biological Psychology, 14, 53-98.

O'Gorman, J. G. (1979). The orienting reflex: Novelty or significance detector.
    Psychophysiology, 16, 253-262.

Öhman, A., & Lader, M. H. (1977). Short-term changes of the human auditory
    evoked potentials during repetitive stimulation. In J. E. Desmedt (Ed.),
    Auditory evoked potential in man: Psychopharmacology correlates of evoked
    potentials. Progress in clinical neurophysiology, 2. Basel: Karger.

Renault, B., Ragot, R., & Lesevre, N. (1980). Correct and incorrect responses
    in a choice reaction time task and the endogenous components of the evoked
    potential. In H. H. Kornhuber & L. Deecke (Eds.), Motivation, motor and
    sensory processes of the brain: Electrical potentials, behavior and clinical
    use. Progress in Brain Research, 54.

Ritter, W., Simson, R., Vaughan, H. G., & Friedman, D. (1979). A brain event
    related to the making of a sensory discrimination. Science, 203, 1358-1361.

Rohrbaugh, J. W., Syndulko, K., & Lindsley, D. B. (1978). Cortical slow negative
    waves following non-paired stimuli: Effects of task factors. Electroencephalo-
    graphy and Clinical Neurophysiology, 45, 551-567.

Rossignol, S., & Jones, G. M. (1976). Audio-spinal influence in man studied by
    the H-reflex and its possible role in rhythmic movements synchronized to
    sound. Electroencephalography and Clinical Neurophysiology, 41, 83-92.

Salamy, A., & McKean, C. M. (1977). Habituation and dishabituation of cortical
    and brainstem evoked potentials. International Journal of Neuroscience, 7,
    175-182.

Semjen, A., Bonnet, M., & Requin, J. (1973). Relation between the time-course
    of Hoffman-reflexes and the foreperiod duration in a reaction-time task.
    Physiology & Behavior, 10, 1041-1050.

Siddle, D. (1979). The orienting response and stimulus significance: Some
    comments. Biological Psychology, 8, 303-309.

Simson, R., Vaughan, H. G., & Ritter, W. (1976). The scalp topography of
    potentials associated with missing visual and auditory stimuli. Electro-
    encephalography and Clinical Neurophysiology, 40, 33-42.

Simson, R., Vaughan, H. G., & Ritter, W. (1977). Scalp topography of potentials
    in auditory and visual discrimination tasks. Electroencephalography and
    Clinical Neurophysiology, 42, 528-535.

Snyder, E., & Hillyard, S. A. (1976). Long-latency evoked potentials to irrele-
    vant, deviant stimuli. Behavioral Biology, 16, 319-331.

Sokolov, E. N. (1960). Neuronal models and the orienting reflex. In M. A. Brazier
    (Ed.), The central nervous system and behavior (pp. 187-276). New York: J. Macy.

Sokolov, E. N. (1963). Perception and the conditioned reflex. Oxford: Pergamon.

Sokolov, E. N. (1975). The neuronal mechanisms of the orienting reflex. In E. N. Sokolov & O. S. Vinogradova (Eds.), Neuronal mechanisms of the orienting reflex (pp. 217-235). Hillsdale, NJ: Erlbaum.

Sokolov, E. N., & Vinogradova, O. S. (Eds.), (1975). The neuronal mechanisms of the orienting reflex. Hillsdale, NJ: Erlbaum.

Squires, K. C., Donchin, E., Herning, R. L., & McCarthy, G. (1977). On the influence of task relevance and stimulus probability on event-related potential-components. Electroencephalography and Clinical Neurophysiology, 42, 1-14.

Squires, N. K., Donchin, E., Squires, K. C., & Grossberg, S. (1977). Bisensory stimulation: Inferring decision-related processes from the P300 component. Journal of Experimental Psychology: Human Perception and Performance, 3, 299-315.

Squires, N. K., Squires, K. C., & Hillyard, S. A. (1975). Two varieties of long latency positive waves evoked by unpredictable auditory stimuli in man. Electroencephalography and Clinical Neurophysiology, 38, 387-401.

Sutton, S., Braren, M., Zubin, J., & John, E. R. (1965). Evoked-potential correlates of stimulus uncertainty. Science, 150, 1187-1188.

Tecce, J. J. (1970). Attention and evoked potentials in man. In D. I. Mostofsky (Ed.), Attention: Contemporary theory and analysis (pp. 331-365). New York: Appleton-Century-Crofts.

Vaughan, H. G., Ritter, W., & Simson, R. (1980). Topographic analysis of auditory event-related potentials. In H. H. Kornhuber & L. Deecke (Eds.), Motivation, motor and sensory processes of the brain: Electrical potentials, behavior and clinical use. Progress in brain research, 54, 279-285.

4

Contingent Negative Variation: Relation to Personality, and Modification by Stimulation and Sedation

P. F. Werre

Since Berger's (1929) discovery of the human electroencephalogram (EEG), inves-tigators have been fascinated by the fact that traces recorded under identical conditions in the same scalp area of an adult reveal great similarities over a period of years, whereas comparable traces taken from different people show remarkable differences. Generally speaking, a person can be distinguished from others by his brain potentials (Travis & Gottlober, 1936). Such observations led to many experiments to determine those relationships between personality and EEG, which could be considered a reflection of the biological foundations of personality.

Many of the earlier studies were concerned with attempts to link EEG variables recorded during a passive situation with personality variables, which of course were obtained during an active situation. These studies yielded problematical results (e.g., Dongier, McCallum, Torres, & Vogel, 1976). In contrast, the results of experiments designed to explore relations between personality vari-ables and EEG variables related to an active event appear to be more promising. An example of this is the work of Buchsbaum and Silverman (1968), who found that people who demonstrate a reduction in the experienced intensity of stimulation, as inferred from their performance on a kinesthetic figural after-effect pro-cedure, also show a comparable tendency on a visual cortical evoked potential procedure. Thus, reducers show an amplitude decrease with strong stimulation, whereas augmenters show the reverse. Latency measures indicated a comparable interaction. There could therefore be a correlation between the intensity and latency functions of sensory evoked potentials and the personality dimension of augmenting-reducing. Another example was presented by Zuckerman, Murtaugh, and Siegel (1974). They found that the amplitude of a specific component of the visual evoked potential is positively correlated with stimulus intensity in the case of subjects' scoring high on the disinhibition subscale of Zuckerman's (1971) Sensation Seeking Scale, whereas in the case of low-disinhibition the relation between amplitude and stimulus intensity shows an inverted-U relation.

In this chapter, we emphasize potentials related to an event needing somewhat more cerebration, that is, a foreperiod reaction time task. Walter, Cooper, Aldridge, McCallum, and Winter (1964) were the first to describe how such a task usually generates a contingent negative variation (CNV) between the warning and imperative stimuli (for a general review, see Callaway, Tueting, & Koslow, 1978).

The author gratefully acknowledges the valuable comments of R. H. C. Janssen and H. Mattie.

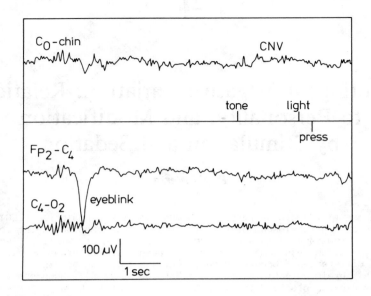

FIGURE 1. The upper trace, a vertex-to-chin derivation, depicts the slow upward
(= relative negativity at the vertex) wave, marked contingent negative variation
(CNV), contingent with the foreperiod reaction time task ("after the tone there
will be a light which has to be extinguished as quickly as possible by pressing
a button"). The middle trace, a right-frontal-to-central derivation, was used
to control for eye movements. The right-central-to-occipital derivation, the
lower trace shown, was used to monitor alpha rhythm.

Also of interest to us were the studies by Walter (1964) and McCallum (1969),
demonstrating differences in CNV properties among normal subjects, neurotic
patients, schizophrenics, and psychopaths. Figure 1 (top) illustrates a single
CNV recorded from the vertex, because the CNV generally has its maximal amplitude over the central part of the scalp. Such clear potentials are not usually
observed on single trials, because the relatively low-voltage CNV is frequently
submerged in other cerebral activity. Therefore, the majority of studies,
including the ones under consideration here, rely on data from summated or
averaged trials (presented at random and selected to avoid contamination by
eye or other relatively large noncerebral potentials). In our studies we
restricted ourselves to a vertex electrode, with the chin as reference.

CONTINGENT NEGATIVE VARIATION AND PERSONALITY

The paucity of normative data led us to investigate first the relationship
between personality and CNV in normal subjects. As frame of reference we chose
Eysenck's (1967) personality theory, because it is clearly formulated and
enables prediction of both psychological and physiological observations.

In the experiment, on which we shall focus first, 118 naive healthy students
(mean age about 23 years, mainly males) participated (Werre, Faverey, & Janssen,
1973, 1975). To obtain the main physiological variable -- maximal CNV amplitude

(summation of 20 CNVs not contaminated by artifacts) -- the subjects were examined separately in the morning for about 2 h. After the electrodes had been applied, the student was seated in a comfortable chair in a sound-dampened cubicle. Opposite the student there was a screen with a fixation point for the eyes, to limit eye movements. The student was required to perform a constant foreperiod reaction time task (a short tone was followed after 2 s by a light, which had to be extinguished as quickly as possible by pressing a button), first in the standard way, next under three stressful conditions; then the experiment ended with a condition identical to the first. The stressful conditions were: (a) distraction (counting numbers, presented by means of a loudspeaker, in addition to the reaction time task described already); (b) equivocation (the second stimulus was randomly omitted in 50% of the trials); (c) a condition in which the subject was required to initiate the trials himself by pressing another button. We review here the data obtained only during the beginning, distraction, and end conditions.

During the same experiment, a performance measure was recorded, that is, mean reaction time in the CNV paradigm.

The following personality variables were determined on another day, shortly before the day of the experiment: (a) extraversion, as measured by the ABV, a questionnaire that is the Dutch counterpart of Eysenck's EPI (Wilde, 1962); (b) neuroticism, also as measured by the ABV; (c) habitual action preparedness, as measured by the HAB questionnaire, which was developed by Dirken (1970) to determine the degree of task orientation, energy, and eagerness to work (it has a positive correlation with extraversion and a negative one with neuroticism); (d) intelligence, as measured by the GIT, a Dutch intelligence test (Snijders & Verhage, 1962).

Factor analysis demonstrated several of the expected effects. Since various investigators had reported lowering of CNV amplitude by a variety of arousal augmenting events (e.g., McCallum & Walter, 1968), extraverts were presumed to have higher CNVs than introverts (who are on the opposite end of the same continuum as extraverts). For, according to Eysenck, extraverts are characterized by relatively low levels of arousal and relatively high levels of inhibition as compared with introverts, and vice versa. In analogy, a negative correlation was thought to exist between neuroticism and CNV amplitude. Moreover, neurotic patients were shown by McCallum and Walter to have lower CNVs that normals, and their CNVs were practically gone when their arousal levels were further heightened by way of a distraction condition. A positive correlation was expected between habitual action preparedness and CNV, because the HAB questionnaire measures, to some degree, stable extraversion versus unstable introversion. No assumptions were made in regard to intelligence test scores. The prevailing view regarding reaction time was that CNV and reaction time were negatively correlated. For other predictions the reader is referred to the original studies.

The following factor-analytic method was used. Principal components derived from the matrix of correlations were transformed into Minres-factors, according to a program developed by Harman (1960). These factors were rotated to simple structure by means of the Varimax method. Because an orthogonal solution is not always optimal in personality research, it was decided to rotate the Varimax factors to oblique structure by means of Promax (Hendrickson & White, 1964). In Table 1 the Promax factor structure of the two significant factors is presented for the beginning, distraction, and end conditions (for the results of the two other central conditions, see Werre et al., 1973). Only the subtests Number and Word fluency of the intelligence test were used; another factor analysis had demonstrated that only these subtests were related to CNV amplitude. The nonrelated subtests were: Vocabulary, Formboards, Destination, Induction and deduction, Gestalt completion, Spatial relations and orientation, and Word squares.

TABLE 1. Promax structure of beginning condition (A), distraction condition (B), and end condition (C).

	A			B			C		
	I	II	h^2	I	II	h^2	I	II	h^2
Extraversion	0.25	0.51	0.26	-0.20	-0.44	0.20	0.13	0.44	0.19
Neuroticism	-0.03	-0.16	0.03	-0.04	0.23	0.07	-0.02	-0.21	0.04
HAB	0.25	0.69	0.49	-0.13	-0.72	0.53	0.08	0.77	0.60
Number	0.34	0.23	0.12	-0.27	-0.27	0.11	0.22	0.25	0.09
Word fluency	0.36	0.32	0.16	-0.23	-0.30	0.11	0.18	0.28	0.09
CNV	0.36	0.50	0.27	-0.26	-0.24	0.09	-0.26	0.02	0.07
RT 1	-0.76	-0.39	0.58	0.95	0.25	0.92	—	—	—
RT 2	-0.78	-0.29	0.62	0.68	0.20	0.47	—	—	—
RT 1 + 2	—	—	—	—	—	—	-0.99	-0.13	1.00

Note: HAB = habitual action preparedness questionnaire; CNV = contingent negative variation; RT 1 = mean reaction time of the first series of 10 trials; and RT 2 = mean reaction time of the second series of 20 trials. From Contingent negative variation and personality by P. F. Werre, H. A. Faverey, and R.H.C. Janssen, 1973. Psychiatrische Kliniek, Rijksuniversiteit Leiden, 1973. Copyright by Werre et al.

If we consider the beginning condition (Table 1, A), we can identify the first factor as a Speed factor. This indicates that the quicker one reacts in the standard CNV paradigm, the faster one can add figures or think of animal words within a given time period. The second factor, CNV-extraversion, demonstrates that the more extraverted and action-prepared one is, the higher is one's amplitude and vice versa. The correlation between the two factors was 0.52, indicating the close relationship between CNV and speed. In other words, the data indicate that there was:

1. A positive correlation between extraversion and CNV amplitude.
2. No correlation between neuroticism and CNV amplitude.
3. A positive correlation between habitual action preparedness and CNV amplitude.
4. A positive correlation between mental efficiency and CNV amplitude.
5. A negative correlation between reaction time and CNV amplitude.

These findings, however, are based on data from the beginning condition. The Promax structures of the distraction and end conditions (Table 1, B and C) again show two significant factors, but the correlation is much lower (0.36 and 0.23, respectively) and the relation between CNV and extraversion is no longer shown (note that the weak relation between CNV and reaction time demonstrated during the end condition is opposite to that previously found: the longer the reaction time, the higher the CNV). Thus, the data obtained during the distraction and end conditions failed to show the aforementioned correlations. This resulted from a considerable decrease of CNV amplitude during the quite exciting distraction condition in both extraverts and introverts (the decrease of the extraverts being considerably larger than that of the introverts). During the end condition, approximately 90 min after the initiation of the experiment, there occurred again a decrease in the case of the extraverts, but the introverts showed some increase. It is our judgment that now reactive inhibition had manifested itself.

Apparently there was an interaction between condition and extraversion. This was explained by the assumption that a nonlinear relationship exists between extraversion (or habitual action preparedness) and the CNV or, more generally stated, between CNV and the excitation-inhibition balance of the central nervous system that underlies manifest personality (Figure 2).

EFFECT OF STIMULATION AND SEDATION ON THE CONTINGENT NEGATIVE VARIATION

This section deals mainly with the data obtained during an experiment in which three groups of eight naive healthy males (mean age about 24 years) were tested twice with an interval of 1 week, one group receiving 10 and 20 mg chlordiazepoxide, another receiving 150 and 300 mg caffeine, and a control group receiving placebo and no-drug treatment (Janssen, Mattie, Plooij-van Gorsel, & Werre, 1978). During each session, the CNV was recorded five times: first prior to drug administration, then in four postdrug measurements, each of these measurements being distinguished in a condition with and without white noise. Before the first session, the extraversion score was determined with the ABV.

Two approaches can be taken in reconsidering the results of this experiment. First, we shall concentrate on the data of both sessions obtained prior to drug administration. Two situations can be distinguished, that is, the first versus the second session and the without-white-noise versus the with-white-noise condition. With respect to the former, one could have predicted an interaction between session and extraversion if the results of the first experiment had been taken into account (see Figure 2). With respect to the latter, an interaction between condition and extraversion could have been envisaged, especially if it is taken for granted that the white noise used in this experiment caused somewhat less excitation than the distraction condition did in the first experiment (cf. Figure 2). This implies that the mean amplitude of the extraverts will hover then somewhere around the top of the curve, meaning no big CNV change, whether positive or negative, between the without-white-noise and with-white-noise conditions. The results of an analysis of variance (Table 2; see also Figure 3) demonstrate that there are significant interactions between session and extraversion as well as between condition and extraversion.

The second approach concentrates on the manipulation of the excitation-inhibition balance not by way of conditions but by way of drugs. According to Eysenck's (1957) drug postulate, depressant drugs increase cortical inhibition and decrease cortical excitation, thus producing extravert behavior; stimulant drugs decrease cortical inhibition and increase cortical excitation, thus producing introvert behavior. As follows from this postulate, it was hypothesized that the CNV increases under the extraverting drug chlordiazepoxide and decreases under the introverting drug caffeine. This hypothesis was significantly verified comparing the data obtained before and during administration of the chlordiazepoxide group with those of the caffeine group (Figure 4). However, making comparisons within

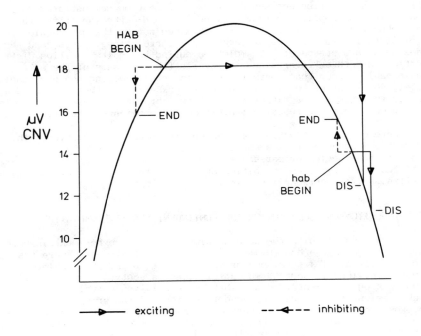

FIGURE 2. Hypothetical relation between observed mean contingent negative
variation (CNV) amplitudes (vertical axis) of high- (HAB; n = 35) and low-
(hab; n = 33) action prepared subjects, and the excitation-inhibition balance
of the central nervous system (horizontal axis). As the HAB questionnaire
measures to some degree stable extraversion versus unstable introversion,
the high-action prepared subjects are thought to occupy the left, inhibition
leg of the inverted-U curve, whereas the low-action prepared subjects are
presumably situated on the right, excitation leg of the curve. During an
excitatory condition (marked DIS; in this case a distraction task was added
to the standard foreperiod reaction time task) and during an inhibitory
condition (marked END; repetition of the standard task at the end of the
experiment) subjects are thought to move in opposite directions away from
the position (marked BEGIN) they occupied during the beginning condition.
From "Contingent negative variation and personality" by P. F. Werre,
H. A. Faverey, and R. H. C. Janssen, 1975. Nederlands Tijdschrift voor
Psychologie, 30, 277-299. Copyright by Van Loghum Slaterus, Deventer.
Reprinted by permission.

TABLE 2. Analysis of variance of the contingent negative variation (CNV)
measurements. Recorded prior to drug administration for two groups (introverts and extraverts) during two sessions, each under two conditions (with
and without white noise).

Comparison	SS	df	MS	F
Between subjects	1512.16	23	65.75	
Groups (A)	12.96	1	12.96	0.19
Subjects within groups	1499.19	22	68.15	
Within subjects	946.00	72	13.14	
Sessions (B)	89.37	1	89.37	9.43*
AB	88.52	1	88.52	9.33*
B × subjects within groups	206.41	22	9.38	
Noise (C)	57.09	1	57.09	5.35**
AC	48.36	1	48.36	4.53**
C × subjects within groups	234.72	22	10.67	
BC	12.27	1	12.27	1.47
ABC	25.13	1	25.13	3.00
BC × subjects within groups	184.13	22	8.37	

Note. From "The effects of a depressant and a stimulant drug on the contingent-
negative variation" by R. H. C. Janssen, H. Mattie, P. C. Plooij-van Gorsel,
and P. F. Werre, 1978. Biological Psychology, 6, 209-218. Copyright by
North-Holland, Amsterdam. Reproduced by permission.

* $p < .01$; $F_{.01; 1,22} = 7.95$

** $p < .05$; $F_{.05; 1,22} = 4.30$

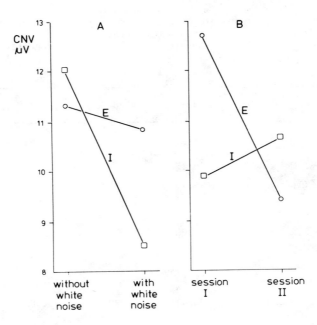

FIGURE 3.   Section A demonstrates the interaction between extraversion and white
noise (see Table 2, Groups × Noise). The significance found (p < .05) indicates
that both personality groups differently responded to the noise condition.   An
a priori test showed introverts (n = 8; squares) to have a significantly lower
mean value during exposure to white noise than without white noise (t = 3.07,
p < .05, df = 14), whereas for extraverts (n = 16; circles) the difference was
minimal and not statistically significant (Tukey's t ratio, one-tailed test).
The interaction between extraversion and session is shown in section B. As can
be seen from Table 2, the effect of sessions proved to be highly significant.
An a posteriori test did not show a significant difference between sessions for
introverts (F = 0.52), but for extraverts a significant F ratio was obtained
(F = 18.46, p < .01, df = 1,22).

groups, only the decrease between the measurements before taking caffeine and
the first measurement after administering this drug was significant. As expected,
no trend emerged during placebo and no-drug sessions. There was also no difference between these sessions.

CONCLUDING REMARKS

Tentatively, it is concluded that certain conditions differentially affect the slow
wave, which is contingent with a constant foreperiod reaction time task, for different groups of people. In our experimental setting, the personality variables
extraversion, habitual action preparedness, and mental efficiency were able to
discriminate these groups, whereas the variable neuroticism failed to do so.

One of the conditions, which was found to have such a clear differential effect
on the CNV, was the one that exists when isolated, motivated, young adult students

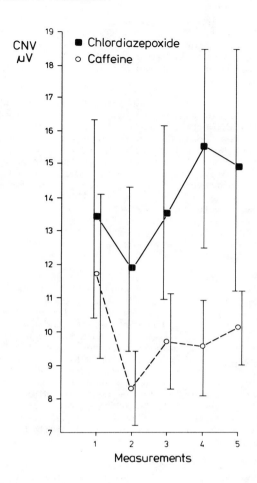

FIGURE 4. Mean contingent negative variation (CNV) amplitude 15 min before (measurement 1) and 30, 60, 90, and 150 min, respectively (measurements 2-5), after administration of 20 mg chlordiazepoxide (n = 8; squares) and 300 mg caffeine (n = 8; circles) in the absence of white noise. Vertical lines denote standard error of the mean. From "The effects of a depressant and a stimulant drug on the contingent negative variation" by R. H. C. Janssen, H. Mattie, P. C. Plooij-van Gorsel, and P. F. Werre, 1978. Biological Psychology, 6, 209-218. Copyright by North-Holland, Amsterdam. Reprinted by permission.

perform a constant foreperiod reaction time task, which is novel to them, in the morning. Then there is a positive correlation between mean CNV amplitude and extraversion, habitual action preparedness, and mental alertness and efficiency, and a negative correlation between CNV amplitude and reaction time. Our first study showed that the mean CNV differences between (stable) extraverts and (unstable) introverts and between high- and low-action prepared subjects were significant.

Conditions that did not lead to CNV differences, at least between groups differentiated with the personality scores used, were those that existed when the students were repeating the standard task and when they were performing a second
task in addition to the standard one (respectively, the end and distraction conditions of the first experiment).

This approach owes much to Gale (1973). He asked the question whether it is
reasonable to expect the EEG of extraverts to be always differentiable from that
of introverts and for the difference always to be in the same direction, as
opposed to the idea that the EEG is like a fingerprint. He compared this with
task performance and gave the work of Colquhoun and Corcoran (1964) as an example:
they showed how time of day and group or individual testing on attentional tasks
can reverse such relationships. In other words, under certain conditions, extraverts perform better than introverts, and under certain conditions they perform
worse. On the basis of such evidence, he assumed that the activity of the nervous
system is differentially affected by experimental conditions, and because the
EEG is a reflection of central nervous activity, it is not surprising that the
EEG should vary also. The problem is whether the variation observed is explic-
able in a systematic manner. In this way he was able to present a post hoc
attempt to reconcile contradictions in studies of extraversion and the EEG.

In passing it should be mentioned here that in the first experiment the central,
more stressful, conditions could have been responsible for the differences
observed between the beginning and end conditions, because mainly for technical
reasons balancing of conditions did not take place. The same holds for the
effect of the beginning condition on the distraction condition. The results
of the second experiment, however, support the idea that repetition indeed leads
to disappearance of the previously mentioned correlations (see Figure 3, B).
Also with respect to the distraction effect, the data from the second experiment
(those shown in Figure 3, A) support the general idea that distraction leads to
a CNV-amplitude decrease. In addition, if the nonlinear model is correct, in
the case of the distraction condition the low mean CNV values are thought to
indicate that extraverts as well as introverts are very much excited, whereas
in the case of the end condition the statistically equal mean CNV values are
thought to mean that extraverts are preponderantly inhibited and introverts
excited (see Figure 2).

Partial confirmation was found when psychiatric patients (24 males, no medication
or cerebral pathology) were brought into a situation similar to the beginning
condition of the first experiment (Plooij-van Gorsel & Janssen, 1980). The experimental set-up was the same, with the exception of an interstimulus interval
of 4 s, enabling distinction of Orienting and Expectancy components of the CNV.
Here, too, extraverts (based on ABV scores) were found to produce higher O and
E waves than were introverts. Nakamura, Fukui, Kadobayashi, and Kato (1979)
also demonstrated a significant positive correlation between CNV and extraversion
(measured with the Japanese version of the MPI) in old people. In addition they
found a negative correlation with neuroticism.

The results of the pharmacological study are according to expectations, but not
impressive. It is possible that this is the consequence of using the linear,
and not the nonlinear model. Had we used the latter, then the effects would
have been studied on extraverts and introverts separately. In the case of the
extraverts, one could have predicted that the sedative would have caused a CNV
decrease and the stimulant some increase or decrease (depending on the dose),
whereas in the case of the introverts opposite effects could have been predicted
to occur: an increase by the sedative, a decrease by the stimulant. We hope
that in the future such knowledge will help in treating patients with psychoactive drugs.

The hypothetical inverted-U relation between the CNV and the excitation-inhibition balance shown in Figure 2 is reminiscent of the classical activation theory idea that there is an optimal level of activation -- that performance is optimal somewhere in the middle of the activation continuum. The conditions under which a certain (optimal) performance level is reached differ from person to person and from task to task, and our results suggest that the height of the CNV could be related to this level. In any case, the negative correlation between CNV and reaction time and the positive correlation between CNV and mental efficiency (both indicators of performance level) found during the beginning condition point in that direction. It was the extraverts who were at that moment probably near optimal activation. The results also remind us of the way in which people differ in looking for more stimulating (radio, stimulant, thrilling or opposing company, etc.) or more restful (silence, sedative, familiar or comforting company, etc.) surroundings, and in handling themselves internally (whether consciously or unconsciously) in a comparable manner, for example, feeling and thinking about calming or exciting events. This is dependent too, of course, on what is demanded, if such should be the case. It should be added here that it would be naive to assume that people always aim at reaching the degree of activation that the experimenter is inclined to call optimal. For instance, (neurotic) defense mechanisms, comparable to the ones that lead in normal life to oversedation (e.g., day sleeping, excessive drinking of alcohol) or overstimulation (e.g., continuous quarreling, drinking excessive amounts of coffee), can come into operation, hampering optimal performance.

The nonlinear model presented here is, by the way, not the only model relating CNV to psychological constructs (e.g., Werre, 1982). Tecce (1972), for instance, presented a two-process theoretical model, consisting of an attention hypothesis (the magnitude of CNV bears a positive monotonic relation to attention) and an arousal hypothesis (the magnitude of CNV bears a nonmonotonic, inverted U, relation to arousal level).

If the nonlinear model is correct, then discrepancies between our data and some mentioned in the literature can be reconciled. For instance, Ashton, Millman, Telford, and Thompson (1974) described a CNV magnitude (a measure that takes into account both amplitude and latency) enhancing effect of caffeine and a reducing effect of nitrazepam (a benzodiazepine, as chlordiazepoxide is), a result opposite to ours. The explanation could be sought by comparing the experimental conditions. A striking difference is that in the case of the Ashton et al. experiment, three subjects and several observers sat together in the subject room. Also, there was some bodily contact between subjects and observers (to count the radial pulse). It is clear that these circumstances could have a different effect on the excitation-inhibition balance as compared with our isolated subject situation. The social reassuring circumstances could have placed the majority of subjects on the left, inhibition, leg of the inverted-U, whereas our more stressful isolation probably did the opposite. Thus, the opposite points of departure on the inverted-U curve could explain why the results of their study and of our study are opposed.

Another enigma is that reported by Tecce and Cole (1974) regarding the effect of amphetamine: 13 out of 20 normal women showed a decrease and the remainder an increase in CNV amplitude. The authors considered a variety of factors that might have accounted for the difference found, but none of them did. However, they did not look at personality differences. Because personality differences appear to be an important factor, we can comment on their results as we did on the results of our own pharmacological study (see previous section). In other words, extraverts and introverts should be considered separately because they occupy different positions in the nonlinear model. Thus, it is possible that the women who showed the CNV increase (and felt more alert) were the more extraverted ones of the group, whereas those who showed the decrease (coupled with what the

authors called "paradoxical" drowsiness, which is after all a reaction form of
several overexcited individuals) were the most introverted subjects of the group.

Ashton et al. (1974) also reported on the dual action of a drug, or, more exactly,
of the complex stimulus cigarette smoking, on the CNV. They found that some
smokers showed consistent increases and others consistent decreases in CNV magnitude immediately after smoking. They stated that correlations of the percentage
change in CNV magnitude with rate of nicotine intake and with degree of extraversion suggested that, in extraverts, the rate of nicotine intake was slower
and associated with a CNV increase, whereas in introverted smokers the rate was
faster and associated with a CNV decrease. They interpreted this as reflecting
stimulant and depressant effects of nicotine, referring to the literature: in
animals small doses of nicotine increase arousal and electrocortical activity
while higher doses sometimes have the opposite effect. However, in the case of
such a complex stimulus interpretation of results is a hazardous enterprise.
For instance, one could argue that there is a pharmacologically induced excitatory effect, at least on certain central nervous system levels to which CNV is
related. More or less opposed, the (depth) psychological soothing effect of
smoking could induce inhibition in these or other levels. Thus, in the case of
the (inhibited) extravert the excitatory nicotine effect of smoking will be the
principal value, but in the case of the (excited) introvert there would be inhibitory psychological effects. The latter is suggested by the data of Ashton
et al.: the introverts showed a faster rate of intake than did the extraverts.
In other words, the extraverts might execute their smoking in such a fashion
that the excitatory action, which is accompanied by CNV increase (on the left
side of the inverted-U), prevails. The introverts, on the contrary, smoke differently, presumably in order to enhance the inhibitory effects. The latter
do not counteract the excitatory nicotine effect sufficiently, as indicated by
CNV decrease (on the right side), but their overall subjective, that is, calming,
effect is apparently to the introverts' preference.

In all, the results underline the importance of individual and conditional differences and their interaction for experimentation. A consequence of these
results is that we are now studying the effects of a stimulant, a sedative, and
a placebo on extraverts and introverts separately, in an experimental setting
that is as much as possible similar to the one we used previously, but with the
addition of a questionnaire, designed to get some information about introspective
experience during the experiment. Notwithstanding the restriction mentioned
here, the latter might be useful as an indicator of activation.

REFERENCES

Ashton, H., Millman, J. E., Telford, R., & Thompson, J. W. (1974). The effect of
    caffeine, nitrazepam and cigarette smoking on the contingent negative variation
    in man. Electroencephalography and Clinical Neurophysiology, 37, 59-71.

Berger, H. (1929). Über das Elektrenkephalogram des Menschen (Erste Mitteilung).
    Archiv für Psychiatrie Nervenkrankheiten, 87, 527-570.

Buchsbaum, M., & Silverman, J. (1968). Stimulus intensity control and the
    cortical evoked response. Psychosomatic Medicine, 30, 12-22.

Callaway, E., Tueting, P., & Koslow, S. H. (Eds.). (1978). Event-related brain
    potentials in man. New York: Academic Press.

Colquhoun, W. P., & Corcoran, D. W. J. (1964). The effects of time of day and
    social isolation on the relationship between temperament and performance.
    British Journal of Social and Clinical Psychology, 3, 226-231.

Dirken, J. M. (1970). De vragenlijst voor habituele aktiebereidheid. Groningen: Wolters-Noordhof.

Dongier, M., McCallum,W. C., Torres, F., & Vogel, W. (1971). Psychological and psychophysiological states. In G. E. Chatrian & G. C. Lairy (Eds.), The EEG of the waking adult (Vol. 6A). In A. Rémond (Ed.), Handbook of electroencephalography and clinical neurophysiology. Amsterdam: Elsevier.

Eysenck, H. J. (1957). Dynamics of anxiety and hysteria. London: Routledge & Kegan Paul.

Eysenck, H. J. (1967). The biological basis of personality. Springfield, IL: Charles C Thomas.

Gale, A. (1973). The psychophysiology of individual differences: Studies of extraversion and the EEG. In P. Kline (Ed.), New approaches in psychological measurement. London: Wiley.

Harman, H. H. (1960). Modern factor analysis. Chicago: University of Chicago Press.

Hendrickson, A. E.,& White, P. O. (1964). Promax: A quick method for rotation to oblique simple structure. British Journal of Statistical Psychology, 17, 65-70.

Janssen, R. H. C., Mattie, H., Plooij-van Gorsel, P. C., & Werre, P. F. (1978). The effects of a depressant and a stimulant drug on the contingent negative variation. Biological Psychology, 6, 209-218.

McCallum, W. C. (1969). Application à la pathologie: Distraction chez les anxieux. In J. Dargent & M. Dongier (Eds.), Variations contingentes négatives (Vol. 52). Congrès et colloques de l'Université de Liège.

McCallum, W. C., & Walter, W. G. (1968). The effects of attention and distraction on the contingent negative variation in normal and neurotic subjects. Electroencephalography and Clinical Neurophysiology, 25, 319-329.

Nakamura, M., Fukui, Y., Kadobayashi, I., & Kato, N. (1979). A comparison of the CNV in young and old subjects: Its relation to memory and personality. Electroencephalography and Clinical Neurophysiology, 46, 337-344.

Plooij-van Gorsel, P. C., & Janssen, R. H. C. (1980). Contingent negative variation (CNV) and extraversion in a psychiatric population. In Barber, C. (Ed.), Evoked potentials. Proceedings of an international evoked potentials symposium, Nottingham 1978. Lancaster: M.T.P. Press.

Snijders, J. Th., & Verhage, F. (1962). Voorlopige handleiding bij de Groninger Intelligentie Test. Swets en Zeitlinger, Amsterdam.

Tecce, J. J. (1972). Contingent negative variation (CNV) and psychological processes in man. Psychological Bulletin, 77, 73-108.

Tecce, J. J., & Cole, J. O.(1974). Amphetamine effects in man: Paradoxical drowsiness and lowered electrical brain activity (CNV). Science, 185, 451-453.

Travis, L. E., & Gottlober, A. (1936). Do brain waves have individuality? Science, 84, 532-533.

Walter, W. G. (1964). Slow potential waves in the human brain associated with expectancy, attention and decision. Archiv für Psychiatrie Nervenkrankheiten, 206, 309-322.

Walter, W. G., Cooper, R., Aldridge, V. J., McCallum, W. G., & Winter, A. L. (1964). Contingent negative variation: An electric sign of sensorimotor association and expectancy in the human brain. Nature, 203, 380-384.

Werre, P. F. (1982). Aspects of the relationship between electroencephalographic and psychological variables in normal adults. In R. Broughton (Ed.), Henri Gastaut and the Marseille school's contribution to the neurosciences. Proceedings of the 25th and final Colloque de Marseille. Amsterdam: Elsevier/North-Holland.

Werre, P. F., Faverey, H. A., & Janssen, R. H. C. (1973). Contingent negative variation en persoonlijkheid. Psychiatrische Kliniek, Rijksuniversiteit Leiden.

Werre, P. F., Faverey, H. A., & Janssen, R. H. C. (1975). Contingent negative variation and personality. Nederlands Tijdschrift voor de Psychologie, 30, 277-299.

Wilde, G. J. S. (1962). Neurotische labiliteit gemeten volgens de vragenlijst-methode. Amsterdam: Van Rossen.

Zuckerman, M. (1971). Dimensions of sensation seeking. Journal of Consulting Clinical Psychology, 36, 45-52.

Zuckerman, M., Murtaugh, T., & Siegel, J. (1974). Sensation seeking and cortical augmenting-reducing. Psychophysiology, 11, 535-542.

5

Dynamics of AEP and Heart Rate as Indicators of Individual Arousal Level and Learning

N. N. Danilova

Individual differences in arousal level have been studied by many investigators, as is clear from contributions to this volume. The principal notion within this approach is that a person's level of arousal regulates his or her life in a significant fashion. There are data indicating that the arousability of a person is a factor in determining occupational choice and that individual differences in arousal level account in part for variations in efficiency of performance. A focus of attention in research is the relationship between arousability and the basic properties of the nervous system, such as the strength and weakness of nervous processes. According to Pavlov and his followers, these properties constitute the essential physiological basis of temperamental traits. Thus a number of studies have been concerned with electrophysiological correlates of arousability, that is, the electroencephalogram (EEG) and vegetative indexes. But few of these studies are concerned with arousability and the average evoked potential (AEP) during task performance in general and learning in particular.

The present investigation is concerned with these two physiological variables and strength and weakness of the nervous system. The subject is required to identify a target stimulus from among nontarget stimuli; the interstimulus interval ranged from 1-3 s, that is, beyond the range of subjective accuracy in time estimation, thus making the task difficult. Mastery of the task of differentiating time intervals is interpreted as a learning process in this experiment, and a model of times involved must be formed in memory. Two groups were set up, differing in nervous system strength, as measured by the Strelau questionnaire. Time estimation and physiological indexes were both expected to be discriminated on the basis of the questionnaire score.

METHOD

The two temperament groups contained 5 subjects; each subject performed two experiments with a 1-week interval between sessions; both occipital and vertex EEG were measured with monopolar leads, electrocardiogram (ECG) and right-hand flexor electromyogram (EMG) were taken. Evoked potentials were averaged over 100 trials using an LP 4050 analyzer. Four separate evoked potentials were derived for each of the four light flash sequences for each session. Learning efficiency was measured by the number of correct responses. There were three sessions in Experiment I:

• Session 1 contained four blocks with different light flashes (.35, .5, .6, and .8 cps); there were 10 flashes per block, presented over intervals of 10 - 15 s.

- In Session 2, the subject was required to differentiate the blocks by frequency and to react with a hand movement when the block in question was equivalent to a target presented before the session.

- In Session 3, the subject was instructed to react to nontarget stimuli.

Experiment II was similar to Experiment I, but excluded the first Session and target presentation before the Session; thus there were two sessions only, Sessions 4 and 5.

RESULTS

All subjects found identification of the target very difficult, and none performed the task in either experiment without error. Both groups, however, learned to differentiate the time intervals, strong nervous system subjects being superior in both speed and efficiency at both the beginning and end of the experiment. These differences in mean error are shown in Figure 1, and they are significant; these differences are reflected in a faster heart rate for the strong subjects, as shown in Figure 2; although not significant, the

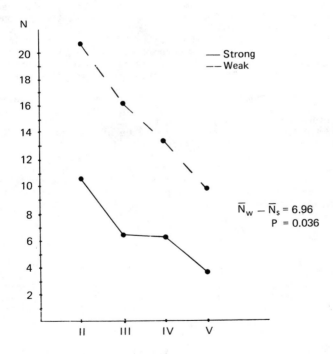

FIGURE 1. Mean error scores as a function of training in the differentiation of time intervals. Ordinate: mean errors; abcissa: Session within the experiment. N_w = mean number of subjects with weak nervous systems; N_s = the same, for strong.

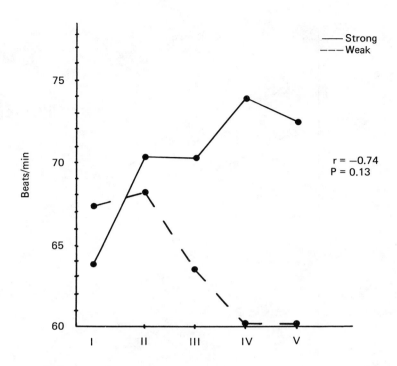

FIGURE 2.   Dynamics of heart rate change for subject with strong and weak nervous systems.   Ordinate: mean heart rate;   abcissa: Session number.

changes indicate differences in heart rate dynamics during the course of learning. There were also differences in the N150 and P200 components of the evoked potential; strong subjects had a higher amplitude in the former and lower in the latter, in contrast to the weak subjects, at both leads.

In addition, there were different relationships among the components of the evoked potentials for the two groups: in the weak group a negative correlation held between N150 and P200, referred from vertex to baseline (r = -.81, p < .001); that is, the higher the positivity of P200, the higher the negativity of N150. In weak subjects ECG frequency increased as the amplitude of both components increased within the vertex AEP (r = .85). For the strong subjects the correlation between the two components at the occiput was significant (r = .78, p < .001); as P200 increased in amplitude, so N150 shifted to positivity. Thus the dynamics of both components shift in the same direction, either positively or negatively. The positive shift in the AEP of the occiput was positively correlated with an increase in heart rate, the highest correlation being with early shifting (N150, r = .61, p < .001; P200, r = .58, p < .001). Thus it was found that in strong subjects, a decrease in the number of errors in the process of learning is associated with an enhancement of heart rate and an increase in the positivity of both components of the occipital AEP. In the weak group, however, the decrease in errors is accompanied by a reduction in heart rate and a decrease in the positive amplitude of P200 and the negative amplitude of N150. In Figure 3 these relationships are shown, measured with reference to the baseline.

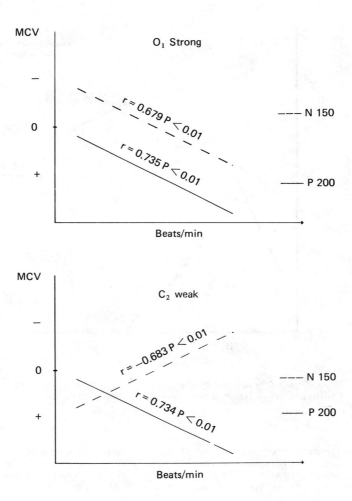

FIGURE 3. Relationships between errors, heart rate and average evoked potential
(AEP) components. Ordinate: amplitude of AEP components referred to baseline
and mean heart rate; abcissa: mean errors. Different leads are shown for subjects with strong and weak nervous systems.

Thus strong and weak subjects differ during the course of learning both in
efficiency and in arousal. Successful learning in strong subjects is associated
with an increase in arousal level, whereas the reverse holds for weak subjects.

DISCUSSION

The data indicate that strong and weak subjects appear to use different ways of
solving the problem of differentiating interstimulus intervals. One possible

source of such differences is variation in the regulation and control of a functional state, which is optimal for the problem to be solved. The level of functional state, or the level of activation at which the subject performs the task, is much higher in strong subjects. Such a view is confirmed by higher heart rate, which in several studies correlates positively with muscular tone (e.g., Obrist, Webb, Sutterer, & Howard, 1970). The shift in positivity of the occipital AEP and the positive correlation with heart rate also support the interpretation that strong subjects are characterized by a much higher level of neurophysiological energy than are weak subjects. That the reverse holds for the weak group is confirmed by a decrease in heart rate during the task and a lessening of the positivity of the vertex AEP.

Another possible cause of differences is the tendency of weak subjects to use mainly verbal operations during information processing. According to data obtained by Golubeva and her co-workers (1980), subjects with strong, more arousable, and labile nervous systems tend to have the first signaling system, whereas those with weak, inert, and less arousable nervous systems tend to have the second signaling system. Their data also show that subjects who perform better on verbal tasks have a more arousable left hemisphere, and subjects who perform better on nonverbal tasks are characterized by higher indexes of arousability and strength within the right hemisphere.

Such data suggest strongly that weak subjects in our experiments use mainly verbal operations; that is why the dynamics of learning in these subjects are so strongly associated with the dynamics of the vertex AEP (P200), an area involved in integration, including verbal activity. The strong subjects who tend to have an artistic type of mentality and nonverbal intelligence seem to use verbal operations to a lesser extent and process information mainly by means of modality-specific systems under given experimental conditions. Our experiments demand fine-grained discrimination and prove to be more difficult for weak subjects. Sokolov's notion of the localized orienting reflex (OR) is consistent with the data showing positive shift in the P200 in the occiput of strong subjects and its decrease in the vertex in weak subjects. The generalized responses emerging at the beginning of the experiment (in Session 2) may be seen as general OR. This is shown by an increase in AEP positivity at P200 in both O_1 and C_z derivations. This correlates with heart rate increase in strong subjects and decrease in weak subjects. N150, on the other hand, increases during the general OR at O_1 and C_z, but only in weak subjects.

Our results are consistent with those of Stelmack, Achorn, and Michaud, who showed that the auditory evoked potential (whose components N117-130 are an analog of the N150 of the visual evoked potential: Goff, Matsumiya, Allison, & Goff, 1977) is more pronounced in introverts than in extraverts. Frigon (1976) showed that introverts are characterized by a weaker nervous system. The growth of N150 in weak subjects only might indicate that this group has a more pronounced OR. This point of view coincides with the interpretation of the AEP negative shift as an expression of the OR (Näätänen & Michie, 1979). Bearing in mind the data of Gray (1967), showing a higher level of anxiety in weak and introverted subjects, we may suggest that an increase in N150 amplitude really points to an enhancement of the OR, and above all, its passive defensive components. The reference list also presents other studies that explore psychophysiological data relating to temperament.

Thus we see that the use of EEG and autonomic indexes permits us to define the qualitatively different mechanisms of arousal regulation during the process of learning in people with weak and strong nervous systems.

REFERENCES

Farley, F. (1979). Recent developments in a theory of the internal-external
    stimulation-seeking motive. Paper presented at the International Conference on
    "Temperament, need for stimulation and activity," Warsaw (Grzegorzewice),
    September 10-14, 1979.

Frigon, J. I. (1976). Extraversion, neuroticism and strength of the nervous
    system. British Journal of Psychology, 67, 467-474.

Gale, A. (1979). Some psychophysiological paradigms for measuring the effects
    of traits and situations. Abstracts of International Conference on "Tempera-
    ment, need for stimulation and activity," Warsaw (Grzegorzewice), September 10-
    14, 1979.

Goff, C. D., Matsumiya, I., Allison, T., & Goff, W. R. (1977). The scalp topo-
    graphy of human somatosensory and auditory evoked potentials. Electroencephalo-
    graphy and Clinical Neurophysiology, 42, 57-76.

Golubeva, E. A. (1975). Electrophysiological research in nervous system proper-
    ties and some individual traits of human memory. Unpublished doctoral disser-
    tation, Moscow University.

Golubeva, E. A. (in press). Individual traits of human memory (psychophysiological
    investigation). Pedagogika (Moscow).

Gray, J. A. (1967). Strength of the nervous system, intraversion, condition-
    ability and arousal. Behavior Research Therapy, 5, 151-169.

Näätänen, R., & Michie, P. T. (1979). Early selective-attention effects on the
    evoked potential: A critical review and reinterpretation. Biological Psychology,
    8, 81-136.

Obrist, P. A., Webb, R. A., Sutterer, I. R., & Howard, I. L. (1970). The cardiac-
    somatic relationship: Reformulations. Psychophysiology, 6, 569-587.

Reykowski, J. (1974). A theoretical analysis of the relationship between tempera-
    ment and personality. Paper presented at the conference "Temperament and per-
    sonality," Warsaw, October 1974.

Stelmack, R. M., Achorn, E., & Michaud, A. (1977). Extraversion and individual
    differences in auditory evoked responses. Psychophysiology, 14, 368-374.

Strelau, J. (1974). Experimental investigations of the relation between reactivity
    as a temperament trait and human action. Paper presented at the International
    Conference "Temperament and personality," Warsaw, October 1974.

Strelau, J., & Sosnowski, T. (1979). The dynamics of psychophysiological changes
    under hypoxia and sensory deprivation in subjects with different anxiety and
    reactivity levels. Abstracts of International Conference on "Temperament, need
    for stimulation and activity," Warsaw (Grzegorzewice), September 10-14, 1979.

Schönpflug, W. (1979). Human action as a means of self-regulation. Abstracts of
    International Conference on "Temperament, need for stimulation and activity,"
    Warsaw (Grzegorzewice), September 10-14, 1979.

Zuckerman, M. (1979). Biological foundations of the sensation seeking tempera-
    ment. Abstracts of International Conference on "Temperament, need for stimula-
    tion and activity," Warsaw (Grzegorzewice), September 10-14, 1979.

6

Personality and Regulatory Functions

Anton Uherík

Personality may be understood as a complex, individualized, psychophysiologically open feedback system that ensures a characteristic intra-individual interaction with the environment through a specific mechanism of reflex and conscious (voluntary) regulation.

Regulatory processes have their reflection in the activation level of the organism; thus they may be traced precisely in changes in activation level.

In its widest sense, activation level (AL) is understood as a certain state of mobilization of physiological and mental functions. Hence, a change of activation will also mean a change of mobilization of these functions.

Activation level is considered to be an important organismic variable, which, thanks to Duffy (1951, 1957), has been put into a hypothetical and general relation with the outcome of activity, a relation known as the inverted-U curve.

The degree of activation, however, stands in a complex relation with the level of regulatory functions. A low activation level need not be equivalent to a depression of the regulatory function. This is related to the well-known fact that the effect of a stimulus depends on the meaning the stimulus has for the subject. This then implies that the most important regulator of AL is personality. And since personality represents an integration of properties of the nervous system and mental traits, it may be assumed that properties of the basic nervous processes -- excitation and inhibition, as well as the regulatory interventions into these processes through mental regulation -- will become manifest in changes in AL. In other words, man's psychophysiological traits are manifested in these changes.

We do not assume that a linear relationship exists between properties of the nervous system and mental or personality traits, especially not concerning regulatory properties with an evident voluntary component.

However, we do assume a neurophysiological determination of mental properties in the sense of their existence and development, though not in the sense of absolute determinism which a priori excludes a feedback effect of the mental processes on the neurophysiological substrate.

REGULATORY FUNCTIONS AND BIOELECTRICAL SKIN REACTIVITY

An electrophysiological indicator of activation changes that is generally

acknowledged is bioelectrical skin reactivity (BSR).   The BSR phenomenon proper
has its own interpretative background, which has gradually built up over entire
decades around the questions, What is BSR? and What does it indicate and through
what mechanisms does it enable us to trace activation changes in the organism?
There exists at present sufficient evidence to consider BSR as a sensitive
indicator of the dynamics of the basic nervous phenomena, excitation and inhibition or, as Darrow (1967) called it, as an index of cerebral functions.

Other authors have investigated the relationship between AL changes as manifested
in the properties of the nervous system and personality traits (Eysenck, H. J.,
1966; Roessler, Burch, & Childers, 1966).   Consequently, solutions have been
proposed within the typological concept of personality, through a study of problems of interindividual and intra-individual specificities in AL changes (dynamics
of nervous process).   From a methodological viewpoint, it is important to discover certain regularities within the AL patterns themselves, AL being represented by the dynamics of the basic nervous processes.   The present contribution
is concerned precisely with this problem, extended to include the relation of AL
patterns to extraversion and perceptual performance.

Method

In our investigation we used equipment constructed in our laboratory for BSR
recording (Uherík, 1967), consisting of a universal portable voltamperometer
recorder (VAREG), provided with a compensatory amplifier for low-voltage values
and current; in addition, we used Wheatstone's resistance bridge as a source of
direct exosomatic current, whose constant value was checked with a milliampero-
meter and adjusted by means of a wire potentiometer.

The AL as reflected in the BSR was continuously recorded in controls as follows:

1. At the start of the experiment, in values of the basic skin conductivity.
2. Under conditions without external stimulation, where we recorded the intra-
    signal, or spontaneous reactions.
3. Under conditions of sound stimulation.
4. In a task situation induced by the application of a modified association
    experiment and the need to solve arithmetical tasks.

The BSR was recorded on the index and middle fingers of the right hand by means
of electrodes.   The recording was carried out, as the experiment required, with
the subjects either sitting or lying down.   The population included 275 healthy
subjects, age 4-40 years; 27 psychotic patients age 25-70 years; and 137
patients with endocrine disorders, age 25-45 years.   Eysenck's Personality
Inventory (EPI), a modified numerical square, T-illusion, and reversible figure
(Schröder's steps) were administered.

When evaluating the BSR recording as an indicator of AL changes, we took into
account the amplitude of reactions, the time of the recovery phase in the reaction curve, and the occurrence of intrasignal reactions.   These parameters
enabled us to judge the dynamics of the basic nervous processes, the role of
excitation and inhibition in AL, and the compensation mechanism of reactivity
regulation.

Results

The data from all the experimental variants with application of different
stimulus modalities may be summarized as follows:

1. The AL traced in the BSR reflects the relationships between stimuli, effects of motivational factors, pharmacological effects, and pathological states.

2. The decreasing reaction phase, recorded continuously in repeated 3-10 sessions at various time intervals, proved to be the most significant parameter of interindividual and intra-individual peculiarities in AL changes.

3. From all the electrodermograms obtained, it was possible to sort out seven samples (patterns) of AL changes (see Figures 1 - 3), which were assessed from the viewpoint of stability and lability of the nervous system and con-sidered as an indicator of a certain characteristic of the primary component of temperament.

4. The patterns obtained for the AL changes bear no relation to the perceptual achievements (performance) of the subjects.

5. The patterns of activation changes do not constitute a typological fixed system. They compose a dynamic model of individual interaction having some common marks for a certain population sample.

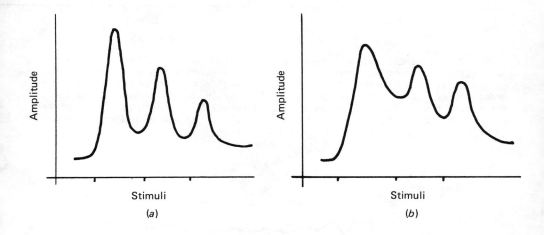

FIGURE 1. Bioelectrical skin reactivity patterns (a and b), illustrating activa-tion changes that express reactivity adequate to stimulation, an effective influ-ence of the compensatory mechanism consisting in a rapid onset of the parasympa-thetic inhibitory process. This becomes manifest not only in the descending phase of every specific reaction, but also in a decline in reaction amplitudes during repeated stimulation and also in the absence of spontaneous (intrasignal) reactions. These patterns illustrate a relatively good stability of the central nervous system, and a satisfactory adaptability adequate to the strength, mobility, and balance of the basic nervous processes -- excitation and inhi-bition.

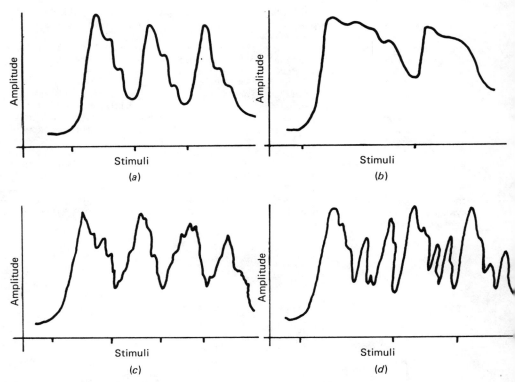

FIGURE 2. Bioelectrical skin reactivity patterns (a-d), illustrating the
lability of the central nervous system. This is manifested in a predominance
of the excitatory process and an absence of a direct compensatory mechanism.
Reaction amplitudes following repeated stimulation do not decrease, and the
descending phase of the curve is either absent or bears signs of the occurrence
of spontaneous reactions. The patterns testify to a lack of balance of the
basic nervous processes and poor adaptability.

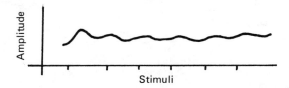

FIGURE 3. Bioelectrical skin reactivity pattern illustrating lability of the
central nervous system, in the sense of weakness of the excitation process, an
inadequate reactivity, imbalance of the basic nervous phenomena, and inadequate
function of the compensatory mechanism.

PERSONALITY DIMENSIONS AND BIOELECTRICAL SKIN REACTIVITY

Over the past several years a considerable amount of research has been reported on the strength-sensitivity property of excitatory processes (Nebylitsyn, 1966; Teplov & Nebylitsyn, 1966). Sensitivity has been theoretically linked with weakness, that is, lack of strength or endurance of the nervous system. An inverse relationship between strength and sensitivity was clearly established in a study by Nebylitsyn (cited by Siddle et al., 1969). Some investigators (Eysenck, H. J., 1957, 1962, 1966; Gray, 1964, 1967; Mangan & Farmer, 1967) have attempted to relate Russian typological properties to Western personality diemnsions. H. J. Eysenck, for example (1966), proposed that the Pavlovian "strong" nervous system is related to the extraverted personality and the "weak" one to the introverted personality. The Eysencks' work (1967a, 1967b) suggests the association of sensitivity with a high level of cortical arousal by introverts, and differences between introverts and extraverts were interpreted by using Pavlov's concept of transmarginal inhibition. The extraversion-introversion dimension in connection with the strength-sensitivity property was also studied by S. L. Smith (cited by Gray, 1969) and D. R. Haslam (cited by White et al., 1969), who found that introverts had lower sensory thresholds than did extraverts. Gray (1967) mentioned that introverts are weaker and reach the threshold of transmarginal inhibition more quickly than extraverts.

Many authors stress that the intra-individual physiological pattern of reactivity should be investigated within a study of the biological basis of personality (Dahlstrom, 1970, Lacey, 1967; Lazarus, 1967; Shapiro, 1970). However, no systematic investigation of the basic parameters and characteristics has been attempted.

In the past, one of our studies was aimed at analyzing the relationship between extraversion and dynamism of basic nervous processes. The results obtained have shown that there is no such relationship (Halmiová & Uherík, 1969).

Load Situation Conditions

Our next study was designed to examine personality traits and BSR in conditions of a load situation. Eleven introverts and ten extraverts with extreme values on the scoring scale were chosen by means of EPI. The results of this research have confirmed, with high statistical significance, the hypothesis of a relationship between introversion and weak nervous system in terms of an increased BSR. On examining the shape of the BSR curve, mainly the recovery phase of the curve, and the frequency of reflex changes in time, including resistance value of deviation, we found either a fairly similar or a completely different picture of reactivity in the two groups. At that time we concluded that personality traits modified performance in the given experiment and showed themselves to be relatively independent of the properties of the nervous system.

After 7 months, the same subjects took part again in the experiment, where different variables than those in the previous study were introduced, to analyze in addition the relationship between extraversion and neuroticism and properties of nervous processes. In this experiment, the subject had to judge acoustic stimulus intensity, which was objectively constant; but the instruction required three kinds of judgment, that is, whether the intensity was the same, lower, or higher compared with an intensity applied at the beginning of the session. Using these conditions, we were interested in the relation between BSR at the point where the subject's answer was "the same," "higher," or "lower." The results showed no relationship between subjective judgment and the measures of BSR. This result was probably due to the degree of security in judgment about the intensity. Then a qualitative analysis of BSR was made and compared with BSR patterns of the

same subjects in the first experiment conducted 7 months earlier. We expected
relatively consistent patterns of BSR by introverts and extraverts to occur even
under different experimental conditions. This hypothesis was not confirmed.
Similarly, as in the first experiment, we found comparable patterns of BSR in
extraverts and introverts; i.e., similar patterns of BSR were observed in extraverts and introverts (Uherík, 1971a).

Sleep Deprivation Conditions

In our next study (Uherík, 1971b), 4 subjects took part in experiments involving
96 hr of sleep deprivation. The BSR and heart rate (HR) to 55-dB and 110-dB
intensity sounds were recorded 24 hr before sleep deprivation and then every
24 hr during deprivation. Subjects reached extreme values on the scale of extraversion-introversion and neuroticism when EPI was administered. In addition,
Taylor's MAS, as modified by Fenz and Epstein (1965), was applied.

The results of this research showed an inconsistent effect of sleep deprivation
in all subjects. No relationship was found between patterns of BSR during sleep
deprivation and extraversion and neuroticism. Scores on the anxiety scale, likewise, showed no relationship to reactivity patterns under conditions of sleep
deprivation. The BSR and HR appeared as independent processes. After 72 hr
of sleep deprivation for 3 subjects, nonadequate reactivity with respect to
stimulus intensity on the initial presentation of the stimulus occurred, that
is, higher reactivity to low intensity of stimuli and low reactivity to high
ones. In 1 subject, inverse reactions to the stimulus of high intensity were
found.

BSR Over Time

One of our further investigations was directed to the dependence of the pattern
of BSR on stimulus situation, personality dimension, and time. The subjects
were 26 men, age 18 - 21 years, who obtained extreme scores on extraversion-
introversion and neuroticism as measured by the EPI. They were divided into
groups on the basis of BSR records by five independent judges, according to pre-
determined criteria. The experiment was repeated with every subject at 3-day
intervals, with the conditions being kept relatively constant. The results
obtained failed to support the assumption according to which introversion would
represent weakness of the nervous system and extraversion would be equivalent
to strength of nervous system.

Self-regulation

In the next research, 11 subjects, age 16 - 62 years, having the ability to control their own activation state, have taken part. At least 2 years of experience
in self-regulation were required. The study included two experiments. Each
experiment had three phases. In the first one, subjects were not to influence
their activation voluntarily (state of spontaneous activation). The second
phase included a state of relaxation. The third phase involved a state of increased mobilization (higher sensitivity to stimuli). In addition, the EPI and
Cattell's PQ were administered. No relationships between patterns of BSR and EPI,
except for factor Q 3 f from Cattell's questionnaire, were found.

DISCUSSION AND CONCLUSION

What might be the interpretation of the results of BSR pattern analysis of extreme extraverts and introverts, which failed to produce unequivocal support for the hypothesis that extraverts have a strong nervous system, low reactivity, and a better adaptation mechanism than have introverts?

In the first place, the principal reason seems to reside in the different methods of research and the disparate criteria applied in the definition of personality traits, on the one hand, and properties of the nervous system, on the other. Another reason might be the differences in the definition of personality, where personality is often presented without any consideration being paid to the important autoregulatory ability of the human organism (e.g., Eysenck, S. B. G., & Eysenck, H. J., 1967a).

Earlier we mentioned the influence of the self-control mechanism. Fuhrer and Baer (1969) also stressed the influence of cognitive processes in experiments with human subjects. Lazarus (1967) suggested that the coping process (or as Lacey and co-workers put it, the orientation with respect to the stimulus) influences the physiological pattern of reaction. This would mean that to understand and predict the physiological pattern, we would have to know the nature of coping and, conversely, that the coping processes can be inferred from the pattern of reaction. As regards Lazarus's opinion, coping processes are dependent on the cognitive processes of appraisal. He holds that not all personality characteristics influence coping by the mediating cognitive process, but that many do.

One of the studies of Lacey, Kagan, Lacey, and Moss (1963) and our data (Uherik, 1973a, 1973b, 1975, 1976, 1978; see also Uherik & Šebej, 1978, 1979) suggest the influence of the coping process on physiological pattern of reaction. Thus we may say that the pattern of autonomic nervous system activity as reflected in the BSR is determined by the nature of the coping process. The role of situation variables in coping depends on factors within the psychophysiological structure, some of these variables being important in influencing appraisal.

As regards the statement that the inhibitiom process is dominant in extraverts and the excitation process in introverts, we hold a different view. Similar or completely different patterns of BSR in the introverted or extraverted groups may be due to some more complex characteristics of introversion and extraversion traits. In introverts, not only the excitatory but also the inhibitory processes may predominate. This depends, except for the conditions mentioned previously, on interindividual differences existing in introverts and extraverts as regards the function of the mechanism regulating reactivity at the level of mental activity.

The results concerning an absence of any relation between patterns of activation and perceptual performance render questionable the hypothesis concerning the dependence of the results of activity on the measure of activation, which concurs with the findings of Darrow (1967), who draws attention to the relative independence of a subject's mental activity from BSR as an indicator of AL changes. Our results raise the problem of the specific and nonspecific AL and the individual measure of its effect on the results of the subject's activity. A solution of this problem might elucidate the hypothetical relationships, established by Duffy (1957), between the AL and the results of activity.

The divergence between our results and data reported by other authors (Marton & Urban, 1966; Roessler et al., 1966) is probably due to the different values in the considered polarity scale of personality tests and a lack of uniformity in the reactivity indexes, as well as problems inherent in the methods used.

Our results, however, agree with those of Roessler et al. (1966) concerning similar trends of BSR under conditions of application of different stimulus variables. Our conclusions on the recovery phase, or its duration, are in agreement with the data of Wolfensberger and O'Connor (1967). We believe that it is precisely this descending phase of response in which we see the function of compensatory and regulatory mechanisms of reactivity, which can be the starting point for the solution of the effect of volitional processes and motivation -- not only at the level of perceptual performance and promptness, but also in the ability to control and regulate its own AL, as was observed by Stern and Lewis (1968).

In conclusion, only systematic and repeated experiments in which the same subjects take part can bring more clarity into the question as to what are the personality traits and what characteristics the properties of the nervous system and function of self-control have in experimental conditions. Then perhaps we will know more about the relationships between personality traits and properties of the nervous system and their relation to the mechanism of self-control.

REFERENCES

Dahlstrom, W. G. (1970). Personality. Annual Review of Psychology, 21, 1-43.

Darrow, C. W. (1967). Problems in use of the galvanic skin response (GSR) as an index of cerebral function: Implications of the latent period. Psychophysiology, 4, 389-396.

Duffy, E. (1951). The concept of energy mobilization. Psychological Review, 58, 30-40.

Duffy, E. (1957). The psychological significance of the concept of "arousal" or "activation." Psychological Review, 64, 265-270.

Eysenck, H. J. (1957). The dynamics of anxiety and hysteria. London: Routledge & Kegan Paul.

Eysenck, H. J. (1962). Conditioning and personality. British Journal of Psychology, 53, 299-305.

Eysenck, H. J. (1966). Conditioning, introversion-extraversion and the strength of the nervous system. Paper presented at the meeting of the International Congress of Psychology, Moscow.

Eysenck, S. B. G., & Eysenck, H. J. (1967a). Salivary response to lemon juice as measure of introversion. Perceptual and Motor Skills, 24, 1047-1053.

Eysenck, S. B. G., & Eysenck, H. J. (1967b). Psychological reactivity to sensory stimulation as a measure of personality. Psychological Reports, 20, 45-46.

Fenz, W. D., & Epstein, S. (1965). Manifest anxiety: Unifactorial or multifactorial composition. Perceptual and Motor Skills, 20, 773-780.

Fuhrer, M. J., & Baer, P. E. (1969). Cognitive processes in differential GSR conditioning: Effects of a masking task. American Journal of Psychology, 82, 168-181.

Gray, J. A. (1964). Strength of the nervous system as a dimension of personality in man. In J. A. Gray (Ed.), Pavlov's typology. Oxford: Pergamon Press.

Gray, J. A. (1967). Strength of the nervous system, introversion-extraversion, conditionability and arousal. Behavior Research and Therapy, 5, 151-169.

Halmiová, O., & Uherík, A. (1969). Eysenck's personality dimensions and properties of the nervous system. Studia Psychologica, 2, 116-124.

Lacey, J. I. (1967). Somatic response patterning and stress: Some revisions of activation theory. In M. H. Appley & R. Trumbull (Eds.), Psychological stress -- Issues in research. New York: Appleton-Century-Crofts.

Lacey, J. I., Kagan, J., Lacey, B. C., & Moss, H. A. (1963). The visceral level: Situational determinants and behavioral correlates of autonomic response patterns. In P. H. Knapp (Ed.), Expression of the emotions in man. New York: International Universities.

Lazarus, R. S. (1967). Cognition and personality factors. In M. H. Appley & R. Trumball (Eds.), Psychological stress -- Issues in Research. New York: Appleton-Century-Crofts

Mangan, G. L., & Farmer, R. G. (1967). Studies of the relationship between neo-Pavlovian properties of higher nervous activity and Western personality dimensions: I. The relationship of nervous strength and sensitivity to extraversion. Journal of Experimental Research in Personality, 2, 101-106.

Marton, M., & Urban, J. (1966). An electroencephalographic investigation of individual differences in the process of conditioning. Paper presented at the meeting of the International Congress of Psychology, Moscow.

Nebylitsyn, V. D. (1966). Some questions relating to the theory of the properties of the nervous system. Paper presented at the meeting of the International Congress of Psychology, Moscow.

Roessler, R., Burch, N. R., & Childers, H. E. (1966). Personality and arousal correlates of specific galvanic skin responses. Psychophysiology, 2, 115-130.

Shapiro, D., & Schwartz, G. E. (1970). Psychophysiological contributions to social psychology. Annual Review of Psychology, 21, 104-107.

Siddle, D. A. T., Morrish, R. B., White, K. D., & Mangan, G. L. (1969). A further study of the relation of strength-sensitivity of the nervous system to extraversion. Journal of Experimental Research in Personality, 3, 264-267.

Stern, R. M., & Lewis, N. L. (1968). Ability of actors to control their GSRs and express emotions. Psychophysiology, 3, 294-299.

Teplov, B. M., & Nebylitsyn, V. D. (1966). Results of experimental studies on properties of the nervous system in man. In A. N. Leontev, A. R. Luria & A. A. Smirnov (Eds.), Psychological research in the USSR (D. Rottenberg, Trans.), Moscow: Progress Publishers.

Uherík, A. (1967). A new apparatus for continuous recording of bioelectrical skin reactivity. Studia Psychologica, 4, 298-300.

Uherík, A. (1971a). Personality traits and intraindividual patterns of bioelectrical skin reactivity. Studia Psychologica, 13 (4), 301-307.

Uherík, A. (1971b). Sleep deprivation, some electrophysiological indicators and personality traits. Studia Psychologica, 13 (3), 214-222.

Uherík, A. (1973a). Methodological problems of psychophysiological research of human subjects. Studia Psychologica, 15, 213-228.

Uherík, A. (1973b). Some psychophysiological problems of self-regulation. Studia Psychologica, 15, 309-313.

Uherík, A. (1975). Interpretation of bilateral asymmetry of bioelectrical skin reactivity in schizophrenics. Studia Psychologica, 17, 51-60.

Uherík, A. (1976). Autoregulation and bilateral asymmetry of bioelectrical skin reactivity. Studia Psychologica, 18 (2), 158-165.

Uherík, A. (1978). Effect of conditioning on lateral differences in bioelectrical skin reactivity. Studia Psychologica, 20, 11-21.

Uherík, A., & Sebej, F. (1978). Effect of autogenic training on lateral differences in bioelectrical skin reactivity. Studia Psychologica, 20, 294-299.

Uherík, A., & Sebej, F. (1979). Effect of hypnotic suggestion in bilateral asymmetry of bioelectrical skin reactivity. Studia Psychologica, 21, 91-97.

White, K. D., Mangan, G. L., Morrish, R. B., & Siddle, D. A. T. (1969). The relation of visual after-images to extraversion and neuroticism. Journal of Experimental Research in Personality, 3, 268-274.

Wolfensberger, W., & O'Connor, N. (1967). Relative effectiveness of galvanic skin response latency, amplitude and duration scores as measures of arousal and habituation in normal and retarded adults. Psychophysiology, 4, 345-350.

7

Dynamics of Psychophysiological Changes under Hypoxia and Sensory Deprivation in Subjects with Different Reactivity and Anxiety Levels

Jan Strelau, Tytus Sosnowski, and Włodzimierz Oniszczenko

The concept of reactivity worked out in our laboratory states that individual differences with respect to this feature (regarded as a relatively stable intensity with which a person reacts to stimuli) co-determine preferences for stimulation (see Strelau, 1974). Without going into details, we may say that highly reactive people with a high stimulation processing coefficient are characterized by a low demand for stimulation. On the other hand, low-reactive people with a low stimulation processing coefficient have a high demand for stimulation. This regularity has been demonstrated in a series of experiments (Strelau, 1983).

Preferences for stimulation in persons differing in level of reactivity should reveal themselves either in psychophysiological variables that inform us about the organism's state of arousal or in the effectiveness of behavior.

In providing a situation of sensory deprivation and a situation of threat resulting from the state of hypoxia, we predicted that highly reactive subjects would show greater psychophysiological changes under threat, this being a highly stimulating condition. In low-reactive subjects, these changes would be more pronounced in the sensory deprivation condition, that is, a state of low stimulation that does not meet the subjects' stimulation need.

Our earlier research on nervous system type revealed that there is a correlation between level of anxiety and strength of nervous system (Strelau, 1969). In terms of empirical indexes, strength of nervous system corresponds to our concept of reactivity. We found that a weak nervous system (i.e., a high level of reactivity) correlates with a high level of anxiety, and vice versa.

On this evidence it may be assumed that trait anxiety is an individual variable that may considerably modify the psychophysiological state of people in high- and low-stimulating situations. Anxiety is commonly defined as being directly related to individual differences with respect to reactions to a definite type of highly stimulating situation, namely, threat. There is, however, some evidence indicating that anxiety may also differentiate the reactions of people in situations of sensory deprivation (see Zuckerman, 1975).

METHOD AND EXPERIMENTAL PROCEDURE

To answer the question of how the dynamics of psychophysiological changes are manifested under hypoxia and sensory deprivation in subjects of different

---

This research was supported by the Polish Academy of Sciences, Grant MR-I-29.

reactivity and anxiety levels, we conducted an experiment in which the following variables were controlled: (a) reactivity, (b) anxiety, (c) psychophysiological changes, (d) hypoxia, and (e) sensory deprivation. The level of reactivity was assessed by Strelau's Temperament Inventory (TI) and also by the alpha index as a measure of bioelectric brain activity (negative correlation with reactivity as measured by STI; see Strelau & Maciejczyk, 1977).

Trait anxiety was measured with the X-2 scale of Spielberger's State-Trait Anxiety Inventory (STAI) in its Polish adaptation.

Subjects were subdivided along the median, both with respect to their reactivity level and trait anxiety, into high- and low-reactive characteristics and into those showing high and low anxiety levels.

The following psychophysiological changes were recorded: state anxiety (measured on scale X-1, STAI), heart rate, and skin resistance.

Two experimental conditions were used: threat and sensory deprivation.

In the first condition subjects were placed (two at a time) in a low-pressure chamber (LPC) where, by lowering the pressure (state of hypoxia), a physical situation was created resembling that at an altitude of 5,000 m. The subjects remained in this chamber for about 50 min. The following features of the experimental situation seem worth considering: physical and psychological discomfort resulting from hypoxia at 5,000 m, physical threat induced by the anticipation of discomfort or sudden collapse, social threat induced by the prospect of failing to cope with the experimental situation, and the novelty of the imposed situation.

Three variables were controlled during the experiment in the LPC: state anxiety, heart rate, and electrical skin resistance.

State anxiety was measured twice: just before the onset of "elevation" and just after arriving at "ground level." The heart rate was measured at the same points in time. Skin resistance was sampled nine times at various stages of the experiment: during "elevation" (records I - III), at 5,000-m "altitude" (IV - VI), and at "ground level" (VII - IX).

The tests in the sensory deprivation condition lasted 6 hr and were conducted individually. Subjects sat in the deprivation chamber (DC) in reclining seats of the airliner type. The tests were performed in darkness, and throughout the experiment white noise was emitted. The freedom of hand and body movements was restricted by belts. The situation in the DC fulfilled the requirements of low stimulation, especially when compared with tests conducted in the LPC.

The same measurements were made in the DC as in the LPC. State anxiety was measured immediately before and after the period of deprivation. Heart rate and skin resistance were measured 14 times during the experiment in the following way:

· During the first and the sixth hour of the experiment; every 15 m.

· Half-way through the experiment; every 60 m.

· Once the subjects had been told that the experiment was over.

Each subject was tested on two consecutive days. The subjects were soldiers in military training and cadets of an officers' training school, their age varying between 18 and 24 years. Altogether, 60 subjects were tested in this experiment; but for technical reasons complete results were obtained for only 37 subjects, and only these are considered in our analyses.

RESULTS

The results of the experiment were analyzed in two ways. First, the variations in the recorded psychological and psychophysiological indexes -- in level of anxiety, in heart rate, and in basic skin resistance -- were examined for the two experimental conditions. Then we analyzed differences in these indexes, as recorded in the groups differing in reactivity and anxiety.

Figure 1 presents changes in heart rate in the DC for the entire tested group. As shown in this figure, the heart rate is clearly and systematically falling during the first 4 hr of the experiment (especially during the first 45 min; then, however, the tendency is disturbed. The means of records VIII and IX (the lowest heart rate) show significant differences (p < .05)[1] when compared with the means of records I - VI. The difference between record XIII (the end of the sixth hour of the experiment) and record XIV (when the subjects had been told that the experiment was completed) is likewise significant (p < .05).

In the LPC, two measurements of the heart rate were made: one before the "elevation" and the other just after "returning to the ground." No significant differences were observed between the measurements.

Skin resistance measured in kilohms was the second psychophysiological variable. Since it is assumed that skin resistance is negatively correlated with arousal, the vertical axes of the figures (Figures 2 - 7) were marked accordingly: the lowest resistance (which corresponded to the highest level of arousal) was marked at the top of the axis, and the highest resistance at the bottom. The curve of the changes of skin resistance in the DC for the entire tested group is U-shaped and characterized by a rapid decline during the first 45 min of the experiment, and then by a gradual increase, most pronounced during the final 45 min of the experiment.[2]

Between record IV (the highest resistance) and records I, II, and VIII, XI, XII, XIII, and also between records XIII and XIV ("experiment completed"), there are significant differences (p < .05).

Also in LPC, distinct changes in the same variables were recorded in the course of experiment. The highest resistance was observed in record V (altitude 5,000 m) and the lowest in the final measure. The differences between record V and records I, II, III, and VII, VIII and IX are statistically significant (p < .05).

The data on trait and state anxiety for the entire tested group are presented in Table 1. As can be seen from the table, in all cases except for the record preceding LPC, the mean values of anxiety are close to each other and the differences between them are not statistically significant. However, the mean state anxiety value recorded before LPC is higher than the remaining ones. It differs significantly from the mean value recorded after LPC and from the initial state anxiety level (p < .05).

---

[1]All differences between the means were tested with Student's t test for correlated and noncorrelated data.

[2]The curves of skin resistance for the entire tested sample in DC and LPC were not presented due to lack of space. However, they can be traced indirectly to Figures 2 - 7, as they always run in between the curves for the HR and LR, and the high- and low-anxiety groups.

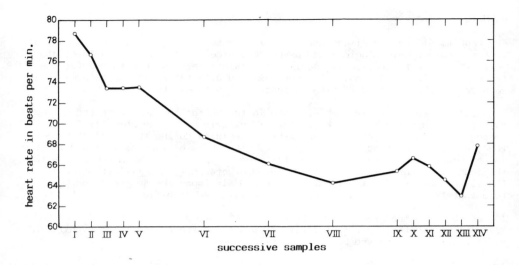

FIGURE 1. Mean measures of heart rate in the deprivation chamber for the entire tested sample.

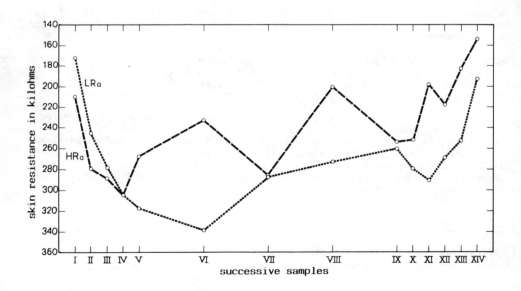

FIGURE 2. Mean measures of skin resistance in the deprivation chamber for groups of high (HR_a) and low (LR_a) reactivity, according to the alpha index.

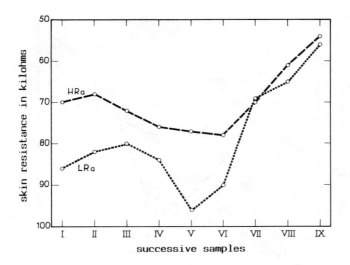

FIGURE 3.   Mean measures of skin resistance in the low-pressure chamber for groups of high (HR_a) and low (LR_a) reactivity, according to the alpha index.

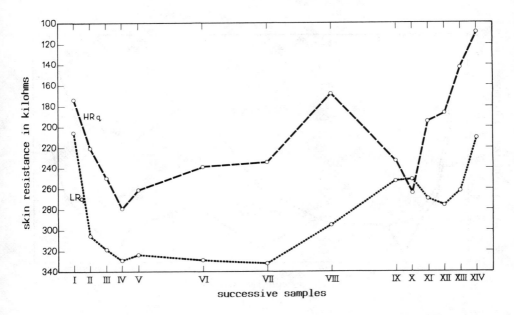

FIGURE 4.   Mean measures of skin resistance in the deprivation chamber for groups of high (HR_q) and low (LR_q) reactivity, according to the Temperament Inventory.

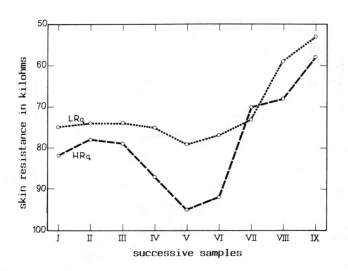

FIGURE 5. Mean measures of skin resistance in the low-pressure chamber for groups of high (HR) and low (LR) reactivity, according to the Temperament Inventory.

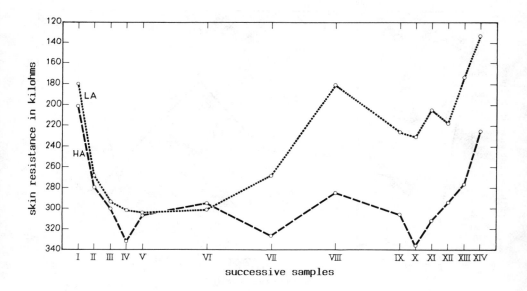

FIGURE 6. Mean measures of skin resistance in the deprivation champter for groups of high (HA) and low (LA) level of trait anxiety.

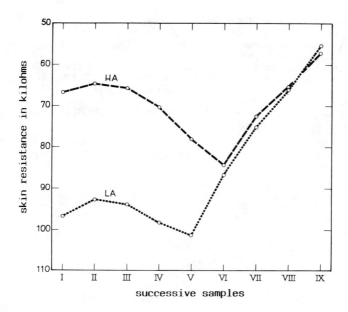

FIGURE 7. Mean measures of skin resistance in the low-pressure chamber for groups of high (HA) and low (LA) level of trait anxiety.

TABLE 1. Mean anxiety indexes in the entire sample.

Measures	Initial level		State anxiety in low-pressure chamber		State anxiety in deprivation chamber	
	Trait	State	Before	After	Before	After
Results	35.9	32.5	35.0	31.5	32.8	32.8

Note. Differences between initial level of state anxiety and levels in the low-pressure chamber were significant (p < .05).

In discussing the results of the entire group, attention must be drawn to the differences in skin resistance and heart rate in the two experimental situations. The lowest mean value of skin resistance in the DC is 183 kilohms (record XIV) whereas the highest value of skin resistance in the LPC is 89 kilohms (record V). The difference is significant at $p < .01$. Similar differences were noted with regard to heart rate. The mean values of the two records done in the LPC are 78 and 76 heart beats per minute, while the mean values obtained in DC vary from 79 (record I) to 63 heart beats (record XIII). The differences indicate that the two experimental conditions vary greatly in terms of the psychophysiological indexes controlled in this experiment.

In our analysis of the differences between the groups differing in reactivity and trait anxiety, we concentrated on skin resistance, because only insignificant differences in heart rate were recorded.

In the DC the highly reactive subjects (HR) revealed lower skin resistance on all records but the first four (see Figure 2). The alpha index was used as a measure of reactivity. Similarly, HR subjects, as compared with low-reactive (LR) persons, attained lower skin resistance indexes in LPC -- on all records but record VII (see Figure 3).

A similar direction of differences between the means was observed in the DC when the STI was used for measuring reactivity -- the HR group was characterized by lower indexes of resistance on 13 of 14 records (see Figure 4.)

The differences were in opposite direction in the LPC: in 8 out of 9 measures, the LR group obtained lower indexes of resistance than did the HR group (see Figure 5

An analysis of the results attained by the groups with high and low anxiety revealed a reversed direction of differences between the means in the two experimental situations. In the DC, starting with record VII, distinctly lower level of skin resistance in the low-anxiety (LA) group (see Figure 6) was noted; however, in the LPC, at the initial stage of the experiment (records I - V), a lower level of resistance was observed in the high-anxiety (HA) group (see Figure 7). The differences between the means of records I - IV in LPC for the high- and low-anxiety groups are statistically significant ($p < .05$).

The differences in state anxiety between the high- and low-anxiety groups are shown for all five records of Table 2. As anticipated, a higher level of anxiety was observed in the HA group. The differences observed in all five measures are statistically significant at $p < .05$.

TABLE 2. Mean state-anxiety indexes in high- and low-anxiety groups.

Measures	Initial Level	Low-pressure chamber		Deprivation chamber	
		Before	After	Before	After
High anxiety (N = 19)	37.0	39.7	34.0	37.4	36.4
Low anxiety (N = 18)	27.2	30.5	27.6	27.2	28.6

Note. Differences between high- and low-anxiety groups were significant ($p < .01$).

DISCUSSION

Limitations of space cause us to concentrate on a comparative analysis of the groups differing in reactivity and anxiety.

The results obtained in the LPC, which reveal a systematic (though statistically insignificant) lower skin resistance in HR subjects, suggest that these people found the LPC condition more stimulating than did LR subjects. This is in agreement with our prediction. It is more difficult to account for the fact that in the DC condition, excluding the first four measures, a similar result was obtained, namely, a consistently (though statistically insignificant) lower skin resistance in HR subjects. If we were to follow Zuckerman's (1975) suggestion that in the early stage of deprivation the novelty of the situation adds weight to the stimulation-seeking factor, whereas later, with the increasing ambiguity of the situation the anxiety factor begins to dominate, then it would be possible to account for the peculiar shape of the skin resistance curve. However, the results obtained in the deprivation situation by subjects distinguished on the basis of their trait anxiety invalidate this interpretation.

In neither situation do the heart rate measurements permit us to speak of differences between the HR and LR groups. The same holds for the groups distinguished on the basis of trait anxiety.

Generally speaking, the results of the HA and LA groups are more differentiated than those obtained by HR and LR subjects. This may be due to the fact that threat was a dominant characteristic of our experiment.

In accord with evidence in the literature we found, on all measures HA subjects showed higher state anxiety than did LA subjects. This means that the X-1 scale, while actually measuring state anxiety as evoked by the experimental situation, reflects the independent variables under study to a lesser extent. Only at the pre-experimental LPC stage did state anxiety reach a higher level than in other situations. Several authors (Shedletsky & Endler, 1974; Spielberger, 1977) have shown that most of the familiar tests measuring trait anxiety (e.g., STAI or MAS) are chiefly measures of individual readiness to react with state anxiety to social threat, being less suited to provide predictions of behavior in situations involving physical or other types of threat. If we accept this point of view, it becomes comprehensible why in our experimental situations, which may be considered difficult, we found some significant differences between the HA and LA groups as far as state anxiety is concerned and why the scale of these differences did not vary significantly across the different measurements under the influence of the particular experimental situation.

The data on skin resistance suggest that the differences in the dynamics of this variable in the LPC and the DC depend on the level of trait anxiety. The relatively low skin resistance in the high-anxiety group in the early stage of the LPC experiment indicates that in the initial stage of the experiment the level of trait anxiety was a differentiating factor for the level of emotional arousal in the tested subject.

No differences between the HA and LA groups could be found in the second stage of the experiment. This is interesting in view of the lower skin resistance characterizing the two groups in the final stage of the experiment. We are presumably confronted with two mechanisms responsible for changes in skin resistance in the first and the second stage of the experiment.

The data obtained in the DC situation also reveal systematic though statistically insignificant differences between the high- and low-anxiety groups as far as skin resistance is concerned. These differences appeared after 3 hr and lasted until the end of the experiment. We are thus led to the conclusion that in the second stage of the experiment LA subjects exhibit higher emotional arousal than HA subjects. The finding runs counter to the previously mentioned statement by Zuckerman (1975) and it may be the result of discomfort caused by the sensory-stimulation deficit, which is more acutely experienced by subjects with low trait anxiety in the second stage of the experiment.

In conclusion, we find that irrespective of what is taken into account, reactivity or anxiety, our results consistently show that the DC situation is significantly less stimulating than the LPC situation. The psychophysiological state of the subjects is specific in these two conditions and depends on whether we consider differences in reactivity or in anxiety.

REFERENCES

Shedletsky, R., & Endler, N. S. (1974). Anxiety: The state-trait model and the interactional model. Journal of Personality, 42, 511-517.

Spielberger,C. D. (1977). State-trait anxiety and interactional psychology. In D. Magnusson & M. S. Endler (Eds.), Personality at the crossroads: Current issues in interactional psychology. Hillsdale, NJ: Erlbaum.

Strelau, J. (1969). Temperament i typ układu nerwowego (Temperament and type of nervous system). Warszawa: Państwowe Wydawnictwo Naukowe.

Strelau, J. (1974). Temperament as an expression of energy level and temporal features of behavior. Polish Psychological Bulletin, 5, 119-127.

Strelau, J. (1983). A regulative theory of temperament, Australian Journal of Psychology, 35, 305-317.

Strelau, J., & Maciejczyk, J. (1977). Reactivity and decision-making in stress situations in pilots. In C. D. Spielberger & I. G. Sarason (Eds.), Stress and anxiety (Vol. 4). Washington: Hemisphere.

Zuckerman, M. (1975). Sensation seeking and anxiety, traits and states, as determinants of behavior in novel situations. Paper presented at the meeting of the Conference on Dimensions of Anxiety and Stress, Oslo, June - July, 1975.

II

PERSONALITY
AND PERFORMANCE

8

Reactivity and Performance: The Third Side of the Coin

Tatiana Klonowicz

The problem of psychological and psychophysiological costs -- the neglected third side of the coin -- has arisen in connection with research on the relationship between temperament and performance. According to Tomaszewski (1963), the course of performance depends on the equilibrium between the acting subject and the demands of the task and the working environment. The balance might be endangered by environmental change, lack of tools to perform the task, lack of knowledge, or other personal factors. It has been argued that temperament is an important regulator of this equilibrium. Pavlov (1928) asserted the existence of the "invalid type." According to Pavlov, certain features of the higher nervous processes of this type make adaptation extremely difficult, if not impossible, thus impairing performance. This unenviable destiny was in store for those with a weak nervous system.

In the early 1960s, Teplov (1961) noticed that temperament does not necessarily determine the final outcome, that is, the result of ongoing activity. It has been shown that an appropriate organization of performance -- the individual style of activity -- enables people to achieve equal results, irrespective of their temperaments. Individual style of activity is determined by temperament, and the term appropriate means suitable for the individual organization of activity. Teplov's argument received strong empirical support in the Soviet Union (cf. Strelau, 1969) and elsewhere. For instance, Strelau and his co-workers (1974) have demonstrated that reactivity is the origin of relatively stable individual differences in the organization of goal-directed activity.

In other words, according to Pavlov, some task demands can never be satisfied by certain temperaments, whereas according to Teplov and others, an equilibrium between a person's capacities and the task demands can be maintained, owing to the individual style of activity.

The pessimistic (Pavlovian) and optimistic (Teplovian) concepts share several assumptions, and perhaps the most important is that in both cases attention is focused on the discrepancies between man and his environment (task) as reflected in level of performance. As long as satisfactory results are obtained, the

This project was begun with the unpublished data obtained by Materska and Klonowicz (1972-1973) and the preliminary study by Klonowicz (1974b). The study is partially based on a M Sc dissertation of the author's student, M. Czyzkowska. The author is grateful to Dr. M. Materska for her constructive counsel. The project was supported by IFIS PAN Grant 11.8.

environment or the task would be regarded as fitting. It has been argued
(Klonowicz, 1980) that more attention should be paid to the third side of the
coin: the psychological and/or psychophysiological costs of work.

The term cost has been defined as work-induced changes in human functioning.
It applies to a variety of phenomena, both subjective (boredom) and objective
(fatigue), their range, and duration. It has been argued that individual differences in goal-oriented activity may be expressed in the results, the specific
organization of activity, and the magnitude of costs.

Although most of the arguments are still of a hypothetical character, it has
been shown (Klonowicz, 1974a) that under monotonous conditions high-reactive
persons perform better and with lower costs than do low-reactive people, whereas
under stress due to overload, the situation is reversed. In the third task used
in this study, both groups achieved identical results, but the high-reactive
people had to pay a bigger price for coping with task demands. Although these
results corroborated the hypotheses, the study was not fully satisfactory.
Individual style of activity was not controlled; therefore, the influence of
this factor on both level of performance and costs remained obscure.

The present research was designed to provide further information related to
these issues. It has been hypothesized that individual differences in reactivity
(moderator variable) differentiate the individual's response (i.e., level of
performance and costs) to the working environment and task demands. The following specific hypotheses have been formulated:

1.   Provided that the subject is given the opportunity to make use of his
     individual style of activity, level of performance will not be influenced
     by level of reactivity.

2.   Equality in terms of performance will be more costly for the high-reactive
     persons.

3.   Imposed working conditions, that is, organization of activity antagonistic
     to the temperamentally determined individual style, will have more effect
     on high-reactive (lower level of performance and higher costs) than on low-
     reactive persons.

Were we to recognize the beneficial effect of individual style of activity, both
high- and low-reactive people should benefit by it. According to the third
hypothesis, high-reactive persons are supposed to be less resistant to adverse
working conditions and less able to adjust to a suboptimal change. In line
with Eliasz's supposition (1981) that high-reactive people display lesser plasticity of adaptation, the third hypothesis suggests that the imposition of certain antagonistic rules pertinent to the temperamentally determined basic
properties of the individual style of activity will affect high-reactive people
to a greater degree.

The third hypothesis differentiates the adverse effects of the imposition of
working conditions (style of work), but the fourth hypothesis bears on the
beneficial aspects of this manipulation.

4.   Irrespective of declared preferences, both high- and low-reactive persons
     should benefit from the imposition of working conditions concordant with
     their temperamentally determined capacities.

Style of activity is a result of two factors: temperament and individual experience (learning). It can be easily imagined that in some people the second
factor takes the upper hand over the first, thus forming a style of work

antagonistic to what presumably is the optimal one. The question arises whether this style could be regarded as optimal from the point of view of costs and performance, and the answer may be relevant to training procedures.

METHOD

Subjects

Four hundred college students were given Strelau's Temperament Inventory (TI). Ninety-seven high-reactive (+R) and 98 low-reactive (-R) subjects were then selected on the basis of their reactivity scores (the lower and upper quartiles of the sample, mean scores: +R = 31.6; -R = 62.4).[1] For Part 2, when the subjects were assigned to eight subgroups, an attempt was made to match the selected subjects across the experimental conditions in terms of their reactivity scores (see Table 1).

Design

The experiment consisted of two parts. In Part 1 all subjects completed two similar tasks: construction of two simple models. Each task was presented with

TABLE 1. Experimental design for Part 2

Group	Reactivity[†] (mean score)	Instruction	Relation of instruction to preferences
1	+R = 32.3	Algorithmic	Agreement
2	+R = 33.1	Algorithmic	Disagreement
3	+R = 32.6	Heuristic	Agreement
4	+R = 33.2	Heuristic	Disagreement
5	-R = 61.9	Algorithmic	Agreement
6	-R = 62.4	Algorithmic	Disagreement
7	-R = 62.6	Heuristic	Agreement
8	-R = 62.1	Heuristic	Disagreement

[†]+R (-R) = high (low) level of reactivity.

---

[1] Part 2 was completed by 89 high-reactive and 95 low-reactive subjects.

either algorithmic (A, detailed, step-by-step descriptions of all the operations) or heuristic (H, general description of the result) instructions.[2]

At the termination of these tasks, given in random order, the subjects were asked about their preferences as to the instruction to be given in Part 2. For Part 2 the subjects were assigned to perform a simple task under each of four experimental conditions. Independent variables in Part 2 were the instruction (either A or H) and the relationship of the instruction to the previously expressed preferences (the instruction either agreed or disagreed with the preferences).

Procedure

The subjects were tested individually. For Part 1 the game "Little Mechano" was used. The two models chosen for this experiment required an identical number of operations and were similar in terms of difficulty. To familiarize the subjects with the experimental procedure, all the data essential for Part 2 were already collected at this stage (e.g., recording of all the operations). In Part 2 the subjects were to form an eyelet in a 2.5 × 2.5 - cm square of self-adhesive plaster. The sequence of operations included cutting a square from a plaster with scissors, finding the center of the square, making a hole in the center, inserting a metal rivet into the hole, and flattening the rivet to form an eyelet (only the main operations are listed here).

RESULTS

Reactivity and Preferences for Type of Instruction

The results obtained in Part 1 were used in two ways: (a) as preliminary information necessary to control the dependent variables in Part 2 (see Table 1), and (b) as information on the determinants of the individual style of activity.

Of 97 high-reactive subjects, 63 preferred the algorithmic and only 34 the heuristic instruction. In the low-reactive group, the preferences for type of instruction were reversed: 56 of 98 subjects preferred the heuristic, and 42 the algorithmic instruction. With chi square = 9.566, we may conclude that instruction preferences are strongly associated with level of reactivity ($p < .01$).

At the same time, the preferences of 35% of high-reactive and of almost 43% of low-reactive subjects contradict the theoretical assumptions as to the working conditions best fitting their temperamental capacities. Thus, although temperament prevails, there are still other than temperamental determinants of a person's preferences as to the organization of working process (e.g., habits acquired through training or imitation of others).

Performance and the consequences of the misfit between a person's capacities and the working conditions

Three indexes of goal-directed behavior were taken into account. Their value has been tested in the earlier work of Materska (1975).

---

[2]The instructions were prepared on the basis of theoretical and empirical data (Klonowicz, 1974b; Strelau, 1969, 1974) revealing the main properties of individual style of activity associated with either low or high reactivity. Thus the experimental procedure allowed the manipulation of the individual style of work variable through imposition of a particular style (organization of activity).

Performance on the task was evaluated in terms of quality of result. The quality index (Q) was calculated as a sum of weighted ratings made by competent judges who evaluated the main features of the result (shape, localization of the hole, and fastening of the eyelet).

At the same time, quality is understood here as a standard that subjects tend to achieve, and hence it serves as a regulator of activity. To attain the desired result, the subjects have to perform several operations, that is, to put in some effort. Effort -- evaluated as the ratio of the sum of all the operations performed (operations repeated included) to the quality -- is the measure of costs, that is, of subject's use of his energy and knowledge to attain the result. The proposed index yields the information on operational costs (the effort expended to obtain a value of one weighted point) and represents the subject's investment of his skills, forces, and knowledge. To facilitate calculations, the ratio number of operations/quality was multiplied by 100.

The misfit between a person's capacities and working conditions depends largely on coping strategies, which help -- either directly or indirectly (e.g., cognitive reassessment) -- to overcome the difficulties. The third index used in the present study -- plasticity (P) -- belongs to the category of direct means of coping with obstacles and is a measure of the person's tendency to correct errors. The index is calculated as a ratio of corrections (corrective operations) to the number of errors (multiplied by 100). In line with what had been said about effort, it is assumed that the quality, as a regulatory standard, plays an important part here as well.

The results are presented in Table 2. The scores of eight groups of subjects were compared to determine the role of: (a) preferences (i.e., the effect of the discrepancy between the preferences and the instruction received: (b) type of instruction (A vs. H), and (c) level of reactivity.

TABLE 2. Mean scores on three dependent variables: Quality of work (Q), Effort (E), and Plasticity (P)

Group	$+RA_{at}$	$+RA_{dt}$	$+RH_{at}$	$+RH_{dt}$	$-RA_{at}$	$-RA_{dt}$	$-RH_{at}$	$-RH_{dt}$
N	29	17	14	29	21	29	27	18
Q	21.09	20.55	16.46	14.76	22.04	20.86	16.83	15.86
E	70	77	94	108	78	96	91	82
P	64	43	36	29	44	42	55	47

Note. +R (-R) = high (low) level of reactivity; N = size of sample; A,H = type of instruction: algorithmic (A), heuristic (H); and at (dt) = agreement (disagreement) between the instruction received in Part 2 and previously expressed preferences.

Quality. The analysis of the data was conducted by means of Student's t test. The main finding was that the performance measure showed evidence of a strong situational effect (type of instruction), the other two variables (preferences and reactivity) being of no importance. This allows us to combine the data across the groups differing in either reactivity level or preferences, but separately for the two types of instruction. The mean scores for these combined data are, respectively, 21.14 (algorithmic) and 15.88 (heuristic instruction). A between-group analysis of variance indicates that the algorithmic group showed superior performance: $F(1,182) = 35.530$, $p < .01$.

Thus, this is a clear case of the influence of instruction on level of performance. Because the instructions reflect the main properties of the styles of activity typical for either low-reactive (heuristic) or high-reactive (algorithmic) people, it might be concluded that in both groups the level of performance depends solely on the working conditions.

Operational costs: Effort. Because of the skewness of the data, the median test was used to determine the role of independent and moderator variables. Because the preferences did not seem to affect this index, the data were then combined across the groups differing in their preferences but separately for the groups with different reactivity levels and different instructions. The results are presented in Table 3.

As the figures in Table 3 indicate, the costs, as measured by effort, are determined by both variables taken into account, that is, reactivity and instruction. The effect is particularly evident in high-reactive subjects: when working under adverse conditions (with the heuristic instruction), they are forced to invest significantly more effort than are low-reactive subjects working under the same conditions ($p < .01$) and to invest significantly more effort as compared with their counterparts working with an algorithmic instruction ($p < .01$). Although the instruction effect is demonstrated for high-reactive subjects only, it is worth noting that in general the algorithmic instruction demands less effort.

TABLE 3. Operational costs (effort) according to type of instruction and reactivity level

Instruction	+R	-R	χ^2
Algorithmic	71	56	1.772
Heuristic	124	74	12.626
χ^2	14.405	2.492	

Note. +R (-R) = high (low) level of reactivity.

TABLE 4.   Comparative analysis of plasticity scores in eight groups of subjects (values of chi square beyond or close to the critical level)

Group	$+RA_{at}$	$+RA_{dt}$	$+RH_{at}$	$+RH_{dt}$	$-RA_{at}$	$-RA_{dt}$	$-RH_{at}$	$-RH_{dt}$
$+RA_{at}$	--	4.121**	7.840***	13.172***	3.704*	4.566**	NS	NS
$+RA_{dt}$		--	NS	NS	NS	NS	NS	NS
$+RH_{at}$			--	NS	NS	NS	3.967**	NS
$+RH_{dt}$				--	3.082*	NS	8.048***	4.263**
$-RA_{at}$					--	NS	NS	NS
$-RA_{dt}$						--	NS	NS
$-RH_{at}$							--	NS

Note. +R (-R) = high (low) level of reactivity; A,H = type of instruction: algorithmic (A), heuristic (H): at (dt) = agreement (disagreement) between instruction received in Part 2 and previously explained preferences.

  * .10 > p > .05
 ** p < .05
*** p < .01

Plasticity. The same procedure was adopted to determine the effect of instruction, preferences, and reactivity on plasticity. The mean scores of eight groups of subjects are presented in Table 2, and their comparative analysis is contained in Table 4.

As the figures in Table 4 indicate, with one exception (+R group in A conditions), the plasticity index is higher in low-reactive subjects. Furthermore, it may be seen that in low-reactive subjects, no significant changes in plasticity arise with changes in working conditions, whereas in high-reactive subjects every departure from optimal conditions leads to a more or less pronounced decrease in plasticity.

DISCUSSION

The results of this study confirm and extend those obtained by Klonowicz (1974b) and Strelau (1974). Because the performance measures were shown to depend on external conditions, these data offer renewed evidence of the possibility of achieving equal results irrespective of level of reactivity. Thus, at least for certain categories of task, appropriate working conditions seem to guarantee a high level of performance.

At the same time, the data on two other dependent variables reveal that level of reactivity mediates the impact of working conditions. Equality is costly, both in terms of subjective effort (operational costs) and in terms of plasticity. It appears that experimental manipulations affected high-reactive persons to a greater

degree: the beneficial as well as the adverse effects of the imposed working conditions are more pronounced in high-reactive subjects. Thus, the data corroborate
the hypotheses related to the behavior of high-reactive persons (1, 2, 3, and 4).

The interaction of the low level of reactivity and the experimental conditions
led to no changes in either operational costs or plasticity. This lack of effect
of task demands on low-reactive subjects confirms the 1st, 2nd, and 3rd hypotheses.
The adverse conditions introduced in this study were still within the capacities
of this group; therefore, the question of the exact role of individual style of
activity in low-reactive people remains open.

Finally, let me draw attention to the meaning of the two indexes of the misfit
between individual capacities and environment. Whereas operational costs as
measured by effort are bound up with the task, the second index -- plasticity --
seems of broader significance. Plasticity reflects the tendency to cope with
obstacles arising in the course of activity. The low plasticity index may
express the person's helplessness, his lack of power to affect the events. The
question arises whether such feelings of helplessness are more easily evoked in
high-reactive persons. This hypothesis is the starting point for future work.

REFERENCES

Eliasz, A. (1981). Temperament a system regulacji stymulacji (Temperament
    and the system of stimulation control). Warszawa: Państwowe Wydawnictwo Naukowe.

Klonowicz, T. (1974a). Reactivity and fitness for the occupation of operator.
    Polish Psychological Bulletin, 5, 129-136.

Klonowicz, T. (1974b). Wpływ poziomu reaktywności i rodzaju instrukcji na
    wykonywanie prostych zadań konstrukcyjnych (Effect of reactivity level and
    type of instruction on performance in simple construction tasks). In
    J. Strelau (Ed.), Rola cech temperamentalnych w działaniu (The role of tem-
    peramental traits in activity). Wrocław: Ossolineum.

Klonowicz, T. (1980). Person-environment fit at work: An attempt to evaluate
    the costs of adaptation. Polish Psychological Bulletin, 11, 249-255.

Materska, M. (1975). Kształtowanie sie struktury czynności pod wpływem instrukcji
    (The effect of instruction on structural features of actions). Warszawa:
    Wydawnictwa Uniwersytetu Warszawskiego.

Pavlov, I. P. (1928). Lectures on conditioned reflexes: Twenty-five years of
    objective study of higher nervous activity (behavior) of animals. New York:
    International Publishers.

Strelau, J. (1969). Temperament i typ układu nerwowego (Temperament and type
    of nervous system). Warszawa: Państwowe Sydawnictwo Naukowe.

Strelau, J. (1974). Experimental investigations on the relation between reactivity
    as temperament trait and human action. Paper presented at the meeting of the
    International Conference on "Temperament and Personality," Warsaw, September,
    1974.

Teplov, B. M. (1961). Problems of individual differences. Moscow: Izdatelstvo
    Akademii pedagogicheskikh nauk RSFSR (in Russian).

Tomaszewski, T. (1963). Wstep do psychologii (Introduction to psychology).
    Warszawa: Państwowe Wydawnictwo Naukowe.

9

Nervous System Properties and Coding Processes

Olga Halmiová and Elena Šebová

Efforts at determining the biological factors underlying certain personality traits are as old as scientific research itself, and considerable attention has been devoted to this problem in psychology over the past century. In dealing with differential problems, Soviet psychologists based their research on Pavlov's views, adopting man's neurophysiological properties as their frame of reference. The transition from the study of types to an investigation of properties of the nervous system contributed significantly to the development of this conception, which has proved to be the most fertile among current biological theories. Its priorities derive from the fact that it takes as its starting point the central nervous system as a regulatory system of the human organism.

Research on the properties of the nervous system may be assigned to four roughly drawn, partly overlapping stages (Bazylevich, Alexandrova, Zhorov, & Rusalov, 1977):

- Stage I includes a comparison of bioelectrical specificities of the regulatory system and the retrocentral area of the brain.

- Stage II involves a determination of those indicators among parameters of the frontal areas that reflect directly the basic complexes of the regulatory system of the brain.

- Stage III comprises a follow-up of the strength of the regulatory system of the brain in humans (functional endurance, work capacity, absolute thresholds, and cerebral evoked potentials).

- Stage IV represents research on the psychological correlates of various specificities of the regulatory system.

Hence, at present, two principal groups of problems are being pursued, in relation to previous findings. First, basic properties are being reinvestigated, with a verification of the methods for their determination and their relationship to mental processes, particularly those of activity. Second, attempts are being made to determine some principal holistic properties that would not be defined on the basis of partial data only. These properties are being investigated principally from the point of view of the systems approach.

The effect of properties of the nervous system appears to be of significance in various types of activity -- in learning, work, and sports activity, as well as in tasks designed to explore basic mental processes, for instance, memory, thinking, and motivation (e.g., Danilov, 1973; Golubeva, 1975; Gorozhanin, 1977; Soloveva, 1971).

Our experiments were designed to determine to what extent interindividual differences in various memory tasks are conditioned by these properties. Some significant correlations have been found in a study of the effect of load on performance
in memory tasks and in a study of retention of meaningful and meaningless material.

The effect of the strength of the subject's excitation processes and of activation
level on performance in recall tasks was examined in two experiments.   From previous studies it was assumed that (a) people with weak excitation processes would
perform worse in tasks of increasing difficulty than those with strong excitation
processes; (b) activation level (measured in terms of bioelectrical skin reactivit
BSR -- also known as galvanic skin response) would decline with increasing task
difficulty; and (c) performance would not differ in the two groups if the items
to be remembered were presented under noiseless conditions, whereas an enhanced
level of activation induced by intensive white noise would negatively affect performance in the weak group as compared with the strong group. It was further
assumed that the application of the subjective scales of "certainty-uncertainty"
(Kovác, 1968) would increase these differences between two groups even further.

EXPERIMENT I

Method

Strelau's Temperament Inventory (TI) (1969) was used to select 14 (from a total of
100) subjects with extreme values of strength and weakness of excitation processes.

The BSR was recorded continuously throughout the experiment with the aid of
electrodes attached to the index and the middle finger of the left hand.

Five sets of 20 currently used, two-syllable words each were presented at the
rate of 1 word every 2 sec, and participants had to recall them with a certain
delay; hence, they had to retain a small group of continually changing words.
In the first set they recalled 1 word after hearing the next word; in the second
set after presentation of the next 2 words (i.e., the first after hearing the
third, etc.), and so on, until in the fifth set they had 5 intervening words
(i.e., they recalled the first word after the sixth had been.
The experiment was terminated by a 3-min relaxation phase during which BSR continued to be recorded.

The words were presented aurally with a tape recorder in a monotonous female
voice, and the test was carried out individually with each person.

Results and Discussion

The subjects were selected with Strelau's TI and his mode of rating, account
being taken solely of the strength and weakness of excitation processes: 7 subjects within the score range of 20-35 (weak excitation processes) and 7 within
the score range of 70-85 (strong excitation processes). The suitability or
otherwise of such methods as this to determine properties of the nervous system
has elicited considerable discussion, particularly in connection with the ongoing
trend set by Soviet authors who determine these properties with measures of
evoked brain potentials. Although no direct relationship can exist between our
knowledge of the physiological bases and mental specificities, it is clear that
this physiological basis does exert an influence on human behavior. Strelau
(1969) verified the various items of the scale, and the method is deemed adequate
for our purpose -- if the given properties of the nervous system are understood
as the basis of the temperamental traits.

Performance in five memory situations was compared for both groups. The results are summarized in Figure 1. It is evident that there are practically no differences between scores in the first, the easiest memory task (with one intervening word). In the second and the third tasks (with two and three intervening words, respectively) the differences are for the most part in favor of the strong group. The difference was the greatest in the fourth task (with four intervening words), being also statistically significant (t = 2.395; p < 0.05). The fifth task proved to be practically unmanageable: subjects were incapable of remembering a group of five constantly changing words; thus performances by the two groups were again closer. But though scores achieved by the weak group showed a minor decline between the fourth and fifth tasks (0.8 word), those achieved by the strong group showed a substantial decrease (3.3 word). Hence, subjects of the weak group reached the lower limit of performance already in the fourth task, and those of the strong group in the fifth one.

The results support our hypothesis. Subjects with weak excitation processes performed worse throughout the entire experiment than did those with strong excitation processes. Although the differences in performance in the simple task were minimal, a substantial increase in task difficulty caused a strong drop in performance in the weak group. This supports our assumption of a lower working capacity of subjects with weak excitation processes in load situations. As regards the discussion about the suitability of Strelau's TI, it might be observed that similar results were obtained in experiments of this kind in which subjects were assigned to groups according to the method of the "law of strength" elaborated by Nebylitsyn (Halmiová, 1971).

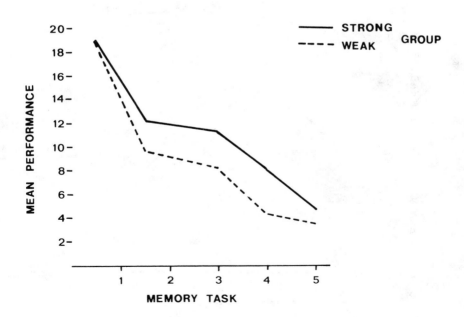

FIGURE 1. Mean performance in the various memory tasks for subjects with strong and weak excitation processes (continuous curve: strong group; dashed curve: weak group).

As a measure of the activation level of psychophysiological data, we made use of BSR, where, from among a number of possible indicators (length of curve, amplitude, number of deviation) we took into account only the length of curve (A), corrected according to the formula introduced by Uherik (1965):

$$A = \frac{L - L_0}{t} \cdot \frac{R_0}{R}$$

where

L = length of curve;

L_0 = the abscissa from the start to the end of the experimental situation;

t = the duration of the experiment;

R_0 = the smallest resistance recorded in each of the subjects during the course of the experiments; and

R = the resistance in the relevant experimental situation

Figure 2 shows the size of activation level (A) in the various memory tasks. In the group with strong excitation processes, A and memory performance proved to be reciprocally independent, whereas in that with weak excitation processes, a

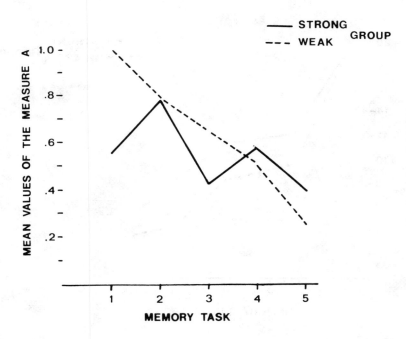

FIGURE 2. Activation level (A) measured with the aid of bioelectrical skin reactivity (BSR) in the various memory tasks for subjects with strong and weak excitation processes (continuous line: strong group; broken line: weak group).

relation of statistical significance was found between a decrease in memory achievement and a decrease in activation (r = 1.000; p < 0.01).

Neither the adaptation nor the relaxation phase showed any intergroup differences in the activation level (t = 0.697 in the adaptation and 0.441 in the relaxation phase). In the first memory task, the initial activation level in the weak group was significantly higher than in the strong group (t = 2.199; p < 0.05), but declined during the course of the experiment as the task difficulty increased. In the strong group the activation level varied independently of performance. Our hypothesis was confirmed for subjects of the weak group only.

The results of our experiments thus imply that subjects with weak excitation processes are most strongly activated at the start of the experimental situation, but a simple memory task results in a significant rise of their activation level in comparison with that of the strong group. These results give support to the theory that "weak" subjects react more sensitively to stimuli than do "strong" subjects, but the latter are more resistant to load (Teplov, 1962).

EXPERIMENT II

Method

Thirty subjects aged 20-21 years were paired by the method based on the law of strength. This method measures reaction time (RT) to sound stimuli of varying intensity, it being assumed that RT is adequate to the stimulus intensity in the strong group of subjects, whereas the weak group tends to respond regardless of stimulus intensity. (The method has been described in more detail by Halmiová, 1971).

Subjects heard two simple texts replayed from a tape recorder containing eight family names each (four common and four rare). The first text was presented in a noiseless atmosphere, the second amidst intensive white noise (80 dB), but so that it was still comprehensible. The common and the rare family names were selected from a telephone directory and were randomized in the texts.

Subjects were instructed to listen to the texts carefully; to remember the names; and, at the end of the presentation, to enter the names in an answer sheet, assigning in addition the degree of their subjective certainty according to a 3-point scale to each name.

Results and Discussion

An evaluation of the global results (from 30 subjects) permits us to state that recall with lower activation level (under noiseless conditions) was higher by 29.3% than that with an enhanced activation level (under conditions of noise). As to differentiation between common and rare names, performance in the first condition (noiseless) amounted to 3.0 items for common and 2.3 items for rare names. In the second condition (noise) the scores were 2.6 items and 1.2 items, respectively. Hence, though performance for rare names under noiseless conditions was 30% lower than for common names, under conditions of noise it was lower by 55%. It is clear that, regardless of activation level, recall of common items was superior to that of rare ones. Similar results were obtained when the subjects were divided into groups of weak and strong excitation processes. Figure 3 shows that our hypothesis of superior performance by the strong group under conditions of enhanced activation failed to be borne out. No statistically significant differences were noted between the two groups; the (just noticeable) trends point rather toward an opposite tendency -- the weak group showed lower

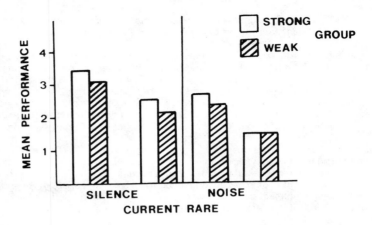

FIGURE 3. Mean achievements by subjects with strong and weak excitation processes under noiseless and noise conditions, with common and rare stimuli.

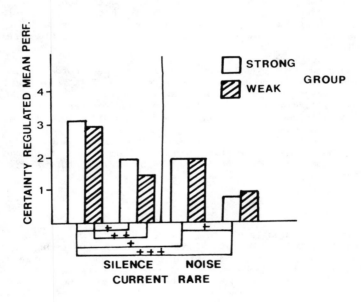

FIGURE 4. Certainty-conditioned mean performance by subjects with strong and weak excitation processes under noiseless and noise conditions, with common and rare stimuli.

  + p < .05
 ++ p < 0.01
+++ p < 0.001

performance during the experiment; under conditions of noise, both groups had equal recall scores for the rare stimuli. A control by means of the subjective measure of certainty underlined these findings, as seen in Figure 4. Subjects in the strong group achieved higher scores, controlled by the subjective measure of certainty (under noiseless condition), but lower scores in comparison with the weak group. This gives support to the earlier findings regarding a higher subjective certainty of subjects with strong excitation processes (Kovác & Halmiová, 1973). A comparison of the actual performance with the measure of certainty showed subjective certainty to be higher by 16% in the strong than in the weak group.

DISCUSSION

Our hypotheses have been confirmed only in part. In the first experiment, involving load in the memory task, we found significantly differing performance by the two groups. In the second experiment we assumed only an increased activation level, which did not create adequate conditions for the groups to differ. However, the results seem to concur with data from the literature. Strelau (1978), for instance, arrived at similar conclusions: although performance by subjects with strong and weak excitation processes (or with low and high reactivity) differed in the experimental tasks involving stress in current learning (and also working) activity, the resulting achievements of the groups were the same. He understands high reactivity as weakness of the excitation processes and vice versa, and determines it by methods based on a principle similar to ours, that is, he relates response strength to various levels of stimulus intensity.

Support has been obtained, however, for a phenomenon already known from other experiments, namely, that differences in performance become less evident in the final results than in the course and style of activity performed in both groups. The second experiment brought evidence of a more even performance for the different variables of the memory tasks in the weak group. Performance by the strong group differed significantly under three variables of the experiment: subjects responded differently to common and rare stimuli under noiseless conditions and enhanced activation, whereas performance by the weak group varied only under noiseless conditions for common and rare stimuli.

The results of our two experiments, though not fully consistent, cannot be considered to be contradictory; they complement each other and contribute to an overall clarification of the determinants of individual differences in memory processes. Research on the relations between properties of the nervous system, activation level, and memory processes is considered to be important because of the data it may generate concerning memory performance and, in our view, represents an effective way for setting up theories in psychology.

Kovác (1978) holds that the systems approach manifests itself in psychological experiments in an interfunctional apprehension (i.e., in an investigation and interpretation of various psychological phenomena in intrapsychic affinities, in relation to the entire complex of stimulus and organismic variables). Such an approach permits psychological scientific facts to be inferred from data of psychological experiments in a greater measure than has been the practice heretofore of classical experimenters.

REFERENCES

Bazylevich, T. F., Alexandrova, N. I., Zhorov, V. A., & Rusalov, V. M. (1977). Some results of investigation into the general properties of the nervous system (in Russian). Voprosy psikhologii, 3, 33-45.

Danilov, V. A. (1973). Diagnostics of a manifestation of the strength of the
nervous system in mental-linguistic activity (in Russian). Voprosy psikhologii,
3, 150-154.

Eysenck, M. W. (1976). Arousal, learning and memory. Psychological Bulletin, 83,
389-404.

Golubeva, B. A. (1975). Electrophysiological investigation of the properties
of the nervous system and certain individual specificities of human memory
(in Russian). Unpublished manuscript, Moscow.

Gorozhanin, V. S. (1977). Control of movement activity as a problem of differential psychology (in Russian). Voprosy psikhologii, 1, 137-142.

Halmiová, O. (1971). Short-term memory and the strength of the nervous system.
Ceskoslovenská psychológia, 15 (5): 444-450.

Kovác, D. (1968). Subjective uncertainty-certainty: Set or regulator of behavior?
In A. S. Prangishvili (Ed.), Collection of papers dedicated to the 85th anniver-
sary of V. Usnadze (pp. 186-198, in Russian). Tbilisi, Mecmereba.

Kovác, D. (1978). The principle of interfunctionality in psychology. Ceskoslovenská psychológia, 22: 506-511.

Kovác, D., & Halmiová, O. (1973). Is there a direct relation between emotional
stability and strength of nervous processes? Studia Psychologica, 15, 314-320.

Nebylitsyn, V. D. (1972). Fundamental properties of the human nervous system.
New York: Plenum Press.

Schwartz, S. (1974). Arousal and recall: Effect of noise on two retrieval
strategies. Journal of Experimental Psychology, 102, 896-898.

Soloveva, S. A. (1971). Mutual relationships between the type of nervous system,
neuropsychic tension, and intensity of motives in memory processes (in Russian).
Paper presented at the meeting of the Soviet Psychology Association, Tbilisi.

Strelau, J. (1969). Temperament i typ układu nerwowego (Temperament and type of
nervous system). Warsaw: Państwowe Wydawnictwo Naukowe.

Strelau, J. (1978). Rola cech temperamentu w rozwoju psychicznym (The role of
temperament in mental development). Warsaw: Wydawnictwa Szkolne i Pedagogiczne.

Teplov, B. M. (1962). Typological properties of the nervous system and their
significance to psychology (in Russian). Moscow: Nauka.

Uherík, A. (1965). Bioelectrical skin reaction. Bratislava: Slovenská akadémia
vied.

10

Polychronicity and Strength
of the Nervous System as Predictors
# of Information Overload

Richard F. Haase

Information overload can be defined as a situation in which informational input
from environment to individual exceeds a person's capacity to process that information. When a person has the option of engaging in selective attention or
filtering cues, responses may well continue to be adaptive. However, if the
situation is such that all relevant stimuli, although exceeding the capacity of
the person to process these cues, must be processed, then a response decrement
usually results. This response decrement might be conceived of as an inverse
function of the degree of information overload and is typically accompanied by
reports of stress by the person (Broadbent, 1971; Milord & Perry, 1977; Miller,
1961). A great variety of situations in modern life demand maximal performance
of people in highly complex, multiple stimulus situations. In certain of these
complex settings (e.g., air traffic control), less than maximal performance can
have serious consequences, which in turn creates additional stress for those who
must perform such tasks. Thus the identification of psychological parameters
that predict adaptive performance under conditions of information overload presents an important problem area for applied psychology.

It seems clear that there are wide individual differences with respect to performance on multiple cue, information overloaded tasks (Dumont & Vamos, 1975;
Milord & Perry, 1977). Moreover, a host of personality variables might differentiate between adequate and inadequate performance in such situations. Two
such sets of variables that may have important implications here are the factors
of polychronicity and those dimensions of temperament derived from the Pavlovian
conception of strength of the nervous system. Following the original work of
Hall (1966), Haase, Dumont, and Banks (1977) have operationalized the concept
of polychronicity. The Polychronicity Index (PCI) is a paper-and-pencil
instrument broadly defined as a self-report measure of the extent to which a
person reports little or no psychological or behavioral disturbance under conditions of rather intense informational input from a variety of sources. The
Polychronicity construct (and the scale to measure it) is heavily rooted in the
notion of structure imposed on activities and interactions performed in the
everyday environment. The basis of the construct assumes that those persons
who impose strict structure on their activities and interactions do so in an
attempt to characteristically control or reduce information overload, which is
seen as a stressful condition. In contrast to this monochronic style, the polychronic style is presumed to place little structure on activities and interactions.

The assistance of Myriam Kirkpatrick in data collection and tabulation for this
project is gratefully acknowledged.

It is inferred that such people, who report little or no distress from information-overloaded conditions, are less susceptible to the negative effects of stimulus intense, overloaded situations.

The PCI is a factorially complex instrument, measuring five independent dimensions:

1. Information Overload: reports of distress (or lack of it) in situations in which too many inputs are present simultaneously; too much is perceived to be going on at once.

2. Interpersonal Overload: reports of stress from the presence and demands of too many interpersonal interactions, negative reactions to crowding, etc.

3. Change Overload: reports of distress from an environmental situation wherein the stimulus inputs are rapidly changing and fluctuating.

4. Activity Structure: the degree of control preferred over activities, both in type and sequence.

5. Temporal Structure: a preference continuum concerning the scheduling of activities within a temporal sequence.

The first three factors are clearly the most meaningful and reliable, both conceptually and statistically.

Several initial studies have been conducted in which the validity of these constructs has been tested (Haase, Dumont, & Banks, 1977; Haase, Lee, & Banks, 1979). In general one or another of the five factors have been shown to be significantly related to psychological flexibility, tolerance of ambiguity, arousal-seeking tendency, cognitive complexity, intelligence, and measures of trait anxiety. It has also been found that the first three factors of polychronicity share significant common variance with measures of extraversion and neuroticism. This general tendency for polychronicity to be related to the theoretical domain of arousal and flexibility suggests several lines of inquiry. One such line of research is the potential relationship between polychronicity and the Pavlovian constructs of properties of the nervous system and dimensions of temperament derived therefrom.

The Pavlovian constructs of temperament and properties of the nervous system appear to be gaining increasing notice among Western psychologists. The relations among properties of the nervous system, derivative concepts of temperament predicated on these typological features and Western concepts of personality and arousal have seen publication in a scattered group of outlets. The most influential collection of writings, however, appeared with the publications of Gray's (1964) Pavlov's Typology, followed by Nebylitsyn and Gray's (1972) Biological Bases of Individual Behavior. Both volumes have done a great deal to stimulate interest among Western psychologists in the Pavlovian constructs. Moreover, these volumes have clearly elucidated some of the more salient connections between Pavlovian properties and Western dimensions of personality, particularly those of arousal and extraversion.

A reading of the Nebylitsyn and Gray (1972) volume, in particular, would suggest that the concepts underlying the definition of polychronicity may share considerable common variance with the concepts of strength of the nervous system and the temperamental dimensions associated with strength. Furthermore, if both polychronicity and dimensions of temperament are viewed as a subset of a higher-order construct of level of arousal, as suggested by Gray (1964), both sets of variables may have implications for predicting performance in multiple-cue, stimulus-intense, information-overloaded experimental situations. Some early evidence of this pattern has been documented with respect to the factors of

polychronicity. Dumont and Vamos (1975) have found that the factors of polychronicity significantly predict behavior in multiple-cue experimental situations.
In general their findings reveal that the monochronic is likely to adopt a
strategy of attending to a single cue while strategically avoiding other cues
in the situation, even though instructed to attend assiduously to all cues. The
polychronic person, on the other hand, was found to perform in a superior fashion
when the criterion was simultaneous attendance to all cues. In a similar vein,
the research summarized in Nebylitsyn and Gray (1972) would suggest that the
Pavlovian dimensions of temperament may also be highly predictive of performance
in such experimental situations. Several relationships documented in that volume
clearly indicate that strength with respect to excitation is predictive of performance under conditions reflective of multiple-cue information processing,
although typically limited to performance on one variable under conditions of
distraction. We have reasoned that the properties of the nervous system of excitation, inhibition, and mobility may well represent the neurological basis of
polychronicity and, furthermore, that both sets of variables should significantly
predict performance in multiple-cue, stimulus-intense, information-overload
experimental tasks. Inasmuch as the present research represents an exploratory
study in this domain, no predictions beyond these general expectations were put
forth.

An ancillary thrust of this research was to provide additional construct validity
to the questionnaire measure of dimensions of temperament as developed by Strelau
(1972). Constructed as a general measure of nervous system type, the questionnaire has several advantages. The measures of excitation, inhibition, and
mobility derived from the questionnaire are taken here as reflections of the
more basic underlying neurological properties. The central purpose of this research, then, was to assess relationships between temperament dimensions as outlined by Strelau (1972) and polychronicity, and to assess the extent to which
these variables are capable of predicting performance in a multiple-cue experimental task intended to be overloaded.

METHOD

Subjects for the present research were 22 undergraduate students enrolled in
psychology courses at Texas Tech University, Lubbock. The sample was equally
divided between male and female participants and ranged in age from 18-26 years.
Students were tested individually by the experimenter. Upon arrival in the
experimental room, each student was apprised of the nature of the experiment
and the tasks they would perform. After this general introduction to the experiment and answering any questions about the study, the students completed the
Polychronicity Index and Strelau's Temperament Inventory. The order of presentation of the two scales was randomized to counterbalance any effects due to
response set or carryover from one questionnaire to the next. On completion
of the instruments, each student was required to complete the following multiple-
cue task. The task was designed to be maximally demanding. Previous research
with these tasks indicated that they constitute a considerable challenge to the
subject (Dumont & Vamos, 1975). The tasks the students performed in this phase
were performed simultaneously. They were instructed in the nature of the tasks
and were implored to attempt to do as well as they possibly could on all three
tasks at once and not to sacrifice any of the tasks at the outset. The experimental tasks were comprised of the following:

1. The student was asked to follow, with the dominant hand, a standard pursuit
   rotor, which was revolving at a rate of 60 revolutions per minute. The subject was required to keep a stylus in contact with a 1-in circle located on
   the other edge of the revolving rotor. The rotor was connected to a recording

clock that accumulated the number of seconds the stylus was in contact with the 1-in disk. The total time available was a continuous 315 s.

2. In addition to the pursuit rotor, the student was also required to perform a dichotic listening task. In this task two different and competing sources of information were presented. The dichotic material was aurally presented by means of a Sony stereophonic tape recorder on which the disparate informational input were recorded on the two channels. On one channel was recorded a passage from an example of the Graduate Record Examination, representing a verbal comprehension task. The information presented was a quite detailed description and analysis of records kept by federal and credit agencies, sources of information about individuals, and the laws relating to such information and its use. The entire passage took 5 min and 15 sec to present aurally and contained a great many detailed pieces of information. The passage was chosen because it presented information that would be unknown to a majority of the students. The students were told that they would be tested on the information at the end of the session and should pay close attention to the content of the message. At the same time this message was presented in one ear, a second source of information was presented aurally to the opposite ear. This information consisted of a series of spoken random digits ranging from 0 to 9, spaced 1 sec apart. The student's task was to signal the experimenter every time the number 7 was spoken. The earphones were reversed (left-right) for alternate subjects to counterbalance any possible laterality effects.

Data for analysis consisted of the following indexes: (a) the number of correct identifications of the number 7; (b) the number of questions answered correctly about the content of the verbal comprehension passage; and (c) the number of seconds of contact maintained by the student with the pursuit rotor. These three indexes provided the primary multiple-cue data against which the predictive power of the Polychronicity Index and the temperamental dimensions were assessed.

RESULTS AND DISCUSSION

The questions posed in this research are multivariate, that is, Do dimensions of temperament (excitation, inhibition, and mobility), as well as the dimensions of polychronicity, account for significant variance in performance in a multiple-cue, stimulus-intense experimental task? Multivariate methods were applied to these data to explore the potential underlying relationships between dimensions of polychronicity and temperament. Issues of accounting for simultaneous performance on all three tasks were further explored in a series of analyses.

Temperament and Polychronicity

It was hypothesized that inasmuch as the conceptual definitions of polychronicity and the Pavlovian dimensions seemed to be similar, there should be significant common variance between the two sets of variables. Zero-order correlations between the five factors of polychronicity and the dimensions of mobility, excitation, and inhibition are shown in Table 1. Examination of these results reveal one significant point of correspondence. The dimension of mobility and the polychronic factor of Change Overload (Factor III) were found to be significantly correlated in a positive direction ($p < .02$). Change Overload is principally a measure of the extent to which one reports not being overloaded by rapidly changing stimulus inputs. High scorers on this dimension report little difficulty in handling such situations and little behavioral disturbances resulting from them. The factor of mobility is described (Nebylitsyn & Gray, 1972) as being characterized by the speed of transformation and the speed of initiating and terminating nervous processes. The operational definition of

TABLE 1. Intercorrelations of strength, polychronicity, and experimental tasks

	Strength Variable			Polychronicity					Task		
	Mobility	Excitation	Inhibition	PC I	PC II	PC III	PC IV	PC V	Rotor	Numbers	Quiz
Strength of the nervous system											
Mobility		.60	.01	.30	.11	.52	.34	-.13	.28	-.02	.38
Excitation			.33	.30	-.12	.35	.08	-.40	-.16	-.03	.47
Inhibition				-.21	.21	.04	-.22	-.43	-.16	.12	.21
Polychronicity factor (PC)											
PC I					.02	.14	.17	.45	-.31	.01	.29
PC II						.13	-.19	.21	.25	-.17	-.31
PC III							-.09	-.07	-.28	-.17	.29
PC IV								.07	.00	.06	.05
PV									-.10	.05	-.34
Mean	54.8	59.1	55.3	16.6	15.3	16.2	12.4	14.6	136.2	21.3	3.8
Standard deviation	8.6	9.3	12.3	1.5	3.1	2.7	2.4	1.9	63.6	4.2	1.4

mobility via Strelau's (1972) TI describes a behavioral state that requires relatively disorganization or distress. Both the mobility dimension and the Change Overload factor appear to share a common base in this respect. Presumably both dimensions are correlated with the more basic neurological processes attributed to mobility, although the present author is unaware of any published research bearing on this issue. Though a few other relationships among this complex set approach marginal levels of significance, the mobility factor appears to be the most promising. A significant negative relationship between inhibition and Temporal Structure is also reflected in these data (p < .05). The negative relationship would suggest that those participants scoring high on the factor of inhibition also report a strong need for imposing strict temporal structure on their activities. The salience of the mobility factor, however, is further underscored by a significant relationship with the total polychronicity score -- averaged across all five factors (r = .46; p < .05); but it should be noted that this relationship is most likely carried by the relationship between mobility and Change Overload.

Predictions of Multiple Task Performance

The central purpose of this research was to assess the ability of both the Pavlovian dimensions of temperament and the factors of polychronicity to predict performance in a multiple-cue, stimulus-intense experimental task. Inasmuch as simultaneous performance on all three experimental tasks was the critical aspect here, two data analytic strategies were employed. First, overall multivariate relationships between temperament and polychronicity, respectively, and task performance were assessed by canonical correlation.

Canonical analysis between the five factors of polychronicity and the three simultaneous tasks revealed a relatively high relationship (R_C = .79); but, given the sample size in this experiment, it was not found to be statistically significant (X^2 = 19.73; df = 15; p = .18). Similarly the canonical correlation between the dimensions of mobility, excitation, and inhibition, on the one hand, and task performance variables, on the other, was high (R_C = .58) but not statistically significant (X^2 = 12.43; df = 9; p = .19). The sizeable proportions of variance predicted in task performance by both sets of variables would suggest that there is some reliable tendency reflected here. However, the lack of statistical significance indicates that the findings could be a chance phenomenon. Replication of these findings with a larger subject pool would be desirable. It should be noted that with respect to polychronicity, Dumont and Vamos (1975) found canonical correlations at a comparable level, suggesting that the findings may have some inferential validity across samples.

Whereas canonical correlations assess the degree of relationship between multivariate sets of variables, the technique is general and cannot precisely answer the most important questions of whether temperament or polychronicity factors can predict simultaneous performance on the tasks employed in this study.

An index of simultaneous performance is required to provide an adequate answer to this question. To accomplish this, performance on the three experimental tasks was categorized into two levels -- those students who performed above the mean of the total group on at least two or three of the tasks simultaneously and those students who performed above the mean of the group on none or only one of the tasks (nonsimultaneous group). Multivariate analyses of variance were performed contrasting the simultaneous and nonsimultaneous groups on the factors of excitation, mobility, and inhibition, as well as on the five factors of polychronicity in a second analysis.

The two groups differed significantly from one another on the combined linear compound variable representing the five polychronicity factors [Wilk's Lambda $(5,1,20) = .431$, $p < .05$]. From the linear discriminant function, which maximally separates the groups, it was found that the factors of Change Overload, Interpersonal Overload, and Temporal Structure are the key discriminants of differences between simultaneous performers and nonsimultaneous performers. That is, students who report little or no disturbance from rapidly changing informational inputs, who report little tendency to tightly structure temporal sequences of activities, and who are monochronic with respect to interpersonal situations (i.e., dislike crowding, too many people, etc.) are the students who performed maximally under demands to attend simultaneously to the three tasks described previously. In terms corresponding to Pavlovian terminology, such a person is strong with respect to excitation and highly mobile in nervous processes.

Confirmation of this interpretation comes from the multivariate analysis of variance on the three Strelau factors of excitation, mobility, and inhibition. The MANOVA between simultaneous and nonsimultaneous performing groups yielded a Wilk's Lambda $(3,1,20) = .677$, $(p < .07)$. The discriminant function of the factors that maximally separates groups indicates that mobility is clearly the strongest predictor of group performance, followed by excitation. The mobility factor is roughly 7 times more important than inhibition and approximately $2\frac{1}{2}$ times more predictive than excitation. The low discriminant weight for excitation is largely due to the fact that mobility and excitation are redundant in this analysis $(r = .60)$. In addition, follow-up univariate contrasts indicate that mobility significantly differentiates groups $(p < .04)$, whereas excitation and inhibition alone do not $(p > .34$ and $.52$, respectively). To add perspective, of those participants who were rated as highly mobile, 74% were also classified as simultaneous performers, whereas only 17% of the students classified as weak with respect to mobility were classified as simultaneous performers. A similar classification analysis on the factors of polychronicity reveals that 91% of the simultaneous performers were also classified as polychronic, whereas only 18% of the nonsimultaneous performers were so classified.

Of all the dimensions tested in this study, the polychronicity factors of Change Overload, Interpersonal Overload, and Temporal Structure and the Pavlovian dimension of mobility stand out as the most consistent predictors of multiple-cue, stimulus-intense performance on experimental tasks. The data presented here confirm some of the early findings of Dumont and Vamos (1975) regarding the constructs of polychronicity as useful predictors of performance in such stimulus-intense, information-overloaded settings. The constructs appear to tap some dimension (perhaps neurological) that facilitates such performance for some and inhibits it for others. The fact that the dimensions of mobility and excitation also predicted such performance, and the fact that the correlation between factors of polychronicity and strength of the nervous system were verified here as well increases the confidence one might place in a neurological interpretation of the data. The factors of polychronicity have not as yet been assessed in conjunction with neurological measurement. But since such data do exist for the strength of the nervous system dimensions (see Nebylitsyn & Gray, 1972), the reasoning becomes plausible. Only direct experimental test will verify such a hypothesized relationship.

It should be noted that we have made the assumption in this experiment that the task was information overloaded. This assertion seems defensible, especially in light of the fact that many students confirmed this fact after the experimental session.

The link between the Change Overload factor of polychronicity and the mobility factor of the Strelau scale is an important conceptual as well as experimental link. The implication of both measures is that the high-scoring person has the ability to shift rapidly from one task to another without behavioral or psychological disturbance. Presuming that both measured attributes are neurologically based, it would seem that the two dimensions may well be tied together by an arousal interpretation of the data (arousal in the optimal sense). Further research in this domain is warranted. Direct examination of the underlying basis of both mobility and polychronicity would be desirable; the data from this study address this issue only tangentially.

Finally, this study will also help to link more closely the Western personality dimensions with those of the Pavlovian model. It is apparent that both scales are reflecting theoretically similar concepts and behavioral manifestations of these concepts. Future research in both East and West should profit from such scientific correspondence between all-too-often disparate lines of work.

REFERENCES

Broadbent, D. E. (1971). Decision and stress. New York: Academic Press.

Dumont, F., & Vamos, P. (1975). Multimodal stimulus processing and polychronicity. Unpublished manuscript, McGill University, Montreal.

Gray, J. A. (Ed.). (1964). Pavlov's typology. New York: MacMillan.

Haase, R. F., Dumont, F. R., & Banks, D. L. (1977). Development and validation of a scale for the measurement of polychronicity. Unpublished manuscript, Texas Tech University, Lubbock.

Haase, R. F., Lee, D. Y., & Banks, D. L. (1979). Cognitive correlates of polychronicity. Perceptual and Motor Skills, 49, 271-282.

Hall, E. T. (1966). The hidden dimension. New York: Doubleday.

Milord, J. T., & Perry, R. P. (1977). A methodological study of overload. Journal of General Psychology, 97, 131-137.

Miller, J. G. (1961). Sensory overloading. In B. E. Flaherty (Ed.). Psychophysiological aspects of space flight. New York: Columbia University Press.

Nebylitsyn, V. D., & Gray, J. A. (Eds.). (1972). Biological bases of individual behavior. New York: Academic Press.

Strelau, J. (1972). A diagnosis of temperament by nonexperimental techniques. Polish Psychological Bulletin, 3, 97-105.

11

Temperamental and Informational Determinants of Problem Solving in Person-Computer Interaction

Czesław S. Nosal

THE PROBLEM AND RESEARCH MODEL

The purpose of the present study was to evaluate the interrelation between temperamental and intellectual variables in the problem-solving process. A computer system that functions in an interactional mode was used for this purpose. Thus, for the purposes of this study, a problem-solving process involves continual conversation between a person and a computer system. However, the computer system per se was not a direct object of research; it was used only as a convenient basis for measurement. The use of a computer system of the time-sharing type created good observational conditions from the point of view of psychological research.

In psychological research based on cybernetic assumptions, it is stressed that the interactional mode of activity constitutes one of the most important aspects of the functioning of the human intellect (Nosal, 1979; Pask, 1975). The theoretical sense of the idea of "conversation" was thoroughly examined in Pask's book. In a general sense, conversation refers to behavior regulated by symbolic processes and indicates a certain style of cognitive control that we can infer by different time and action indexes, such as reaction time and types of operations and errors committed during the problem-solving process.

Further, the measurement of various aspects of person-computer conversation is important for an investigation such as ours, the purpose of which is the evaluation of the simultaneous influence of many temperamental and intellectual characteristics on problem-solving activity. Furthermore, measurement under real conversation conditions corresponds closely to the definition of temperament as a set of formal traits manifested in the energy level and reaction-time parameters of behavior, in agreement with Strelau's theory (1972, 1974).

The approach preferred by the present author is based on the assumption that problem solving by a person who is cooperating with a computer system is a type of cognitive activity organized in the form of various interaction programs. A simpler form of interaction would be isolated reactive behavior; a more complex form would be goal-directed conversation regulated by symbolic processes. The dynamics of these regulation programs depend on the following sets of variables:

1. The type of task and the form of cognitive set elicited by the instructions and detailed task demands.

2. A person's intellectual dispositions, which in a general sense may be interpreted as fluid and crystallized factors of human intelligence (Cattell, 1971).

3. The temperament type, understood as a given combination of central nervous system (CNS) features.

4. A functional limitation connected with simultaneous temperament-intellectual influences in the context of the task demands.

When taking into consideration the results of psychological analyses of such functional cognitive limitations, we must distinguish clearly between two quali- tatively separate levels of these limitations: (a) limitations connected with processing at an elementary level, that is, identifying or recognizing information in a certain data field; and (b) limitations of a higher order connected with discrimination or integration regulated by complex processes of comprehension, reasoning, and productive thinking; at this level, one-sided criteria such as recognition or reaction time are not important.

These types of limitation in information processing are described in the repre- sentative literature as state- versus process-limited processing (Garner, 1974) or as data- versus resource-limited processing (Norman, 1976).

This interpretation of problem-solving activity during person-computer conversa- tion is especially interesting in the context of temperament theory. Through multicriterion measurement of human cognitive activity, it should be possible to evaluate which type of relation between temperamental and intellectual character- istics plays an essential role in a particular type of situation.

HYPOTHESIS, METHODS OF MEASUREMENT, AND ANALYSIS DESIGN

The basic hypothesis of this study is that indexes of problem solving under person-computer conversation conditions are more closely correlated with CNS features than with intellectual dispositions. In general, this hypothesis does not agree with the kind of psychological interpretation in which the role of intellectual dispositions is overvalued at the expense of other types of char- acteristics, for example, temperamental. If we consider that the environment demands behavior that is adequate and not overly delayed, then the role of functional interaction of temperamental and intellectual characteristics becomes clearer. It seems, however, that temperamental traits play a vital role in dynamic situations that demand continual adaptation to environmental changes in a relatively short period of time.

A homogeneous group of male chemistry students 21-22 years old (N = 20) was selected for investigation. The measurement of problem-solving indexes extended over two sessions during an introductory course in computer programming. The persons tested undertook two tasks:

1. A reproductive task, which consisted in finding an error in a computer program.

2. A productive task, which consisted in initiating a certain program for the first time.

When evaluating the intellectual dispositions of the students, three variables were taken into account; the L variable, which measures the person's mastery of the computer language (FORTRAN), based on a multiple-choice test; the K-variable, which evaluates the person's knowledge of computer programming methods, based on a didactic test; and the R-variable, which measures the person's reasoning ability, based on Raven's Progressive Matrices (43 of the most difficult tasks were selected from this test).

The intellectual dispositions represented by the L, K, and R variables can be interpreted in the context of intelligence theory (Cattell, 1971). We know that reasoning (R variable), based on figural data, possesses maximum factor loading on fluid intelligence. The K variable represents one of the essential aspects of crystallized intelligence. But there is a certain difficulty involved in the interpretation of the L variable because, depending on the degree of memorization of the rules of an artificial language such as FORTRAN, this variable will be closer to the first or second factor of intelligence.

Temperament traits were measured by Strelau's Temperament Inventory (TI: Strelau, 1972). On the basis of this method, four CNS traits can be estimated: E, strength of the excitation process; I, strength of the inhibition process; M, mobility of nervous processes; and B, index of CNS balance expressed as the ratio of the E/I results.

In the experiment, the following set of time/action indexes that give information about the dynamics of the problem-solving process was considered: NO, number of operations; TE, number of thought errors; WE, number of written errors on the computer terminal; GT, global interaction time or the full cycle of cognitive activity; WT, sum of the writing time intervals; TT, sum of the thought time intervals; and EF, index of effectiveness ratio (TE + WE) : NO.

In agreement with the purpose of the research and with the proposed hypothesis, the full set of independent variables included intellectual dispositions L, K, and R and temperamental traits E, I, M, and B. The dependent variables were indexes of problem solving (NO, TE, WE, GT, WT, TT, and EF), identical for both experimental tasks.

From a statistical point of view, this study presents the problem of multiple determination, which occurs when the experimenter intends to estimate the simultaneous influence of numerous independent variables on numerous dependent variables. This type of estimation is made possible by a procedure called canonical analysis (Harris, 1975).

The idea of the canonical variable lies at the root of the procedure under discussion. From a mathematical point of view, the canonical variable is represented by the linear approximative function that is best suited to a set of measurement data. Carrying out a canonical analysis, we look for many maximally correlated pairs of linear functions (canonical variables) having a number equal to the sets of dependent variables. In each such pair, the first function represents the measurement data for the independent variables, and the second function represents the data for the dependent variables. The degree of correlation of each pair of functions is expressed by the so-called canonical correlation (C_R). Furthermore, in canonical analysis we can calculate total and partial canonical determination coefficients. The first coefficient (D_C) describes what percentage of the total variance of dependent variables is simultaneously determined by the set of independent variables. On the other hand, the series of partial canonical determination coefficients indicates the way in which the influence of a given independent variable is distributed among particular canonical variables that represent the dependent variables. Therefore, the procedure of canonical analysis supplies an abundant set of coefficeints that analytically and synthetically describe the interrelations between the experimental variables as a whole.

RESULTS

Reproductive Task

The results of the canonical analysis for the reproductive task are listed in Table 1.

TABLE 1. Influence of temperamental and intellectual variables on different time and action indexes described by canonical coefficients. The reproductive task.

Independent variable	Canonical representation of dependent variable						
	NO	TE	WE	GT	WT	TT	EF
E	37+	03+	01–	01+	40+	12+	06+
I	13+	10+	10+	31+	06–	01+	29+
B	32+	12+	13+	35+	01–	04+	02+
M	03–	21–	10–	08–	33+	22–	01–
R	27–	29–	22–	10–	03–	04–	05–
K	24–	02–	01–	10–	10–	35–	18–
L	01+	30+	02+	40+	14+	07+	06+
Total variance accounted for (%)	46	33	47	58	42	56	45
Canonical correlation (C_R)	.95	.88	.83	.52	.42	.33	.13
Total canonical determination (D_C)				.51			

Note. Numbers in the first 7 rows represent the coefficients of partial canonical determination for the given independent variable (the sum of each row is equal to 100%). The algebraic signs show the direction of the relationships (determination) between the measured features of the given pair of variables.

Independent variables: E = strength of the excitation process; I = strength of the inhibition process; B = index of central nervous system balance expressed as the ratio of the E/I results; M = mobility of nervous processes; R = reasoning ability; K = knowledge of computer programming methods; and L = mastery of computer language (FORTRAN). Canonical representation of dependent variables: NO = number of operations; TE = number of thought errors; WE = number of written errors on computer terminal; GT = global interaction time or full cycle of cognitive activity; WT = sum of the writing time intervals; TT = sum of the thought time intervals; EF = index of effectiveness ratio (TE + WE) : NO .

The principal analytic information in Table 1 is provided by the coefficients of partial canonical determination (the first 7 rows). The last 3 rows contain important synthetic information: the percentage of total variance explained by canonical analysis, canonical correlation values (C_R), and total determination (D_C).

The numbers in the first row represent a standardized distribution of partial determination (percentages) and add up to 100. They show the degree and direction in which trait E influences the particular action and time indexes. For two indexes (NO, WT), there is a singularly high determination: the higher intensity of trait E has an essential influence on the rise in the number of operations (NO) and the lengthening of the writing time intervals (WT). Thus, in both cases, the influence of trait E is in a deteriorating direction.

Comparing the values of partial determination in the following columns (but only on an ordinal scale), we can also estimate which relative rank a given independent variable occupies among other variables of the same type. For example, in the first column, partial determination for trait E has the highest rank, the second highest is trait B, and so on. In the same column, the ranks with determination of traits E and B are higher than the ranks achieved by the intellectual variables R and K. The last two numbers in the first column supply important synthetic information about how much (percentage) of the total variance has been explained. For example, it is 46% for the canonical variable representing NO, with canonical correlation $C_R = .95$. (The shape of complex functions and tables of C_R significance are given by Harris, 1975.)

In general, many interesting tendencies appear in Table 1. It is peculiar, for instance, that temperamental trait I shows a similar direction of influence to the previously mentioned trait E. The high level of CNS inhibition influences the lengthening of the GT interval and the drop of the efficiency index (EF). Similarly, trait B considerably determines two important aspects of thought (NO and GT). An interesting contradictory direction of the influence is revealed in trait M (CNS mobility). Table 1 shows that trait M determines the shorter intervals TT and the level of TE and WE errors. From this, we may conclude that the direction of influence of trait M and of the intellectual variables R and K are similar.

The tendencies associated with all three intellectual variables call for a separate discussion. The character of the influence of the R and K variables is obvious: both variables lower the numerical values in all aspects of the time and action indexes. On the other hand, the direction of influence connected with the degree of mastery of the computer language (L variable) is different. The data in row 7 (Table 1) show that the influence of the L variable is connected with an increase in errors (TE) and longer time (GT). The main factor that explains these seemingly paradoxical directions of dependencies would seem to be the divergence or incongruity between the configurative-conceptual structures representing the problem-solving process and the excessively linear computer language.

By comparing the partial canonical determination values in the second and third columns of Table 1, we may conclude that a large TE number depends mainly on two subsets of variables whose influence runs in opposite directions: L+ and B+ versus R- and M-. In the case of writing errors (WE), the clearest determination is that by the R variable. On the other hand, the synthetic index of performance (EF) is mainly related to the influence of temperament trait I and intellectual variable K.

The occurrence of interaction between temperamental and intellectual characteristics is also noticeable in the scope-of-time indexes (GT, WT, and TT). For example, the intervals WT are considerably lengthened as a result of interaction between two temperamental traits (E and M) and one intellectual characteristic (L variable). Intervals of thinking time (TT) depend mainly on the interaction of the K variable with CNS mobility (trait M). On the contrary, the lengthening of GT intervals is connected with the influence of three variables (L, B, and I), representing an identical tendency.

Generally speaking, the coefficients in Table 1 show that over the whole range of time and action indexes, functional interdependencies appear between the characteristics of temperament and intellect.

Productive Task

Let us now discuss the results that characterize the process of solving the second experimental task (productive task), which is of a different cognitive character. Table 2 contains the essential numerical data; this table is con-structed like Table 1.

Generally, in Table 2 the percentage of explained total variance is more ir-regular. Hence the value of total canonical determination is smaller for the productive task (D_C = .47) than for the reproductive task (D_C = .51, Table 1). However, Table 2 also shows that the two canonical functions correlated with the NO and WE indexes explain a large part of total variance (60%).

The partial canonical determination coefficients in the first row of Table 2 indicate that the high intensity of temperament trait E goes along with shorter TT intervals and a smaller number of TE type errors. This tendency runs counter to the one that appeared in the reproductive task. A possible explanation might be that trait E, depending on the demands of the cognitive task, marks the level of fluctuating versus focused attention.

The numbers in the second and third rows of Table 2 show that a higher degree of CNS inhibition and balance (traits I and B) tends to be connected with lower-ing of the thought indexes. (See in particular two determination tendencies: influence of trait I on indexes TE and TT and influence of trait B on indexes TE and EF.) Both these directions of influence are analogous to those in the reproductive task (with the exception of the influence of trait I and B on index WT).

As shown in the next two rows of Table 2, which respond to diametrically differ-ent characteristics M and R, these characteristics exhibit a similar regularity. A higher level of CNS mobility lowers the number of valid operations (NO) and improves the efficiency (EF); similarly, a greater intensity of reasoning ability is connected with lowering the indexes NO and WT. The direction of influence of variables M and R is analogous to the tendency mentioned earlier in the context of Table 1; the influence of trait M on WT-type errors is an exception. The similarity of the functions suggests an important relationship, the mobility of CNS with the cognitive dimension, which has been little studied so far.

The role of the intellectual variables K and L is particularly clear in relation to the (respective) indexes GT and WT, as well as to NO and EF. Comparing these tendencies with the ones that appeared in Table 1, it is worth emphasizing their internal psychological consistency. In the reproductive task, the students looked for an unspecified error. Under such task conditions, the level of the K variable (knowledge of general methods of computer programming) shows greater disagreement with the more specific knowledge concerning the correctness of the relatively short, linear-type computer language. On the other hand, under condi-tions of a productive task, this disagreement is smaller because the student generates

TABLE 2. Influence of temperamental and intellectual variables on different time and action indexes described by canonical coefficients. The productive task.

Independent variable	Canonical representation of dependent variable						
	NO	TE	WE	GT	WT	TT	EF
E	02+	26–	00	04–	07–	60–	01–
I	02+	24+	13+	01+	04+	52+	04+
B	07+	41+	10+	13+	02+	08+	19+
M	42–	00	15–	03–	12–	01–	27–
R	23–	10–	03–	01–	61–	00	02–
K	07+	03–	05+	57+	22+	04–	02–
L	66+	00	05–	00	06+	06–	17–
Total variance accounted for (%)	61	28	60	24	53	54	44
Canonical correlation (C_R)	.95	.84	.82	.76	.44	.24	.14
Total canonical determination (D_C)				.47			

Note. Numbers in the first 7 rows represent the coefficients of partial canonical determination for the given independent variable (the sum of each row is equal to 100%). The algebraic signs show the direction of the relationships (determination) between the measured features of the given pair of variables.

Independent variables: E = strength of the excitation process; I = strength of the inhibition process; B = index of central nervous system balance expressed as the ratio of the E/I results; M = mobility of nervous processes; R = reasoning ability; K = knowledge of computer programming methods; and L = mastery of computer language (FORTRAN). Canonical representation of dependent variables: NO = number of operations; TE = number of thought errors; WE = number of written errors on computer terminal; GT = global interaction time or full cycle of cognitive activity; WT = sum of the writing time intervals; TT = sum of the thought time intervals; EF = index of effectiveness ratio (TE + WE) : NO .

a general logical outline of the program, which is sequentially realized. It seems that the difference between the demands of the two experimental tasks can be stated in the following way: it is more difficult to find an error in a particular configuration (program) using the linear method of testing that configuration; it is relatively easy to express an already established conceptual structure of the computer program in a linear language. In the context of these statements, it becomes more understandable why in the first task the influence of the R variable on errors in TE and WE is clearly greater than in the second experimental task.

These consistencies in the range of interaction for the intellectual variables increase our confidence regarding the accuracy of the evaluation and interpretation of the tendencies observed in the field of temperamental traits.

DISCUSSION AND CONCLUSION

The aim of our analysis was to determine the relationships between temperamental and intellectual characteristics in the context of problem-solving activity. A comparison of the simultaneous determination of the subset of independent variables shows that temperamental traits play an important regulative role and explain a significant part of the total variance for the different time and action indexes.

How could we explain this role? It is possible to hypothesize that temperament traits B and I determine the style of cognitive activity control. Three basic styles can be distinguished:

1. Conservative interaction, manifested by reaction blocking and delaying; in this case control exists in the form of analyzing the long series of potential consequences of reaction (trait $I > E$, small TE, long TT).

2. Impulsive interaction, manifested in a tendency to rapid reactions and domination of the post-results type of control (trait $I < E$, many TE and WE, long GT containing numerous short TT).

3. Balanced interaction, expressed in using and comparing the results of both mentioned forms of cognitive control ($E \approx I$, high balance of CNS, equalized proportion of the different time intervals and type of errors.

The reported results may also be analyzed in terms of a theory of temperament-intellect relationships. This type of theory does not exist in a fully structuralized form. But giving attention to crystallized versus fluid factors of intelligence, we can find an overlapping field for the fluid factor and the temperamental trait M. It can be inserted as a cognitive characteristic. This supposition receives important support in the presence of correlations between CNS mobility and flexibility/fluency values (Strelau, 1977). Finally, we may conclude that in a functional paradigm, temperamental features play a more regulative role in information processing than is recognized by the classical, dispositional point of view.

REFERENCES

Cattell, R. B. (1971). Abilities, their structure, growth and actions. New York: Houghton-Mifflin.

Garner, W. R. (1974). The processing of information and structure. Hillsdale, NJ: Erlbaum.

Harris, R. J. (1975). A primer of multivariate statistics. New York: Academic Press.

Norman, D. A. (1976). Memory and attention: An introduction to human information processing. New York: Wiley.

Nosal, C. S. (1979). Mechanisms of intellectual functioning: Abilities, cognitive styles, information processing. Wrocław: Technical University Press.

Pask, G. (1975). Conversation, cognition and learning: A cybernetic theory and methodology. New York: Elsevier.

Strelau, J. (1972). A diagnosis of temperament by non-experimental techniques. Polish Psychological Bulletin, 3, 97-105.

Strelau, J. (1974). Temperament as an expression of energy level and temporal features of behavior. In J. Strelau (Ed.), The role of temperament features in activity. Wrocław: Ossolineum.

Strelau, J. (1977). Behavioral mobility versus flexibility and fluency of thinking: An empirical test of the relationship between temperament and abilities. Polish Psychological Bulletin, 8, 75-82.

12

Self-Exposure to Sensory Stimuli in Rats as Activity Motivated by the Sensory Drive

Jan Matysiak

Homeostatic theories of optimal stimulation (Leuba, 1955; Schultz, 1965) assume that any deviance from the optimum motivates the organism to undertake activity that would control the level of incoming stimulation. From this, we would assume that self-exposure to sensory stimuli is an expression of need for stimulation. In other words, need for stimulation motivates an animal to take up activity that results in self-exposure to sensory stimuli (e.g., light). Such an interpretation of the sensory reinforcement phenomenon is confirmed by experimental data showing that activity in the chamber for self-exposure to light increases after the animals have been previously kept in darkness (Roberts, Marx, & Collier, 1958), as well as by those experiments in which prior exposure of continuous light decreased, and prior exposure of pulsatory light removed the augmenting effects of light in the test chamber (satiation). It has also been shown that satiation is a temporary phenomenon (Kish, 1966).

Thus, an organism will undertake activities to enhance the amount of stimulation when its level is suboptimal; by contrast, when stimulation overload occurs, the organism will perform activities to reduce the stimulation flow.

STIMULATION ENHANCEMENT VERSUS REDUCTION

The consequences in the suboptimal stimulation condition seem to be obvious. Empirical data, that is, numerous studies concerning sensory deprivation, provide support for the suggestion that an increase in activity is functional to stimulation deficiency. There is no direct evidence, however, of activities performed to reduce stimulation; in fact, research indicates only that stimulation overload results in a discontinuance of an activity that previously or under different conditions led to a stimulation increase. Also, studies revealing deterioration in functioning or disintegration of behavior under excess stimulation are not helpful as far as active regulation of the level of stimulation is concerned.

On the other hand, activities performed to reduce stimulation are displayed in natural settings as frequently as those aiming at stimulation increment. For example, an animal or a human being will withdraw to a quieter or darker environment when the noise or light is too intense. We might even find active,

The studies were supported by Grant 11.8 from the Institute of Philosophy of the Polish Academy of Sciences.

manipulative behavior (instead of passive avoidance), such as closing the
window if the noise outside is too loud, or turning off excessive light.

Thus, the popular assumption that individuals showing a strong need for stimulation reach higher activity levels than those characterized by a low need for
stimulation, should be revised. Individuals with a strong need for stimulation
will be more active when faced with stimulation deficiency; in such a situation,
they are relatively more understimulated. By contrast, individuals with a low
need for stimulation will show more activity in a stimulation overload condition;
in such circumstances, they are relatively more overstimulated.

It should be emphasized, though, that we deal with different activities in each
condition: in the first one, activity increases stimulation; in the latter,
decreases. Therefore, one can distinguish activity orientation (positive vs.
negative, depending on its enhancing vs. reducing effect on stimulation) as a
dimension of behavior motivated by the sensory drive.

This hypothesis offers a new explanation of data obtained by such investigators
as Barry and Symmes (1963) or Goodrick (1970). The authors suggested that the
lack of group differences in the intensity of turn-on and turn-off responses
provided undeniable evidence of the reinforcing capacity of changes (regardless
of their character).

Such studies are methodologically erroneous: they ignore individual differences
in the need for exposure to stimuli. Thus, the lack of group differences may
be a mere result of the relativity of stimulation levels.

We shall discuss this interpreation at length to clarify the underlying reasoning. If the distribution of the need for exposure to stimuli is normal (which
has been confirmed in our research), we can expect to find similar percentages
of animals with low and high needs for stimulation in two equal samples. If we
now rank the animals according to the level of their activity (separately within
the two groups), we find that individuals with strong need for stimulation will
receive high ranks and those with low need will receive low ranks in the turn-on
group (stimulation deficiency). The ranking in the turn-off group will be
reversed. High ranks will be attributed to low-need individuals; low ranks, to
the high-need ones. This reversal of ranking does not necessarily contribute
to the average activity level in groups. The discussed hypothesis is illustrated
in Figure 1.

According to this reasoning, experimental testing of the hypothesis requires a
certain paradigm, in which the same sample is examined twice. First, the
animals are placed in a turn-on apparatus or, in other words, under a stimulation deficiency condition; next, the same animals are tested in a turn-off
apparatus, that is, under a stimulation overload condition. A negative correlation between results obtained in the two experimental conditions would
support our prediction.

The stimulation deficiency condition is easy to arrange: an initial zero light
intensity seems to be appropriate in the turn-on apparatus. Unfortunately, the
initial light intensity, which should lead to stimulation overload in the
turn-off apparatus, is much more difficult to define. Research provides only
some indirect hints. Henderson (1957) reported gradual diminishing of the
reinforcing effect of light from the point of 53 lux intensity. Russel and
Glow (1976) observed the reinforcing phenomenon at 70 lux and even higher
intensities. Therefore, two experiments were conducted. In the first one,
the intensity of light turned on in the turn-on apparatus and turned off in
the turn-off apparatus was the same and was set at 1.2 lux. In the second experiment, the turned-on light intensity was 3.8 lux and turned-off light, 58 lux.

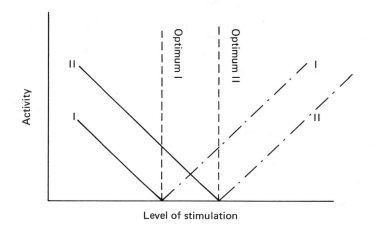

FIGURE 1. Hypothesis of sign of activity.

METHOD

Thirty white male rats (Wistar) were tested in the first experiment. A self-exposure apparatus, described earlier (Matysiak, 1979) was used. The apparatus consists of an ordinary cage (40 × 30 × 20 cm) -- in which rats are usually kept in our laboratory -- built into a .5-cm-thick light-proof plywood box. Two symmetrical 6 × 10-cm levers shaped as shelves were installed inside the cage, 10 cm from floor level. Pressing one (experimental) lever resulted in illuminating the cage as long as the bar was kept down. Depressing the control lever caused no changes. Food and water were available as needed. A small ventilator constantly supplied the cage with fresh air. The turn-off box differed from the turn-on box in one respect: the 1.2 lx illumination was constantly kept on. The rat could turn off the light by pressing the experimental lever. The period of darkness lasted as long as the bar was held down. Measurements in the turn-off apparatus were taken 4 days after the turn-on session.

Twenty-eight rats were subjected to testing in the second experiment. The animals were about 100 days old in both studies. In the second study, the rats were divided randomly into two equal groups. One group was subjected to the turn-on apparatus first and, after a 5-day rest, to the turn-off box. The sequence was reversed in the second group. In both studies, each animal was tested during 24-hr period in both conditions. The following indicators were recorded: the number of times the experimental lever was pressed (NPe) and the number of times the control bar was pressed (NPc). The following, transformed indicator: NPe / NPt (NPt = NPe + NPc) was subjected to statistical analysis. In both studies, Pearson-Bravais correlation coefficients were computed between the NPe / NPt indicators in the two experimental conditions.

RESULTS AND DISCUSSION

Visual Stimulation Studies

The weak, nearly zero correlation obtained in the first study indicates a lack of connection between measurements taken in the turn-on and the turn-off conditions. But then, the same correlation derived from data recorded in the second study reveals a negative relation between the two measurements. The two correlation coefficients are as follows: Study 1, r = -.06, n.s.;   Study 2, r = -.43, p < .05.

Furthermore, the means of the NPe/NPt indicator in the turn-on and the turn-off conditions were compared in both studies. The results are presented in Table 1.

Table 1 shows that in the first study more activity was displayed in the turn-on apparatus; in the second study, in the turn-off condition. The difference between the NPe/NPt indicators was more salient in the second, but still, the differences are significant in both.

These data indicate that the procedure applied in the second study was more appropriate. The animals were tested -- regarding the methodological assumptions -- in two situations: stimulation deficiency (the turn-on apparatus) and stimulation overload (the turn-off apparatus).

The negative correlation is consistent with our hypothesis concerning the two types of activity (positive vs. negative) motivated by the sensory drive. Individuals showing high need for stimulation display more positive activity than do individuals with low needs.   On the other hand, individuals with low need for stimulation achieve higher rates of negative activity than do individuals with a high need.

Table 1.   Mean rates of the NPe/NPt indicator in the turn-on and the turn off conditions

| Study | Condition | | t |
	Turn-on $\overline{X}$	Turn-off $\overline{X}$	
1	.65 ± .05	.58 ± .05	2.64*
2	.58 ± .03	.73 ± .05	7.12**

Note.   NPe = number of times experimental lever pressed;   NPt = number of times control lever pressed.

*p < .01

**p < .001

The data presented in Table 1 are revealing. We must stress their consistency with the results of Glow's study (1970), in which higher levels of activity were also found in the turn–off condition. Both Glow's findings and the dominance of positive activity discovered in our study -- which was contradictory to the outcome of our second experiment -- explicitly confirm the notion of the primary role of light intensity in sensory reinforcement schedules.

The controversy between the two opposite theoretical approaches, distinguishing different major factors in the process of sensory regulation (changes vs. stimulation level) has remained an open issue. Schultz's (1965) concept of sensoristasis supports the hypothesis of changes. Some investigators (Forgays & Levin, 1959; Goodrick, 1970; McCall, 1965) also lean toward this opinion in their studies on self-exposure to light. However, Lockard proposed a competitive hypothesis based on several studies (Lockard, 1963, 1966; Lockard & Lockard, 1964). According to the view of the Lockards, the level of illumination and not changes has a substantial influence on the sensory reinforcement procedure. In his 1966 study, Lockard indicated that changes operate in the initial stage of experimentation only. Later on, the light-intensity factor assumes the dominant role.

Our expectations, while preparing the present studies, were as follows:

1. If stimulation fluctuations are the main determinant, one might anticipate higher stimulating capacities of changes and, consequently, less activity leading to changes, when the discrepancy between the initial state and the outcome of activity increases. Thus, activity in the turn-off apparatus should be lower than in the turn-on box in our second study.

2. If changes in stimulation are the main determinant, then the turn-on and the turn-off conditions should be identical as for their stimulating capacities (assuming the intensity of the turned-on and of the turned-off light would be the same), because the animal's activity alone modifies the degree of changes. Therefore, activities in the two experimental conditions should convey the same meaning in our first study.

3. If stimulation changes are the main determinant, one might predict a positive correlation between measurements taken in the turn-on and the turn-off conditions in both studies, because the animal's activities alone regulate the degree of changes in stimulation. In other words, individuals showing strong need for stimulation would perform more activities than those with low need for stimulation in both experimental conditions, regardless of the intensity of the turned-on and the turned-off light.

We shall now compare our anticipations with our actual findings.

There is a discrepancy between our first prediction and the results of our second study. The level of activity in the turn-off condition was much higher than that observed in the turn-on setting (see Table 1).

According to our second assumption, activity indicators in the two experimental conditions should not differ from each other in the first study. Here, also, data presented in Table 1 do not confirm our expectations. The level of activity was higher in the turn-on condition.

Finally, our third prediction that a positive correlation between measurements in the two experimental conditions should occur in both studies, was not supported. There was no relation between the mentioned measurements in the first study and, instead, a negative correlation was found in our second experiment.

Apparently, our findings cannot be explained from the standpoint postulating the primary role of stimulation fluctuations in sensory regulation.

In fact, our studies support our own hypothesis concerning activity orientation. Our hypothesis is based on the assumption that the arousing capacity of stimuli is determined by their intensity and not by the extent of changes in their intensity. Therefore, our results also confirm this assumption.

Still, we cannot totally deny the significance of changes in satisfying the need for exposure to stimuli. Presumably, changes, just like the novelty factor, have some influence during the initial stage of experimentation. Such evidence was obtained by Lockard (1966). We believe, however, that their role is essentially informational. In other words, an animal gains information about its behavioral control over its environment through inducing changes. It seems logical that changes, understood as information, conseqeuntly function as a source of stimulation. Probably, the stimulating capacity of changes (like novelty) decreases due to gradual habituation.

Visual and Auditory Stimulation Study

In studies to date on sensory reinforcement, it was frequently observed that not only visual stimulation has reinforcing properties. Similar properties are held by stimuli of other modalities, for example, auditory and kinaesthetic. There also exist data testifying to the reinforcing properties of tactile (Richards & Leslie, 1962), olfactory (Berlyne, 1955), and even electric stimuli (Harrington & Linder, 1962). It thus seems that stimuli of any modality may serve as sensory reinforcement; only lack of adequate methods has hindered its manifestation through visual, auditory, or kinaesthetic stimulation.

If, then, need for stimulation refers to any modality, is it reduced for different modalities independently, or is stimulation from different modalities complementary or summative?

Three groups of rats (10 rats each) were studied in a chamber for self-exposure to sensory stimuli. By pressing a bar the visual group could expose visual stimuli (light of 1.2 lux intensity); the auditory group, auditory stimuli (tone of 60 dB and 8000 Hz); and the visual-auditory group, stimuli that were simultaneously both visual and auditory.

The following transformed indicators were subjected to statistical analysis: NPe/NPt, Te/Tt (Te = global duration of pressure on experimental bar; Tt = Te + Tc (Tc = global duration of pressure on control bar); and an additional index of need for stimulation SN = NPe/NPt × Te/Tt.

Table 2 presents data obtained in this study. It was found that rats from the visual and auditory groups exceed the visual-auditory group in both indexes (NPe/NPt and SN), whereas no significant difference between the visual and auditory groups was found.[1] No significant differences were found between groups regarding general activity (NPt). This result points to the higher stimulatory value of a complex stimulus and thus to its lower reinforcing value. Therefore, this result seems to confirm the hypothesis that it is possible to summate stimulation values of stimuli with different modalities.

---

[1] The analysis of variance and Duncan test were applied.

Table 2. Mean values of NPe/NPt, SN, and NPt obtained by the studied groups

Groups	NPe/NPt	SN	NPt
Visual	.57	.34	41
Auditory	.50	.27	24.3
Visual-auditory	.28	.09	34.4

Note. NPe = number of times experimental lever pressed; NPt = number of times both levers pressed; SN = need for stimulation. From "Self-exposition of sensory stimuli of different modalities in rats" by J. Matysiak, 1979, Polish Psychological Bulletin, 10, 159-165. Copyright 1979 by Adapted by permission.

Visual-Auditory-Kinaesthetic Study

The question arises, however, whether the interindividual differences in need for one stimulation modality correlate with the need for other types of stimulation. If the answer is yes, then the sign of the correlation would answer another question: Do individuals with a high need for one (e.g., visual) type of stimulation have an equally high need for auditory or kinaesthetic stimulation? We must not reject the possibility, however, that need for stimulation is a partial feature related to stimulus modality.

An attempt to solve this problem was undertaken in another experiment in which level of need for visual stimulation was compared with that of need for kinaesthetic stimulation measured in the activity wheel. Those two modalities were chosen to avoid repeated measurements on the same apparatus, which would be necessary if comparisons were performed between visual and auditory stimuli.

A group of 30 rats was subjected to a 24-hr study in a chamber for self-exposure to visual stimuli; next, after 14 days, all rats were placed for 24 hr in a normal (breeding) cage with an activity wheel added. In one wall of the cage, just above the floor, a hole was placed through which animals could enter the wheel freely any time they pleased. Wheel revolutions were registered by an electronic meter, started by impulses from a photocell. Animals had constant, easy access to food and water.

Values of Pearson' correlation coefficients between measures of need for visual stimulation and measures of need for kinaesthetic stimulation are as follows (Matysiak, 1979): NPe/NPt, $r = -.51$, $p < .01$; Te/Tt, $r = -37$, $p < .05$; SN, $r = -.48$, $p < .01$; and NPt, $r = .28$, n. s.

As can be seen, all three indexes of need for visual stimulation correlate negatively with need for kinaesthetic stimulation.

One thus may conclude that rats with a high need for visual stimulation display a low need for kinaesthetic stimulation and vice versa. This points to the existence of specific, individual preferences as to modality of incoming stimulation.

Allowing for the fact that all animals were bred in identical conditions, we may suppose that individual preferences with regard to modality of sensory stimulation might be determined by genetic factors.

CONCLUSIONS

The results presented here and speculations about them seem to confirm the usefulness of the sensory drive idea. It helps us to understand behavior that is difficult to explain on the basis of traditional conceptions of elementary drive reduction.

However, the conclusions drawn from these studies should be transposed to the human population very carefully. They ought to be useful rather in formulating research hypotheses, to be verified in experiments with human subjects.

REFERENCES

Barry, H., & Symmes, D. (1963). Reinforcing effects of illumination change in different phases of the rat's diurnal cycle. Journal of Comparative and Physiological Psychology, 56, 117-119.

Berlyne, D. E. (1955). The arousal and satiation of curiosity in the rat. Journal of Comparative and Physiological Psychology, 48, 238-246.

Forgays, D., & Levin, H. (1959). Discrimination and reversal learning as a function of change of sensory stimulation. Journal of Comparative and Physiological Psychology, 52, 191-194.

Glow, P. H. (1970). Some acquisition and performance characteristics of response-contingent sensory reinforcement in the rat. Australian Journal of Psychology, 22, 145-154.

Goodrick, C. (1970). Light- and dark-contingent bar pressing in the rat as a function of age and motivation. Journal of Comparative and Physiological Psychology, 73, 100-104.

Harrington, G. M., & Linder, W. K. (1962). A positive reinforcing effect of electrical stimulation. Journal of Comparative and Physiological Psychology, 55, 1014-1015.

Henderson, R. L. (1957). Stimulus intensity dynamism and secondary reinforcement. Journal of Comparative and Physiological Psychology, 50, 339-344.

Kish, G. B. (1966). Studies of sensory reinforcement. In W. K. Honig (Ed.), Operant behavior: Areas of research and application. New York: Appleton-Century-Crofts.

Leuba, C. (1955). Toward some integration of learning theories: The concept of optimal stimulation. Psychological Reports, 1, 23-33.

Lockard, R. B. (1963). Self-regulated exposure to light by albino rats as a function of rearing luminance and test luminance. Journal of Comparative and Physiological Psychology, 56, 558-564.

Lockard, R. B. (1966). Several tests of stimulus-change and preference theory in relation to light controlled behavior of rats. Journal of Comparative and Physiological Psychology, 62, 415-426.

Lockard, R. B., & Lockard, J. S. (1964). Stimulus change versus preference for light. Psychological Reports, 15, 191-198.

Matysiak, J. (1979). Self-exposition of sensory stimuli of different modalities in rats. Polish Psychological Bulletin, 10, 159-165.

McCall, R. B. (1965). Stimulus change in light-contingent bar-pressing. Journal of Comparative and Physiological Psychology, 59, 258-262.

Richards, W. J., & Leslie, G. R. (1962). Food and water deprivation as influences in exploration. Journal of Comparative and Physiological Psychology, 55, 834-837.

Roberts, C. L., Marx, M. H., & Collier, G. (1958). Light onset and light offset as reinforcers for the albino rat. Journal of Comparative and Physiological Psychology, 51, 575-579.

Russel, A., & Glow, P. H. (1976). Exposure to non-contingent light change in separate sessions prior to light-contingent bar pressing. Quarterly Journal of Experimental Psychology, 28, 403-408.

Schultz, D. P. (1965). Sensory restriction. New York: Academic Press.

13

Temperament Differences in Vigilance Performance as a Function of Variations in the Suitability of Ambient Noise Level

Robert Hockey

The vigilance task has proved a popular testing ground for theories concerning the effects of personality on performance. One reason is the relative simplicity of the situation, coupled with the generally systematic form of the performance function over the duration of the task. In addition, however, the typical decrement in performance over time has come to be regarded, in some ways, as synonymous with a fall in chronic arousal level. Thus, decline in performance has been employed as an "index of arousal by means of which to test personality theories implicating arousal as a factor" (Eysenck, H. J., 1976). It is true, of course, that a number of studies have demonstrated a fall in the level of physiological activation over time (Davies & Krkovic, 1965; O'Hanlon, 1965), but whether this is a cause or a consequence of reduced vigilance is not clear.

EXTRAVERSION–INTROVERSION AND VIGILANCE

The present study examines the role of the temperament dimension introversion-extraversion in vigilance performance, and will question the assumption that differences in performance related to this factor can be attributed to character-istic differences in arousal level (Broadbent, 1963; Corcoran, 1965). Instead, I shall suggest that introverts differ from extraverts primarily in the greater degree of control they exercise over the effects of environmental conditions on their internal state. Their performance, in terms of current cognitive models, may be characterized as essentially "top-down," whereas that of extraverts is "bottom-up."

The vigilance literature contains a number of results that appear to support the arousal theory of extraversion. Extraverts have generally been found to perform at a lower level than do introverts (Bakan, 1959; Bakan, Belton, & Toth, 1963; Davies & Hockey, 1966), whereas they benefit more from an increase in task requirements (Bakan, 1959) or extraneous auditory stimulation (Davies & Hockey, 1966). The most comprehensive evidence comes from experiments by Corcoran (1965, 1972) and by Blake (1971). Corcoran (1965) showed that speed of per-formance on the 5-choice serial reaction task correlated negatively with extra-version but that the correlation was most pronounced under unstimulating condi-tions (low motivation and sleep deprivation). Both Corcoran (Colquhoun & Corcoran, 1964) and Blake (1971) have demonstrated that the superiority of introverts is confined to tests carried out early in the waking day, and in isolation rather than being in groups, though Bakan et al. (1963) failed to find such an interaction.

These data are clearly generally consistent with the hypothesis that extraverts have a lower level of arousal, so that they benefit more from the presence of

high levels of stimulation during the task (Corcoran, 1965).   H. J. Eysenck
(1967) argues that they suffer from "stimulus hunger" and are continually seeking
stimulation to maintain an adequate arousal level. This view certainly receives
support from the observations that extraverts select higher levels (and more
frequent periods) of noise during vigilance tasks (Davies, Hockey, & Taylor,
1969; Hockey, 1972). The main difficulty with the arousal argument, however,
is that it assumes a passive role for the subject in the control of task-related
activity. Whatever his level of extraversion, he is regarded as having no
direct influence over the way in which environmental or task factors are allowed
to affect his performance. This is an unfortunate consequence of the passive
information-processing models of the 1960s and has now been recognized as funda-
mentally wrong. Jerison (1967) has demonstrated for the vigilance situation
that people must certainly be regarded as actively constructing their activity
in relation to task demands. They develop strategies based on both current and
previous task information, as well as long-term goals and priorities. Rather
than considering the differences between introverts and extraverts as the result
of a passive rising and falling arousal process (a view that seems totally un-
acceptable in a more general sense: Hockey, 1979), it is possible to consider
such differences from the point of view of strategic concepts such as these.
A closer look at the data indicates that this may be a useful step to take.
There are very few cases to be found in which introverts are actually impaired
by conditions that are favorable to extraverts. In Corcoran's (1965) study
(Table 2, p. 270), the effect of motivation or sleep loss on both hits and gaps
is very small for introverts, compared with the effects on extraverts; and, in
both cases, the absolute level of performance is higher for introverts under
all conditions. In Blake's (1971) data, the performance of introverts is stable
over the working day and is hardly affected by knowledge of results; both factors, on the other hand, have large effects on extraverts. Interactions of
extraversion with arousal variables seem largely to be based on their having
an effect on extraverts but not on introverts, rather than the two groups'
being affected in opposite directions. Results of our own (Hockey, 1972)
support this view. Performance changes with both 100-dB noise and one night's
sleep loss are consistently greater for extraverts, even though the two sets
of changes are in opposite directions. If introverts are chronically higher
in arousal they should be expected to be more susceptible to changes produced
by conditions thought to produce overarousal even in extraverts. In a number
of such results, introverts perform consistently and well over a range of conditions, whereas the performance of extraverts varies from very poor to very
good, depending on the underlying effect of the variable used to manipulate
arousal level.

The alternative hypothesis is that introverts exercise more internal control
over their activity than extraverts, to the extent that their performance is
relatively less dependent on environmental conditions. This is broadly equivalent
to the top-down strategy familiar from current cognitive models, while extraverts
may be described essentially as bottom-up people. The distinction, like that of
extravert-introvert itself, is, of course, only one of degree. The amount of
top-down control exercised by people will vary with task parameters, practice,
and many other factors for both groups. The following experiment offers a preliminary test of this central idea, and makes use of the observed differences
in noise preferences between the two groups. If people are given free access
to noise during the vigilance task, it may be assumed that they will select a
level that "feels comfortable" and that could be expected to optimize their
performance. A simple model of arousal changes in vigilance tasks is adopted
for the purpose of the study, where noise stimulation may be seen as a means
of "topping up" falling arousal. This view is almost certainly wrong, but does
not materially affect the rationale of the experiment. Whatever the mechanism,
it seems reasonable to argue that the best conditions for work are those one
would pick oneself. A yoked-control procedure is used to compare introverts

and extraverts who select their own noise levels (master subjects) with those who must work in the condition set by others (slave subjects). Furthermore, we can compare three levels of suitability of noise conditions: (a) optimal, self-selected; (b) suitable, selected by a master of the same temperament type; and (c) unsuitable, selected by a master of the opposite temperament type. From this argument, we could predict that this decrease in suitability would have less of an effect for introverts than extraverts, since their performance is less determined by external variation in conditions. From the results of previous work, all effects would be expected to increase with time at work, which might be regarded as itself producing a reduction in internal control (as well as any reduction in arousal level that might result from continuous work of this type).

METHOD

Subjects and Design

Subjects were 48 male undergraduates of the University of Durham aged between 18 and 24 years (median = 19.2 years). They were selected from an original sample of 103, as being the 24 highest and 24 lowest scorers on the Extraversion (E) scale of the Eysenck Personality Inventory (EPI), after equating mean scores on the Neuroticism (N) scale for the two groups. Those having scores of 4 or more on the Lie (L) scale were not used. The students were tested in groups of 3 in a yoked design. Each group comprised a master (either introvert or extravert) and two slaves (one introvert and one extravert). There were thus eight introvert-controlled groups and eight extravert. The slave subjects were designated (for the purposes of analysis only) as being in either a suitable or unsuitable group, depending on whether their temperament matched that of the master. This was designed to provide for three levels of suitability of noise environment, as shown in Table 1, which also summarizes the temperament data.

Table 1. Summary of temperament data for each of the subgroups (mean and range).

Suitability level	Introvert master	E	N	Extravert master	E	N
1	Introvert	7.25 (1-9)	13.62 (7-16)	Extravert	18.50 (14-23)	13.12 (7-15)
2	Introvert	7.38 (2-9)	14.12 (9-16)	Extravert	18.50 (15.20)	14.00 (6-16)
3	Extravert	18.12 (16-22)	12.50 (8-14)	Introvert	7.25 (2-10)	14.00 (5-18)

Note. E = Extraversion and N = Neuroticism on the Eysenck Personality Inventory.

Vigilance Task

The task consisted of eight 4-min periods (combined for analysis purposes into four 8-min periods) in which the students, seated in a lecture theater, saw slides containing a white circular patch on a black ground. Each period contained 160 such events, 1 every 1.5 s. Signals were defined by slightly brighter patches and occurred with a probability of .05, 16 signals in each 8-min period. Slides were presented by two Kodak carousel projectors, set at a 3-s rate and synchronized 180° out of phase, to give 1 slide every 1.5 s. Students were required to indicate their detection of a signal by pressing a button on a hand-held response switch, held below desk level, to prevent any possibility of other students' seeing the slight movement involved. In the control room, at the back of the theater, the experimenter recorded detections from response lights that stayed on until cancelled. The luminance of the signals was set from a pilot study to give an average detection level of about 80% over an 8-min run.

Noise

The noise was broad band noise (60-6 KHz), having an attenuation of approximately 3-5 dB per octave above 1 KHz. It was produced by a Dawe 419C noise generator via a Leak Stereo 70 amplifier and projected into the lecture theater through two sets of 4- × 8-in Wharfedale Bronze loudspeakers positioned at the front of the lecture theater.

Procedure

Each group of 3 subjects was tested together in a large lecture theater, seated well apart with the master in the middle, each having an uninterrupted view of the screen. They were given a 4-min practice session with the noise level set at 55 dB, in which eight signals occurred (the first two of these were pointed out, and they were afterwards told how many signals had occurred). Master subjects were shown how they could reduce the noise level by holding down a spring-loaded button during a 20-s break following each 4-min period after the noise had been increased back up to 100 dB. This was signaled by the lights in the theater, normally set at "dim," being turned up to "full" and the screen going blank. The interval was used to change the magazines on the two slide projectors. After practice, the noise was turned up to a level of 100 dB over a 30-s period. Before beginning the task, this was adjusted by the master to a "comfortable level for carrying out the task." Neither master nor slave subjects were aware that they were being selected on a temperament criterion; they were told that the subject designated (by us) as the master was responsible for controlling the level for all three. The task was then run for eight 4-min periods, with breaks for resetting of the noise level. The students were afterward interviewed informally, and slaves were asked whether the noise level set by the master was too high, too low, or "about right" for them. They were told about the purpose of the experiment and thanked for their cooperation.

Analysis of Data

Detection performance was expressed in terms of probability of detection for each subject in each 8-min period. False positives were very rare (only 7 subjects made even one such response, and only 16 were made altogether). These data are therefore omitted from the analysis; they were distributed across the different conditions. Subjects were classified according to temperament (extravert, E, or introvert, I) and level of suitability (1, 2, or 3) as shown in Table 1. The principal analysis took the form of a $2 \times 3 \times 4$ analysis of variance with repeated measures on the last factor (periods). A second analysis of variance considered the level of noise selected by introvert and extravert masters over the eight 4-min periods.

RESULTS AND DISCUSSION

Noise Level Preferences

Figure 1 shows the mean noise settings of the two groups of master subjects, introverts and extraverts, over the eight 4-min periods. Extraverts clearly select higher levels of noise than do introverts ($F = 29.62$, df = 1,14, $p < .001$), and the preferred level rises steadily over the task session. The overall effect of periods is significant ($F = 3.66$; df = 7,98, $p < .01$) and is located almost entirely in the linear component of the trend ($F = 23.00$, df = 1,98, $p < .001$), the residual being negligible ($F < 1$). The mean level of noise selected before the task had begun did not differ significantly for the two groups ($t = 1.58$, df = 15, $p < .05$) and was, in both cases, lower than all settings during the task. The increase from this setting to the first task setting was, however, much higher for extraverts ($t = 3.27$, df = 15, $p < .01$).

Clearly, the preference level for extraverts is considerably higher than for introverts (about 15 dB), though only during the task. Both groups show increases in preferred noise level over time, but the interaction is not at all significant ($F = 1.10$, df = 7,98, $p > .05$). Examination of individual data reveals that there is, in fact, hardly any overlap between the two groups in terms of selected level, a fact reflected in the low standard errors illustrated in Figure 1. This means that it is valid to assume that incompatible slave-

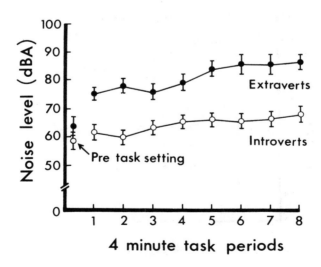

FIGURE 1. Preferred noise level settings of introvert and extravert master subjects (means and standard errors) for each 4-min period. (n = 8 per group) with standard error of means.

master pairings will produce suboptimal noise environments, as defined by the criterion of personal selection. Because introvert and extravert slaves are indistinguishable from their respective masters in temperament characteristics, it is thus very likely that they would choose similar levels themselves if they had control over the noise level. It therefore becomes interesting to ask what effect the enforced suboptimal environmental stimulation has on their detection performance.

Detection Performance

Figure 2 shows the mean detection rates for each combination of temperament and noise suitability. Inspection of the data suggests that (a) introverts perform better than do extraverts, both in terms of level of performance and maintenance of vigilance over the task; (b) there is a systematic decrement in performance with decrease in suitability level, and (c) the decrement with reduced suitability is more pronounced for extraverts than for introverts. Analysis of variance confirms these observations. There are significant main effects of

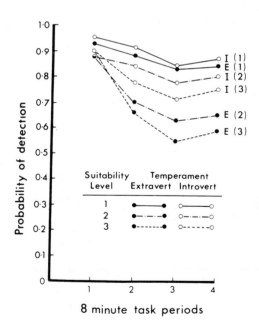

FIGURE 2. Probability of detection as a function of temperament, suitability level, and period of task.

temperament (F = 8.31, df = 1,42, p < .01), suitability level (F = 13.09, df = 2,42, p < .001) and task periods (F = 93.30, df = 3,126, p < .001). The Temperament × Suitability interaction is not significant (F = 1.15, df = 2,42, p > .05), though the interaction of these two variables with periods is significant (F = 2.23, df = 6,126, p < .05).

These results, taken in conjunction with Figure 2, may be interpreted as indi-cating that introverts suffer smaller decrements either with time on the task or with less than optimal noise conditions than do extraverts. Under optimal conditions (master subjects) there is no observable effect of temperament, but differences become progressively more marked as conditions become less optimal.

DISCUSSION

The results offer rather clear-cut support to the hypothesis. Variation in the suitability of noise level during the task has no measurable effect on the per-formance of introverts but a progressive and quite pronounced effect on that of extraverts. While they perform only slightly less efficiently when another extravert is responsible for the noise setting (though still worse than all three introvert groups), their vigilance decrement is markedly greater under the introvert control. Extraverts select levels of noise about 15 dB higher than that selected by introverts when they are given the choice (Figure 1); thus, there seem good grounds for supposing that (a) the poor performance of extraverts under an introvert master is attributable to a suboptimal level of stimulation during the task and that (b) the good performance of the comparable introvert group results from a relative imperviousness to such variations in environmental conditions. The intermediate performance of the compatible slave groups may be seen to reflect the slight variations in preferred level within each temperament group, though this still has a more marked effect on extraverts. Before considering general implications of these data, one further possibility should be raised. In addition to the differences in suitability of noise level inherent in the situation, these are also clearly differences in degree of perceived control. The master not only selects the optimal level of noise for himself, but "feels" a reasonable degree of control over his environment. The incompatible slave condition, on the other hand, is associated with both a per-ceived lack of suitability of noise level and the knowledge that one is powerless to affect the situation. The results could be due, then, to a greater sense of anxiety or frustration under these conditions in extraverts.

How are we to relate this (probable) lack of perceived control in the setting of noise levels to our suggestion of a difference in the degree to which subjects operate a top-down strategy, in which external factors have only a minimal in-fluence on controlled responding? It is possible that the introvert is able to separate the two control problems, effectively concerning himself only with the management of task-directed activity. Any perceived lack of control of external environmental factors would have only minor consequences for such a strategy. The extravert, on the other hand, may be more involved in manipulating the environment to suit his needs for increased stimulation. He may also, whether he actively seeks such stimulation or not, be less able to prevent environmental changes from directly intruding on his attempts to manage the necessary task activity. Clearly, it is not possible to separate these different possibilities in the present situation, though the evidence suggests quite strongly that the poor performance of extraverts in the unsuitable condition did not result from frustration or anxiety about their inability to control the noise level. First, in the posttest interview, there was (interestingly enough) no tendency for these students to indicate that they would have liked a higher level during the task (whereas introverts often reported that they would have preferred a lower one). Second, of course, the difference between the two groups can be seen quite clearly for the suitable condition, where the level can be assumed to be about what each would have set. Finally, it should be emphasized that the students were totally unaware of either their own or other subjects' temperament scores; therefore, they should not have any reason for feeling less in control, for example, in the unsuitable than in the suitable slave condition. Certainly, degree of perceived control over the task conditions has been shown to be an important modifying variable in the effects of noise on performance (e.g., Glass & Singer, 1972). In the present situation, however, it is difficult to see how it could be regarded as biasing the outcome in the particular way we have observed.

Overall, the evidence suggests that introverts and extraverts differ primarily (within the context of tasks requiring sustained attention at least) in the degree to which they can resist variations in environmental conditions and actively control their activity on the basis of internal goals and resources. The top-down control implied here is almost certainly a feature of the attentional behavior of all normal people (Jerison, 1967), though there are good grounds for supposing that it is more prominent in introverted subjects. This is, after all, hardly surprising in view of the long-accepted clinical definition of the intro-vert as having an internal rather than an external basis for his actions. He is defined through his responses to the EPI as one who plans carefully before acting (low impulsiveness) and who avoids unnecessary stimulation (low sociability). These two components are only moderately correlated (Eysenck, S. B. G., & Eysenck, H. J., 1963; Sparrow & Ross, 1964), and this should not be forgotten when interpreting data from performance tests such as the present one. Though the "planning" characteristic of the introvert is clearly what we have in mind in our notion of the strategic control he appears to exercise over his resources, this may not be related in any functional sense to his tendency to select lower levels of noise (or company). It may well be true that the increasing preference for higher levels of noise over the task by groups (Figure 1) does represent a compensatory response to falling arousal, as most theorists would argue, though there is no evidence that this is more marked in extraverts in either these data or those of Hockey (1972). However, separately (if not quite independently) from this, the maintenance of task control of the introvert can be seen to persist more strongly, both over time and over changes in environmental conditions. In the context of sustained task-oriented activity, this would appear to be the more relevant distinction to focus upon.

REFERENCES

Bakan, P. (1959). Extraversion-introversion and improvement in an auditory vigilance task. British Journal of Psychology, 50, 325-332.

Bakan, P., Belton, J. A., & Toth, J. C. (1963). Extraversion-introversion and decrement in an auditory vigilance task. In D. N. Buckner and J. J. McGrath (Eds.), Vigilance: A Symposium. New York: McGraw-Hill.

Blake, M. J. F. (1971). Circadian variations in mental efficiency. In W. P. Colquhoun (Ed.), Biological rhythms and human performance. London: Academic Press.

Broadbent, D. E. (1963). Possibilities and difficulties in the concept of arousal. In D. N. Buckner and J. J. McGrath (Eds.), Vigilance: A symposium. New York: McGraw-Hill.

Colquhoun, W. P., & Corcoran, D. W. J. (1964). The effects of time of day and social isolation on the relationship between temperament and performance. British Journal of Social and Clinical Psychology, 3, 226-231.

Corcoran, D. W. J. (1965). Personality and the inverted-U relation. British Journal of Social and Clinical Psychology, 56, 267-273.

Corcoran, D. W. J. (1972). Studies of individual differences at the Applied Psychology Unit. In V. D. Nebylitsyn and J. A. Gray (Eds.), Biological basis of individual behavior. New York: Academic Press.

Davies, D. R., & Hockey, G. R. J. (1966). The effects of noise and doubling the signal frequency on individual differences in visual vigilance performance. British Journal of Psychology, 57, 381-389.

Davies, D. R., Hockey, G. R. J., & Taylor, A. (1969). Varied auditory stimulation, temperament differences and vigilance performance. British Journal of Psychology, 60, 453-457.

Davies, D. R., & Krkovic, A. (1965). Skin conductance, alpha activity and vigilance. American Journal of Psychology, 78, 304-306.

Eysenck, H. J. (1967). The biological basis of personality. Springfield: Charles C Thomas.

Eysenck, H. J. (1976). Comments on personality and vigilance, The measurement of personality, p. 169. Lancaster, England: M. T. P.

Eysenck, S. B. G., & Eysenck, H. J. (1963). On the dual nature of extraversion. British Journal of Social and Clinical Psychology, 2, 46-55.

Glass, D. C., & Singer, J. E. (1972). Urban stress. New York: Academic Press.

Hockey, G. R. J. (1972). The effects of noise on human efficiency and some individual differences. Journal of Sound and Vibration, 20, 299-304.

Hockey, G. R. J. (1979). Stress and the cognitive components of skilled performance. In V. Hamilton & D. M. Warburton (Eds.), Human stress and cognition: An information processing approach. Chichester, England: Wiley.

Jerison, H. J. (1967). Activation and long-term performance. Acta Psychologica, 27, 373-389.

O'Hanlon, J. F. (1965). Adrenaline and nor-adrenaline reaction to performance in a visual vigilance task. Science, 150, 507-509.

Sparrow, N. H., & Ross, J. (1964). The dual nature of extraversion: A replication. Australian Journal of Psychology, 16, 214-218.

III

APPLIED IMPLICATIONS

14

Psychopathy, Stimulation Seeking, and Stress

Robert D. Hare and Jeffrey W. Jutai

Several investigators have suggested that certain aspects of the psychopath's behavior, including his impulsivity, inability to tolerate routine, proneness to boredom, and antisocial inclinations, are the result of an attempt to maintain an optimal level of arousal by constantly searching for new and varied sensory input. Much of this evidence has been reviewed elsewhere (see Cox, 1977; Hare, 1970; Hare & Schalling, 1978; Quay, 1965; Zuckerman, 1979) and need not be repeated here.

The primary purpose of this chapter is to describe some of our recent research bearing on the relationships between psychopathy, sensation seeking, and reaction to stress in criminal populations. Before doing so, however, a few comments are needed on what we mean by psychopathy and on the procedures used to define it.

ASSESSMENT OF PSYCHOPATHY IN CRIMINAL POPULATIONS

The specific pattern of personality traits and behaviors that defines the syndrome of psychopathy has been well described by Cleckley (1976), whereas recent coverage of the clinical and empirical literature on psychopathy can be found in Reid (1978), Hare and Schalling (1978), and Smith (1978). In the 1980 edition of the American Psychiatric Association's Diagnostic and Statistical Manual of Mental Disorders (DSM-III), the category most closely related to the syndrome of psychopathy is "Antisocial Personality Disorder." Data on the reliability and incidence of this disorder in prison populations, as well as on the relationship between DSM-III and our procedures for the assessment of psychopathy, are available elsewhere (Hare, 1983).

The procedures that we use in the assessment of psychopathy have been outlined elsewhere (Hare & Cox, 1978). In essence, we use interviews and extensive case history data to make global ratings of psychopathy on a 7-point scale. These ratings are very reliable, with correlations between independent sets of ratings routinely being greater than .85. However, the procedures require a considerable amount of experience and rely heavily on the sorts of clinical impressions and judgment that are not easily communicated to other investigators. For this

Preparation of this paper and the research reported were supported by Grant MT-4511 from the Medical Research Council of Canada. The assistance of Janice Frazelle, Judy Bus, Brent McNeill, John Lind, and Sandra Janzen is gratefully acknowledged.

reason, we have recently attempted to make our assessment procedures as explicit as possible and, in doing so, to develop a reliable and reasonably objective method for assessing psychopathy in criminal populations. The first result of this attempt has been the development of a 22-item checklist (see Hare, 1980, for details) and a preliminary manual for use with the checklist (Hare & Frazelle, 1980). The items that make up the checklist are presented in Table 1. A 3-point scale is used to rate inmates on each item, with 0 indicating that the item does not apply to a given inmate, 1 indicating some uncertainty about whether it applies, and 2 indicating that it does apply. The total score, which can range from 0 to 44, is reliable and well correlated with global ratings of psychopathy (Schroeder, Schroeder, & Hare, 1983). The 22 items have been subjected to principal components analysis and varimax rotation, with the first factor to emerge being most relevant to the present discussion of psychopathy and sensation seeking. The items that loaded most heavily on this factor were the following: Item 4, Proneness to boredom/low frustration tolerance (.87); Item 14, Lack of realistic, long-term plans (.83); Item 10, Parasitic life-style (.73); and Item 15, Impulsivity (.71).

TABLE 1.   Items in research scale for the assessment of psychopathy in criminal populations

---

1. Glibness/Superficial charm

2. Previous diagnosis as psychopath (or similar)

3. Egocentricity/Grandiose sense of self-worth

4. Proneness to boredom/Low frustration tolerance

5. Pathological lying and deception

6. Conning/Lack of sincerity

7. Lack of remorse or guilt

8. Lack of affect and emotional depth

9. Callous/Lack of empathy

10. Parasitic life-style

11. Short-tempered/Poor behavioral controls

12. Promiscuous sexual relations

13. Early behavior problems

14. Lack of realistic, long-term plans

15. Impulsivity

16. Irresponsible behavior as parent

17. Frequent marital relationships

18. Juvenile delinquency

19. Poor probation or parole risk

20. Failure to accept responsibility for own actions

21. Many types of offense

22. Drug or alcohol abuse not direct cause of antisocial behavior

---

Note.   From "A research scale for the assessment of psychopathy in criminal populations" by R. D. Hare, 1980. Personality and Individual Differences, 1, 111-119.

PSYCHOPATHY AND NEED FOR STIMULATION

There have been many attempts to "explain" psychopathy. The view that inter-sects most readily with the theme of this volume is that the psychopath "needs" an inordinate amount of varied and exciting stimulation to maintain an optimal level of arousal.

Some of the clinical criteria for psychopathy (e.g., see Cleckley, 1976), as well as several items in our 22-item checklist, bear some relationship to the concept of sensation seeking. For example, three of the items (4, 14, and 15) that define the first factor would seem to involve excessive stimulation-seeking behavior. It is interesting, however, that this behavior, which contributes to the diagnosis of psychopathy, is only weakly reflected in self-report measures of sensation seeking, for example, Zuckerman's Sensation Seeking Scale (SSS). To illustrate this point, data recently collected from two different penal institutions are presented in Tables 2 and 3. In each case independent ratings of psychopathy were made by two experienced investigators using a 7-point scale. The subjects were white, male inmates of two prisons (Oakalla and Mission) near Vancouver. The assessments were very reliable, the correlation between the two

TABLE 2. Pearson product-moment correlations between ratings of psychopathy and SSS scores obtained from white male prison inmates

Prison	Form	N	GEN	TAS	ES	DIS	BS	Total
Oakalla	IV	58	.15	.10	.15	.21	.15	–
Mission	V	114		.18*	.10	.19*	.09	.21*

Note. SSS = Sensation Seeking Scale; GEN = General Scale, Form IV; Total = Total Score, Form V; TAS = Thrill and Adventure Seeking; ES = Experience Seeking; DIS = Disinhibition; BS = Boredom Susceptibility.

*p < .05, one-tailed.

TABLE 3. Estimates of reliability (coefficient alpha) of SSS scores obtained from white male prison inmates

Prison	Form	N	GEN	TAS	ES	DIS	BS	Total
Oakalla	IV	58	.66	.64	.80	.72	.53	–
Mission	V	114	–	.73	.46	.74	.61	.81

Note. SSS = Sensation Seeking Scale; GEN = General Scale, Form IV; Total = Total Score, Form V; TAS = Thrill and Adventure Seeking; ES = Experience Seeking; DIS = Disinhibition; BS = Boredom Susceptibility.

sets of ratings being .86, and .90 for the Oakalla and Mission studies, respectively. As Table 2 clearly indicates, the correlations between the summed ratings of the two investigators and the SSS, though in several cases statistically significant, were quite small. It would appear that the criminal psychopath's need for stimulation is more apt to be revealed in antisocial behavior than in his responses to self-report inventories administered in a prison context. This conclusion is not shared by Zuckerman (1979, pp. 303-307), who refers to two studies in which psychopathic inmates received higher SSS scores than did other inmates. However, there would appear to be a certain degree of circularity involved in these studies, because the psychometric criteria used for psychopathy contained many items that were conceptually similar to those in the SSS. Further, although Zuckerman described these psychometric criteria as being objective, there is little evidence that they are consistently related to measures of psychopathy based on a persistent pattern of behavior over a long period of time (Hare & Cox, 1978). We find none of this surprising; anyone who has worked in a prison setting realizes that there are many reasons for being cautious about taking verbal disclosures of psychopathic criminals at face value and as valid indicators of underlying personality dimensions. This view is shared by Cleckley (1976), who remarked, "The psychopath shows a remarkable disregard for truth and is to be trusted no more in his accounts of the past than in his promises for the future or his statement of present intentions" (p. 341). Although we have doubts about the usefulness of the SSS as a measure of sensation seeking in psychopathic criminals, the reliability of the total score on Form V of the SSS appears to be reasonably good. Table 3 presents Cronbach's (1951) measure of internal consistency reliability, coefficient alpha, for Form IV and V of the SSS; the data are from the Oakalla and Mission institutions referred to in Table 2. The reliability of the SSS-V total score was only slightly lower than that obtained with noncriminals (Zuckerman, 1979). However, the reliability of the Experience Seeking (ES) and Boredom Susceptibility (BS) subscales was generally very low. It appears that doubts expressed by Ridgeway and Russel (1980) about the subscale reliabilities of SSS-V may apply to criminal populations as well as to normal ones.

Need For Stimulation and Antisocial Behavior

Cleckley (1976) said of the psychopath, "Perhaps the emptiness or superficiality of a life without major goals or deep loyalties, or real love, would leave a person with high intelligence and other superior qualities so bored that he would eventually turn to hazardous, self-damaging, outlandish, antisocial, and even destructive exploits in order to find something fresh and stimulating in which to apply his useless and unchallenged energies and talents" (p. 402). The psychopath may not be as talented as Cleckley implied: a recent study on the structure of primary mental abilities in a prison population (Hare, Frazelle, Bus, & Jutai, 1980) found that psychopaths were no more creative or original than were other inmates. Nevertheless, it is quite true that psychopaths engage in a great deal of antisocial behavior, at least in part because of a proneness to boredom and an excessive need for stimulation. It should be emphasized, however, that Low Cortical Arousal and Need For Stimulation models provide only incomplete and oversimplified "explanations" of psychopathy. Such models may be more readily applicable to antisocial and criminal aspects of psychopathic behavior than to what many investigators believe to be the key features of the disorder, namely, lack of empathy, guilt or remorse, a callous disregard for the rights of others, egocentricity, and poor role-taking ability (see Gough, 1948). Though most psychopaths are probably sensation seekers, most high sensation seekers are not psychopaths.

Farley (1973) has argued that delinquency may result from the combination of stimulation-seeking behavior and an absence of socially acceptable channels for this behavior. An extension of Farley's theory to psychopathy might be made by including several of the more important features of the disorder. Most of the processes and characteristics that help to inhibit antisocial behavior in normal people -- concern for others, role taking, and fear of consequences -- appear to play only a small inhibitory role in the dynamics of psychopathy. We might expect far fewer constraints on the sensation-seeking behavior of a person with a strong need for stimulation and, for example, poor role taking ability, than there would be on someone with a similar need for stimulation but good role-taking ability (e.g., see Cox, 1977; Zuckerman, 1979, p. 304). The needs of the former person (and the psychopath) would find easy expression in action, whether the action is considered socially acceptable or not. Applying this argument to actual antisocial behavior, we might expect that the crimes of the psychopathic criminal would be more frequent, varied, and severe than those of other criminals.

Some recent data may be relevant here. They were obtained as part of a follow-up study of prison inmates who took part in at least one of our projects during the years 1964 to 1975 (see Hare, 1978, for details). About 100 psychopaths and 100 nonpsychopaths were involved in the study, although the actual numbers varied somewhat for different analyses. The two groups differed considerably in their criminal history. Briefly, compared with other inmates at the time of study, the psychopaths were first convicted in adult court at an earlier age, were convicted of more crimes, had committed a greater variety of crimes, had spent more time in prison, had used more aliases, had a greater variety of victims, had broken out of prison more often, and had violated the conditions of probation and parole more often. The psychopaths were also more likely to have been convicted of a crime of violence at some point in their criminal careers.

The relationship between psychopaths and violence was explored further in a set of analyses involving 243 white male criminals (see Hare, 1981, for details). Compared with other criminals, the psychopaths were more likely to have been convicted of armed robbery, assault, forcible seizure, and rape. They were also more likely to have used a weapon, to have been involved in fights, and to have engaged in aggressive homosexual behavior in prison. Their records notwithstanding, the psychopaths had been more successful at obtaining parole and probation than had other criminals -- testimony to their ability to manipulate, con, and convince others of their sincere intentions to reform.

We might reasonably interpret at least part of the psychopath's antisocial and criminal behavior in terms of strong stimulation seeking coupled with poor role-taking ability, low empathy, and a lack of inhibitory controls.

PSYCHOPATHY AND STRESS

Lazarus (1976) defined stress as a reaction to demands on the individual that tax or exceed his adjustive resources. The psychopath is frequently described as a person who is relatively free from many of the subjective experiences that we usually associate with psychological stress (e.g., apprehension, guilt, threat, and conflict). In addition, environmental conditions that generate high levels of stress in most people (e.g., excessive task demands and sensory input) may simply serve to produce a more optimal level of arousal in the psychopath.

Anticipatory Anxiety

There is a considerable amount of clinical and empirical evidence that anticipatory anxiety does not have the same motivational properties for psychopaths as it does for others. Indeed, it is possible to attribute much of their antisocial behavior to the failure of cues associated with punishment to produce sufficient

anticipatory anxiety for the guidance of behavior and for the inhibition of
antisocial responses (see Hare & Schalling, 1978, especially the chapters by
Spielberger, Schalling, Hare, and Trasler). It is not clear why premonitory
cues do not seem to have normal signal and motivational properties for psychopaths. One possibility is that they are able to make the appropriate connection
between warning cues and aversive events at the cognitive level but not at the
physiological level. A related possibility is based on the finding that the
anticipation of an aversive stimulus by psychopaths is associated with a large
increase in heart rate but only a small increase in palmar skin conductance
(Hare & Craigen, 1974; Hare, Frazelle, & Cox, 1978; Schalling, 1978), a pattern
that we hypothesize reflects the operation of an efficient coping process
serving to reduce anticipatory fear and the impact of warning cues (see Hare,
1978). Although a recent study by Tharp, Maltzman, Syndulko, and Ziskind (1980)
failed to replicate our heart rate results, it could be argued that the 95-DB
tone used was not particularly aversive; certainly it was far less aversive
than the 120-dB tone used by Hare et al. (1978) and the tolerance-level electric
shocks used by Hare and Craigen (1974).

Some results from a recent study may also have a bearing on the strategies used
by psychopaths to cope with stress (Hare, 1982). The procedure was adapted from
one used by Averill and Rosenn (1972). Prison inmates were given several trials
in which they were told to expect a 120-dB noise within the next few minutes,
and in which they could choose how to spend their time while waiting for the
noise. The inmates were told that while waiting they could listen (through
headphones) to (a) white noise, (b) a recording of a performance by a nightclub
comedian, or (c) a tone that changed in frequency 10 s before the noise, that
is, served as a warning signal. In one condition the noise was unavoidable,
and most of the inmates (46 of 51) chose to listen to the comedian; that is,
they adopted a nonvigilant coping style (Averill & Rosenn, 1972) or were "dis-
tractors" (Miller, 1979). The same three choices were available in the other
condition but this time the inmate was told he could avoid the noise by indicating when the warning signal occurred. Again, most of the inmates (38 of 51)
listened to the comedian and received the aversive stimulus. Thirteen inmates
monitored the channel containing the warning signal, but only 9 of these responded
in time to avoid the noise. We had expected that inmates with a low rating of
psychopathy would be more likely to adopt a vigilant coping style (i.e., to
monitor the channel with the warning signal) than would those with a high rating
of psychopathy, but this did not happen. However, an interesting psychopathy-
physiology relationship has emerged from this study. When the aversive stimulus
could not be avoided, inmates with low and high ratings of psychopathy exhibited
similar patterns of physiological activity while listening to the comedian. But
when the aversive stimulus could be avoided, listening to the comedian was associated with greater electrodermal arousal in inmates with low ratings of psychopathy
than in those with high ratings. That is, a nonvigilant coping strategy was
associated with heightened electrodermal arousal in nonpsychopathic inmates but
not in psychopathic ones. Several other studies have found that nonvigilance
can be more physiologically arousing than vigilance in normal subjects (Averill
& Rosenn, 1972; Hare, 1966), possibly because such a strategy involves a certain
degree of conflict. Our results seem to show that psychopathic criminals can
adopt a nonvigilant coping strategy without experiencing any appreciable conflict
and without undue worry about the fact that such a strategy may have aversive
consequences for them. That is, when psychopaths distract themselves they do
so very efficiently, whereas when others distract themselves they continue to
be aware of the fact that something unpleasant still may happen.

Somatic Anxiety

Schalling (1978) has argued that though psychopaths may be low in Psychic Anxiety
(worry, apprehension, and anticipatory anxiety), they may be high in other aspects

of anxiety, including somatic anxiety and muscular tension. As she puts it, "[Psychopaths] tend to have more vague distress and panic, more cardiovascular symptoms and muscular tenseness, but less worry and anticipatory concern than nonpsychopaths" (p. 89). We have some empirical data on this hypothesis. As part of the Mission study referred to earlier, 56 male prison inmates were administered Schalling's (1978) Multicomponent Anxiety Scale (MCA) IV, and the Fenz-Epstein Multifactorial Scale of Anxiety (MSA; Fenz & Epstein, 1965). The correlations between ratings of psychopathy and Schalling's MCA scales were -.18 for psychic anxiety, -.19 for somatic anxiety, and -.19 for muscular tension (n.s. in each case). The correlations between ratings of psychopathy and the Fenz-Epstein MSA scales were -.23 for feelings of insecurity, -.31 (p < .05) for autonomic arousal, -.23 for muscle tension, and -.30 (p < .05) for the total scale. Contrary to Schalling's hypothesis, psychopathy was associated with a tendency toward low scores on each of the indexes of anxiety.

Because there may be problems with the interpretation of self-report inventory data in criminal populations, it seemed reasonable to look at other ways in which the psychopath's responses to psychological stress might reveal themselves. For example, do psychopathic and other criminals differ in the incidence, severity, and type of psychosomatic complaints? In her longitudinal study of sociopathic personality, Robins (1966) concluded that sociopaths experience many somatic symptoms, including depression, gastrointestinal disturbances, and a high level of anxiety (cf. also, Yochelson & Samenow, 1976, pp. 481-482). The diagnosis of sociopathy, however, was a rather loose one: a subject had to satisfy only 5 of 19 criteria to be considered for inclusion in the category. One of these criteria was the presence of many somatic symptoms (p. 342). Since this particular criterion was a factor in 30% of the diagnoses of sociopathic personality in male subjects (p. 81), the later "finding" (pp. 118-121) that the sociopaths had "a high level of neurotic and somatic symptoms" is hardly surprising.

The relationship between psychopathy and psychological stress in criminals is the subject of one of our current research projects. So far we have studied almost 100 white male inmates; however, analysis of the data from only half of these subjects has been completed, and only some very preliminary findings can be presented at this time. Each inmate received a rating of psychopathy on a 7-point scale and, several weeks later, was given a semi-structured interview designed to obtain as much information as possible on the incidence and severity of a variety of somatic symptoms he had experienced. Thus far we have failed to find any significant relationships between ratings of psychopathy and any of a long list of individual symptoms or groups of symptoms having to do with autonomic, gastrointenstinal, cardiovascular, or muscle tension distrubances.

Although these findings do not support the view that psychopaths have a large number of somatic symptoms, they were based on what each inmate chose to say about himself. We felt that a better source of information would be the inmate's medical file. Prison inmates generally make extensive use of medical facilities; because all inmates in this study were incarcerated in the same institution (Mission), the medical and recordkeeping procedures were more or less the same for each inmate. Although medical records are usually confidential, we were able to obtain permission from the administration, medical staff, and inmates to use the records for research purposes. Analysis of data from the first 46 inmates clearly indicates that there were wide discrepancies between how an inmate described himself in the interview and the picture that emerged from the medical files. These discrepancies were not always consistent, with some symptoms and illnesses being overreported in the interview and others underreported. There were no systematic differences between psychopathic and other inmates in the type, number, or severity of the illnesses or complaints that led them to seek medical treatment. However, it is the practice of the medical staff to make notations about the legitimacy of each complaint. The correlation between these "bogus" complaints and rating of psychopathy was .42 (p < .01, df = 44). Inmates with high ratings of psychopathy made more than four times as many bogus complaints as did those with low ratings of psychopathy. On an individual basis, 14 of 19 (74%) of the inmates with a high rating of psychopathy, 8 of 15 (53%) with a medium rating, and 2 of 12 (17%) with a low rating had made at least one bogus complaint during the preceding year (χ^2 = 10.55, df = 2, p < .01). It was quite evident that the psychopaths made use of the medical facilities primarily to receive special privileges, obtain drugs, and to get out of work, rather than because of genuine illness or symptoms. If we exclude bogus complaints, we are left with the conclusion that psychopaths in prison have fewer symptoms and complaints requiring medical treatment than do other prisoners.

Life Stresses

There has been a considerable amount of research on the contribution of life stresses to physical and psychological well-being (cf. Rahe, 1975). Some researchers have attempted to devise scales designed to assess stress in particular environmental situations. The Hospital Stress Rating Scale of Volicer, Isenberg, and Burns (1977) is one example of such a scale, tailored to aspects of hospitalization. We are also collecting data on the degree of stress that inmates associate with various prison events. Our concern for the present is not so much with how life stress predicts future pathology, but with the possibility that psychopathic and nonpsychopathic inmates may differ in the degree of stress produced by events that occur while they are in prison. We have a list of 56 such events, most suggested by the inmates themselves. Some events are positive (e.g., marital reconciliation, getting out of isolation, and sentence reduced on appeal), whereas others are negative (e.g., death of a close friend, going into isolation, and visitor not showing up). The current version of this Prison Stress Rating Scale is highly reliable, coefficient alpha being .90 with the first 50 subjects. Although we wish to have data for at least 100 prisoners before doing detailed analyses, some interesting trends have already emerged. For example, among the negative events considered to be least stressful are receiving a warning from a staff member, an inmate's attempting suicide, having the cell searched, and having an argument with the staff. Among the negative items considered to be most stressful are having an appeal denied, death of a close friend, receiving an increased sentence on crown appeal, and death of a close member of the family. As far as psychopathy is concerned, the preliminary finding most relevant to the theme of this volume is that inmates with high ratings of psychopathy considered being sentenced to a period of isolation to be much more stressful than did inmates with low ratings of psychopathy.

REFERENCES

American Psychiatric Association. (1980). Diagnostic and statistical manual: Mental disorders (DSM-III), 3rd ed. Washington, D. C., Author.

Averill, T. R., & Rosenn, M. (1972). Vigilant and nonvigilant coping strategies and psychophysiological stress reactions during the anticipation of electric shock. Journal of Personality and Social Psychology, 23, 128-141.

Cleckley, H. (1976). The mask of sanity, 5th ed. St. Louis, MO: Mosby.

Cox, D. N. (1977). Psychophysiological correlates of sensation-seeking and socialization during reduced stimulation. Unpublished doctoral dissertation, University of British Columbia, Vancouver, Canada.

Cronbach, L. J. (1951). Coefficient alpha and the structure of tests. Psycho-metrika, 16, 297-334.

Farley, F. (1973, September). A theory of delinquency. Paper presented at the meeting of the American Psychological Association, Montreal.

Fenz, W. D., & Epstein, S. (1965). Manifest anxiety: Unifactorial or multi-factorial composition? Perceptual and Motor Skills, 20, 773-780.

Gough, H. G. (1948). A sociological theory of psychopathy. American Journal of Psychology, 53, 359-366.

Hare, R. D. (1966). Denial of threat and emotional response to impending pain-ful stimulation. Journal of Consulting Psychology, 30, 359-361.

Hare, R. D. (1970). Psychopathy: Theory and research. New York: Wiley.

Hare, R. D. (1978). Psychopathy and crime. In L. Otten (Ed.), Colloquium on the correlates of crime and the determinants of criminal behavior (pp. 95-132). Arlington, VA: Mitre.

Hare, R. D. (1980). A research scale for the assessment of psychopathy in criminal populations. Personality and Individual Differences, 1, 111-119.

Hare, R. D. (1981). Psychopathy and violence. In J. R. Hayes, K. Roberts, and K. Solway (Eds.), Violence and the violent individual (pp. 53-74). New York: Spectrum.

Hare, R. D. (1982). Psychopathy and physiological activity during anticipation of an aversive stimulus in a distraction paradigm. Psychophysiology, 19, 266-271.

Hare, R. D. (1983). Diagnosis of antisocial personality disorder in two prison populations. American Journal of Psychiatry, 140, 887-890.

Hare, R. D., & Cox, D. N. (1978). Clinical and empirical conceptions of psycho-pathy and the selection of subjects for research. In R. D. Hare and D. Schalling (Eds.), Psychopathic behavior: Approaches to research (pp. 1-22). Chichester, England: Wiley

Hare, R. D., & Craigen, D. (1974). Psychopathy and physiological activity in a mixed-motive game situation. Psychophysiology, 11, 197-206.

Hare, R. D., & Frazelle, J. (1980). Some preliminary notes on the use of a research scale for the assessment of psychopathy in criminal populations. Unpublished manuscript (available from R. D. Hare, Psychology Department, University of British Columbia, Vancouver, V6T 1W5, Canada).

Hare, R. D., Frazelle, J., Bus, J., & Jutai, J. W. (1980). Psychopathy and the structure of primary mental abilities. Journal of Behavioral Assessment, 2, 77-88.

Hare, R. D., Frazelle, J., & Cox, D. N. (1978). Psychopathy and physiological responses to threat of an aversive stimulus. Psychophysiology, 15, 165-172.

Hare, R. D., & Schalling, D. (Eds.). (1978). Psychopathic behavior: Approaches to research. Chichester, England: Wiley.

Lazarus, R. S. (1976). Patterns of adjustment. New York: McGraw-Hill.

Miller, S. (1979). Coping with impending stress: Psychophysiological and cognitive correlates of stress. Psychophysiology, 16, 572-581.

Quay, H. C. (1965). Psychopathic behavior as pathological stimulation-seeking. American Journal of Psychiatry, 122, 180-183.

Rahe, R. H. (1975). Life changes and near-future illness reports. In L. Levi (Ed.), Emotions: Their parameters and measurement. New York: Raven Press.

Reid, W. H. (Ed.). (1978). The psychopath: A comprehensive study of antisocial disorders and behaviors. New York: Brunner/Mazel.

Ridgeway, D., & Russell, J. A. (1980). Reliability and validity of the Sensation-Seeking Scale: Psychometric problems in Form V. Journal of Consulting and Clinical Psychology, 48, 662-664.

Robins, L. N. (1966). Deviant children grown up. Baltimore: Williams & Wilkins.

Schalling, D. (1978). Psychopathy-related personality variables and the psychophysiology of socialization. In R. D. Hare and D. Schalling (Eds.), Psychopathic behavior: Approaches to research (pp. 85-106). Chichester, England: Wiley.

Schroeder, M. L., Schroeder, K. G., & Hare, R. D. (1983). Generalizability of a checklist for assessment of psychopathy. Journal of Consulting and Clinical Psychology, 51, 511-516.

Smith, R. (1978). The psychopath in society. New York: Academic Press.

Tharp, V. K., Maltzman, I., Syndulko, K., & Ziskind, E. (1980). Autonomic activity during anticipation of an aversive tone in noninstitutionalized sociopaths. Psychophysiology, 17, 123-128.

Volicer, B. J., Isenberg, M. A., & Burns, M. W. (1977). Medical-surgical differences in hospital stress factors. Journal of Human Stress, 3, 3-13.

Yochelson, S., & Samenow, S. E. (1976). The criminal personality, Vol. I. New York: Wiley.

Zuckerman, M. (1979). Sensation-seeking: Beyond the optimal level of arousal. Hillsdale, NJ: Erlbaum.

15

Intensity of Interpersonal Aggression in Relation to Neuroticism and Psychopathy

Wanda Ciarkowska and Adam Frączek

By <u>interpersonal aggression</u> we mean aggressive behavior that occurs in the course of social interaction, and committed by the individual in connection with a task he is required to perform (Frączek, 1975, 1979b). A specific method of behavioral aggression measurement was used in all the studies reported. A modified version of Buss' procedure was used (1961), in which the subject's task requires him to administer unpleasant stimuli (i.e., electric shocks of an intensity he chooses) to the interacting partner.

Our thesis is that the stable traits of a person modify his reception of that external stimulation, which is assumed to act as an aggressive cue (Berkowitz, 1974, 1978). Thus in taking neuroticism and psychopathy, as an example, we show that interpersonal aggression dynamics are connected with the question of individual differences.

NEUROTICISM IN REGULATION OF INTERPERSONAL AGGRESSION

<u>Neuroticism</u> here is considered emotional lability, as proposed by Eysenck (1960). Eysenck's view is that neuroticism is a sign of the lability of the sympathetic division of the autonomic nervous system. The Polish version of Eysenck's Maudsley Personality Inventory (MPI) (Choynowski, 1968) was used for the assessment of neuroticism in both studies.

In the first study dealing with the relationship between neuroticism and aggression dynamics (Jodko, 1971), two independent variables were introduced: frustration and stimulation of an aggressive nature. Manipulation with the former variable consisted of a negative evaluation of a task performed by subjects in the experimental group and in a positive evaluation of the control's performance. Manipulation with the variable of external stimulation consisted of the introduction of two types of stimulation: aggressive (fragments of a radio broadcast of a boxing match) and neutral (fragments of an educational radio program for farmers).

Four experimental situations were obtained by dichotomizing the two variables (i.e., frustration vs. lack of frustration, and aggressive vs. neutral stimulation). Buss' procedure, described earlier, was used for assessment of aggression.

The results showed that frustration has a significant effect on aggression intensity, whereas an expected relationship between aggressive behavior intensity and type of external stimulation was confirmed only in the form of a trend. Subjects exposed to aggressive stimulation manifested more pronounced aggression than did those exposed to neutral stimulation, but the difference between the two groups did not reach significance.

Analysis of the relationship between neuroticism and aggression intensity was based on correlations between the variables in question (see Table 1). Obtained correlation coefficients suggest the following: a positive correlation between neuroticism and aggression intensity was found in three situations only: that of frustration ($r = .245$, $p < .10$), aggressive stimulation ($r = .269$, $p < .10$), and interaction of these factors ($r = .668$, $p < .01$). The relationship between neuroticism and aggression intensity is particularly significant in the latter case. Thus, it can be assumed that when both frustration and a stimulus of aggressive nature are manipulated, intensity of manifested aggression relates to level of neuroticism. Besides, the positive sign of the correlations indicates that the higher the neuroticism level, the more the intensity of aggression due to the introduction of frustration or aggressive stimulation.

The second study was concerned with the effect of an emotionally negative stimulus on the intensity of aggressive behavior (Gajda, 1971).

In some subjects a negative emotional response to light in a given color was developed by means of a classical conditioning procedure (electric shocks were used as the unconditioned stimulus). For the remaining subjects, the color was neutral throughout the experiment. To measure the effectiveness of the conditioning procedure, the galvanic skin response (GSR) was monitored. In the second part of the experiment, aggression intensity was assessed by means of the Buss machine. In one group of subjects the apparatus was in the previously conditioned color, and the remaining subjects used an apparatus in a color that was emotionally neutral. According to prediction, aggressive behavior took place only in the former situation in the presence of a stimulus having an emotional value.

Data illustrating the relationship between neuroticism and aggression intensity under particular experimental conditions are shown in Table 2. Analysis of the correlations shows that neuroticism is related to aggression intensity ($r = .138$, $p < .08$) in the whole sample. Moreover, a low positive correlation was found

TABLE 1. Correlation coefficients between neuroticism and intensity of post-frustration aggression

Sample	N	r	p
Total sample	57	.194	n.s.
No frustration	29	.120	n.s.
No frustration + aggressive cue	14	.039	n.s.
Frustration	28	.245	.10
Aggressive cue	27	.269	.10
Frustration + aggressive cue	13	.668	.01

TABLE 2. Correlation coefficients between neuroticism and aggression intensity under experimental conditions

Sample	N	r	p
Total sample	100	.138	.08
No conditioning	40	-.119	n.s.
Conditioning (aversive stimulation)	60	.203	.08
Conditioning + neutral stimulation	30	.059	n.s.
Conditioning + aggressive stimulation	30	.374	.05

between neuroticism and intensity of aggression manifested after prior experience with noxious stimulation (i.e., electric shocks during the conditioning procedure; r = .203, p < .08). A relationship between neuroticism and aggression manifested in the presence of the emotionally negative stimulus (r = .374, p < .05), is particularly interesting. These data justify the conclusion that the higher the neuroticism the stronger is aggression, intensified by the presence of negative emotional stimuli.

Because our correlational analysis has limitations, and the design does not allow for any specification of the mechanism underlying the effect of neuroticism on aggression, we wish to present only tentative conclusions on the basis of our data.

There is a positive correlation between neuroticism and the intensity of aggression evoked either by frustration or by the type of task. The relationship is particularly pronounced in the case of the summation of factors releasing the tendency to aggressive behavior (frustration plus aggressive stimulation in the first study and experience of noxious stimuli plus the presence of a stimulus eliciting a negative emotional response in the second one). This means that neurotic persons (i.e., those characterized by emotional lability) are more susceptible to external influences aimed at manipulating their emotional states.

Our supposition concerning the origins of the positive correlation between neuroticism and aggression intensified by factors affecting emotional processes is that the phenomenon may be explained in terms of sensitivity to external stimulation. The supposition is to some extent supported by data cited by Strelau (1969), showing a negative correlation between neuroticism, assessed by the Eysenck MPI, and the intensity of arousal processes in the nervous system, as measured by the Strelau Temperament Inventory (TI, 1972). In other words, the higher the level of neuroticism, the weaker -- that is, more sensitive -- is the nervous system. Thus, it can be assumed that neurotic people feel frustration more vividly; and, in their case, the presence of the emotional stimulus evokes a stronger negative emotional response.

PSYCHOPATHY AND INTERPERSONAL AGGRESSION

We now turn to an analysis of changes in the intensity of aggressive behavior due to a stimulus of emotional value, in people with either high or low psychopathic traits (Ciarkowska, 1979). For a detailed discussion on the nature of psychopathy, we refer the reader to competent, detailed works on the subject (Cleckley, 1964; Hare, 1970; Hare & Cox, 1978; Hare & Jutai, this volume). We begin with a concise characterization of the research problem before explaining why psychopathy was introduced into research on aggression.

The main objective of the study was to determine the effect on intensity of aggression of an external stimulus, evoking either negative or positive emotional response. The study in question is a continuation and extension of the experiment (described here earlier) on the relation between emotionally negative stimulation and intensity of aggressive behavior. In the first stage of the present study, the initial level of aggression intensity was established. This was followed by classical conditioning procedure, aimed at transformation of an initially neutral stimulus, a yellow light, into a cue of either negative emotional value (lighting up of the yellow lamp was associated with electric shocks), or positive one (the light was associated with cigarettes). The effectiveness of the procedure was controlled by means of GSR recording. In the next stage of the study, the Buss machine was used once again to measure the subject's aggression. Three types of experimental situation, differing in emotional value, were used: in the first one, the subject's aggressive behavior took place in the presence of emotionally neutral stimuli (the apparatus was grey); in the second, a stimulus of negative emotional value was present (i.e., the apparatus was yellow, and the yellow light had been used as the negative conditional stimulus in the previous stage of the experiment); and in the third situation, there was a stimulus of positive emotional value (i.e., the apparatus was yellow, and this color had been used as the positive conditioned stimulus (CS) in the previous stage of the experiment).

The key reason for including the measurement of psychopathy in the research was provided by clinical data and experimental findings indicating a defect in negative emotional responses conditioning in psychopaths (Hare, 1965a, Lykken, 1957). Thus, in the case of highly psychopathic people, the procedure aimed at transformation of an external stimulus into a cue of negative emotional value should be expected to have little effect, or even to have no effect at all. In consequence, the CS should remain emotionally neutral, and so, it would have no influence on aggression dynamics. An assumption was made then that the presence of a stimulus having negative emotional value would increase aggressive behavior intensity only in persons with a low level of psychopathic traits. Because no data were available concerning the course of positive emotional responses conditioning in psychopaths, it was assumed that in all subjects, irrespective of the degree of their psychopathic traits, the external stimulus would be transformed into a cue of a positive emotion. Consequently, a drop in aggression intensity was expected in all subjects as a result of the stimulus in question.

In the light of clinical findings (Cleckley, 1964; Hare, 1979) psychopaths, as compared with other people, are believed to undertake -- more frequently and in a more intense form -- actions resulting in harm, suffering or pain of others. Therefore, a positive correlation was expected to occur between aggression intensity (measured at the beginning of the experiment, before the experimental treatment manipulation) and psychopathy level. In other words, highly psychopathic people were expected to manifest initially stronger aggression than were persons with a low level of psychopathic traits.

For assessment of psychopathic traits intensity, the Pd scale of the Minnesota Multiphasic Personality Inventory (MMPI) (Welsh & Dahlstrom, 1963) was used. Subjects whose scores on control scales (L, F, K) were different from the norm were excluded from the experiment.

Psychopathy score distribution obtained in the sample of 95 convicts serving a prison sentence ranged from 10 to 70 raw points. The distribution was then dichotomized, and convicts whose scores fell in the interval between 10 and 35 points were categorized as those having low psychopathic traits, whereas the remaining subjects were classified as high.

The key data were differences in aggression intensity (expressed in terms of electric shocks duration), measured at the beginning of the experiment and after the manipulation with independent variables. Delta indexes, determining the extent of changes in aggression intensity, were compared by means of Student t-test for correlated pairs. Data obtained from the analysis are shown in Table 3.

First, in the case of convicts with low psychopathy traits a significant decrease in aggression intensity was found when they were given the apparatus eliciting their positive emotional response (t = 7.698, p < .01). When the stimulus evoking negative emotions was present, a significant increase in aggression intensity was observed (t = 4.262, p < .01).

In highly psychopathic convicts the stimulus having positive emotional value resulted, as in the previous group, in a diminished intensity of aggression (t = 3.618, p < .01). The emotionally negative stimulus was found to have no effect on aggression level in these subjects (t = 1.827, n.s.).

TABLE 3. Change of aggressive behavior intensity in subjects with low and high degree of psychopathic features

Situation	Low degree of psychopathy			High degree of psychopathy		
	N	t	p	N	t	p
Control	12	1.353	n.s.	7	1.570	n.s.
Negative emotional stimulation	7	1.920	n.s.	12	1.612	n.s.
Positive emotional stimulation	11	1.792	n.s.	8	1.262	n.s.
Cue with negative emotional value	12	4.262[a]	.01	7	1.827	n.s.
Cue with positive emotional value	9	7.698[b]	.01	10	3.618[b]	.01

Note. Student's t-test for correlated pairs.

[a] Increase in aggression.

[b] Decrease in aggression.

Delta indexes obtained from convicts with high and low level of psychopathic
traits were then compared by means of Student's t-test (Table 4).

Aggression intensity diminished in all convicts, irrespective of their psychopathy level, in the presence of the stimulus of positive emotional value.
Introduction of the stimulus with negative emotional value resulted in an
increase of aggression intensity in both groups, which is reflected in the
positive sign of delta indexes. Nevertheless, the difference between delta
values is statistically significant ($t = 2.300$, $p < .05$). Thus, it can be
said that the increase in aggression intensity, evoked by the stimulus of
negative emotional value, was more pronounced in convicts with a low level of
psychopathic traits.

Generally, the study shows that aggressive behavior of psychopathic people was
only partially due to their relatively strong readiness for this type of
behavior. There was a positive relationship between initial aggression intensity and the level of psychopathic traits ($r = .168$, $p < .10$) for the total
sample ($r = .247$, $p < .10$ for convicts with a low degree of psychopathy;
$r = .430$, $p < .01$ for those with a high degree of psychopathic features)
(Ciarkowska, 1977). Nevertheless, the presence of a stimulus evoking a positive
emotional state served to diminish the intensity of aggressive behavior in all
convicts.

Explanation of the finding that the emotionally negative stimulus did not increase aggression intensity in highly psychopathic persons must be more complex.
The finding supports our hypothesis, but the data obtained did not confirm
premises underlying the hypothesis, because the correlation between the course
of negative emotional conditioning -- percentage of GSR changes -- and the
intensity of psychopathic traits did not reach the level of statistical significance. As it has been already noted, we believe that the content of the
conditioned emotional response can be characterized as anger, because the
response was evoked by a cue signaling occurrence of a weak pain (Reykowski,
1979). In this context it seems paradoxical that people whose behavior is
usually described as impulsive do not express any more marked aggression in a
situation permitting them to abreact anger. In the light of clinical data

TABLE 4. Comparison of changes in aggression intensity due to stimuli with
emotional value in subjects with high and low psychopathy level

Sign of emotional value	Degree of psychopathic features	$\overline{\Delta}$	t	p
Negative	high	.642	2.300	.05
	low	1.010		
Positive	high	- .626	1.127	n.s.
	low	- .749		

(Cleckley, 1964; Storr, 1972), the nature of aggressive behavior of psychopaths is much more often instrumental (being one of the essential ways of gratifying many needs) than emotional. Moreover, anger is believed to be a superficial and transitory emotion. Despite the fact that all convicts responded with anger to the yellow light as a result of conditioning, in highly psychopathic persons the response was not generalized onto the situation in which they could display aggressive behavior. The result in question corresponds to data reported by Hare (1965b) and Lykken (1957), who pointed out that in psychopaths only a direct threat evoked emotional response in the form of fear. For an alternative explanation of our result, we must refer to studies dealing with the psychopath's way of responding to noxious external stimulation. It seems that cardiovascular activity, rather than GSR, is the factor differentiating psychopaths from normal persons (Hare, 1978). As the former was not taken into consideration in our research, we cannot be quite sure whether the lack of difference in GSR indexes obtained from subjects differing in intensity of psychopathic traits really means that we managed to evoke anger as the conditioned response.

In summary, the relationship between psychopathy and interpersonal aggression dynamics is reflected, above all, in the fact that psychopathy determines the manner of reception of external stimulation affecting the emotional process responsible for changes in aggression intensity.

CONCLUSIONS

The following points can be made on the basis of our empirical data concerning the effect of structural traits on interpersonal aggression dynamics. Reception of external stimulation affecting aggressive behavior intensity is modified both by neuroticism and psychopathy. We believe that neuroticism determines, above all, the facility of anger release (i.e., of evoking the emotion responsible for aggression occurrence) by situational factors. Our results allow us to assume, with a certain degree of caution, that in highly neurotic people emotional changes can be evoked more quickly and intensely by means of applying stimulation having emotional value. Activation of emotional processes in neurotic persons, however, does not always result in an increase in their aggression intensity (Eliasz, 1973). The author compared neurotic and normal persons with respect to aggressive behavior dynamics under conditions of slight, moderate, or strong frustration. Neurotic subjects, as compared to normal controls, were found to respond to a moderate increase in frustration intensity with a significantly higher increase in aggression level. Thus far the results confirm our assumption that the neurotic person's response to emotion-evoking stimuli is stronger. However, further increase of frustration strength yielded a drop in the aggression level in neurotic subjects, whereas the reverse relationship was observed in normal controls. It can be supposed that under exposure to exceptionally strong external stimulation, anger in neurotic persons is substituted by fear; therefore, a drop in the aggression intensity is observed, instead of an increase. In other words, high neuroticism can be expected only to a certain extent to promote aggressive behavior in response to specific emotion-eliciting stimulation.

The dynamics of interpersonal aggression due to stimulation having emotional value is affected also by psychopathy. The latter variable turned out to produce probably a specific reception of external stimuli, consisting in a different interpretation of their emotional meaning. A stimulus expected to evoke conditional response of anger had no effect on aggressive behavior intensity in highly psychopathic persons. Psychopathy influences aggression intensity, determining the individual's readiness for learning the emotional value of stimuli (especially the negative one), as well as his capability of emotional responses generalization.

The following general thesis emerges from our discussion: the effect of analyzed structural properties on the dynamics of interpersonal aggression consists in modification of reception of external stimulation significant for aggressive behavior. In other words, the properties in question determine the probability of transformation of the potential readiness for aggression into actual aggressive action.

Both the structural properties and situational factors dealt with in the study were connected, above all, with emotional processes. In our opinion, in future research on the role of structural properties in the course of interpersonal aggression, cognitive mechanisms should be also taken into consideration (Frączek, 1979a; Geller, 1979).

REFERENCES

Berkowitz, L. (1974). Some determinants of impulsive aggression. In W. Hartup and J. DeWit (Eds.), Determinants and origins of aggressive behavior. The Hague: Mouton.

Berkowitz, L. (1978). Whatever happened to the frustration-aggression hypothesis? American Behavioral Scientists, 21.

Buss, A. H. (1961). The psychology of aggression. New York: Wiley.

Cleckley, H. (1964). The mask of sanity. St. Louis, MO: Mosby.

Choynowski, M. (1968). Opracowanie polskiej adaptacji Inwentarza Osobowości H. J. Eysencka (Polish version of Eysenck's Maudsley Personality Inventory). Biuletyn Psychometryczny, 2, 51-95.

Ciarkowska, W. (1977). Rola stymulacji emocjonalnej i cech psychopatycznych w regulacji dynamiki czynności agresywnej (Role of emotional stimulation and psychopathic traits in dynamics of aggressive behavior). Unpublished doctoral dissertation, University of Warsaw.

Ciarkowska, W. (1979). Znaczenie emocjonalne bodźca a natczenie czynności agresywnej (Emotional meaning of stimulus and intensity of aggressive acts). In A. Frączek (Ed.), Studia nad psychologicznymi mechanizmami ozynności (Studies on psychological mechanisms of aggressive actions). Wrocław: Ossolineum.

Eliasz, H. (1973). The dynamics of aggression in neurotics. Polish Psychological Bulletin, 1, 37-42.

Eysenck, H. J. (1960). The structure of human personality. London: Methuen.

Frączek, A. (1975). Mechanizmy czynności agresywnych (The mechanisms of aggressive actions). In I. Kurcz and J. Reykowski (Eds.), Studia nad teoria czynności ludzkich (Studies on human action theory). Warsaw: Państwowe Wydawnictwo Naukowe.

Frączek, A. (1979a). Functions of emotional and cognitive mechanisms in regulation of aggressive behavior. In S. Feshbach and A. Frączek (Eds.), Aggression and behavior change. New York: Praeger.

Frączek, A. (1979b). Czynności agresywne jako przedmiot studiów eksperymentalnej psychologii społecznej (Aggressive acts as a research subject of experimental social psychology). In A. Frączek (Ed.), Studia nad psychologicznymi mechaniz-mami czynności agresywnych (Studies on psychological mechanisms of aggressive actions). Wrocław: Ossolineum.

Gajda, W. (1971). Znaczenie emocjonalne bodźca jako czynnik modyfikujący zachowanie agresywne (Emotional meaning of stimulus as a factor modifying aggressive behavior). Unpublished master's thesis, University of Warsaw.

Geller, S. (1979). Werbalizacja znaczenia emocjonalnago bodźca a natezenie czynności agresywnej (Verbalization of the stimulus emotional meaning and intensity of aggressive act). In A. Frączek (Ed.), Studia nad psychologicznymi mechanizmami czynności agresywnych (Studies on psychological mechanisms of aggressive actions). Wrocław: Ossolineum.

Hare, R. D. (1965a). Acquisition and generalization of a conditioned fear response in psychopathic and nonpsychopathic criminals. Journal of Psychology, 58, 367-370.

Hare, R. D. (1965b). Temporal gradient of fear arousal in psychopaths. Journal of Abnormal Psychology, 6, 442-446.

Hare, R. D. (1970). Psychopathy: Theory and research. New York: Wiley.

Hare, R. D. (1978). Electrodermal and cardiovascular correlates of psychopathy. In R. D. Hare and D. Schalling (Eds.), Psychopathic behaviour: Approaches to research. London: Wiley.

Hare, R. D. (1979). Psychopathy and violence. In J. R. Hare, K. Roberts, and K. Solway (Eds.), Violence and the violent individual. New York: Spectrum.

Hare, R. D., & Cox, D. N. (1978). Clinical and empirical conceptions of psycho-pathy and the selection of subjects for research. In R. D. Hare and D. Schalling (Eds.), Psychopathic behaviour: Approaches to research. London: Wiley.

Jodko, M. (1971). Wpływ frustracji, specyficznej stymulacji sytuacyjnej i niektórych zmiennych osobowościowych na intensywność reakcji agresywnej (Effects of frustration, specific situations stimulation and some personality traits on intensity of aggressive behavior). Unpublished master's thesis, University of Warsaw.

Lykken, D. T. (1957). A study of anxiety in the sociopathic personality. Journal of Abnormal and Social Psychology, 55, 6-10.

Reykowski, J. (1979). Intrinsic motivation and intrinsic inhibition of aggres-sive behavior. In S. Feshbach and A. Fraczek (Eds.), Aggression and behavior change. New York: Praeger.

Storr, A. H. (1972). Human aggression. Harmondsworth, England: Pelican Books.

Strelau, J. (1969). Temperament i typ układu nerwowego (Temperament and type of nervous system). Warsaw: Państwowe Wydawnictwo Naukowe.

Strelau, J. (1972). A diagnosis of temperament by nonexperimental techniques. Polish Psychological Bulletin, 3, 97-105.

Welsh, G. S., & Dahlstrom, W. G. (1963). Basic readings on the MMPI in psychology and medicine. Minneapolis: University of Minnesota Press.

16

Reactivity and Empathic Control
of Aggression

Hanna Eliasz and Janusz Reykowski

One of the most popular approaches in personality research is to distinguish a person's stable traits (dispositions, or factors) that determine observed properties of his behavior (Cattell, 1957; Eysenck, 1953; Guilford, 1959; Zawadzki, 1970). The assumption underlying this approach is that recurring features of the "manifest behavior" are determined by relevant implicit dispositions. In many cases, however, the assumption is not confirmed when subjected to thorough empirical verification (Mischel, 1968); thus, the explanations of behavior seem to be oversimplified.

An alternative model, which has a long history in the Warsaw laboratories, is that there is no one-to-one correspondence between characteristics of internal mechanisms and behavior. Personality mechanisms constitute a system, and attempts at making accurate predictions can be based only on an analysis of the functioning of the whole system, and not on particular traits. This standpoint, which we have called a "theory of regulation" (Tomaszewski, 1975), leads to a different outlook in relation to a number of phenomena. For example, Strelau's (1982) application of this approach to the theory of temperament allowed him to formulate many hypotheses -- unexpected on the grounds of the traditional approach -- which have been supported by empirical data (see reports by A. Eliasz, Vol. 1, and Strelau and Klonowicz, Vol. 2, of the present work).

The model also can be applied to the analysis and explanation of human social behavior (Reykowski, 1975, 1979). In personality theory, the approach was presented by Reykowski and his co-workers as the Regulative Theory of Personality (Reykowski & Kochańska, 1980).

The objective of this chapter is to show how the regulative approach can be applied to the analysis of the concrete phenomenon of the regulation of aggressive behavior. In the traditional model, aggressive behavior would be considered as a manifestation of a specific underlying disposition (i.e., aggressiveness), whereas control of such behavior would require the presence of traits antagonistic to aggressiveness (e.g., empathy). Here, we discuss the relationship between aggression and empathy within the framework of the theory of regulation.

EMPATHY AND AGGRESSIVE BEHAVIOR

The relationship between empathy and aggression has been the object of interest to psychologists for many years (Eliasz, H., 1975; Feshbach & Feshbach, 1979; Frączek, 1977; Freud, 1937; Reykowski, 1977). The term empathy is used in psychological

literature in three senses. First, empathy is considered to be an emotional
process consisting in co-experiencing affective states of another person in
response to his expression or emotive behaviors (Aronfreed, 1968; Stotland,
1969). Second, empathy is regarded as a mainly cognitive process, involving
the ability of putting oneself in the place of another person (Dymond, 1949;
Feffer, 1959). Finally, in recent years attempts have been made to describe
the phenomenon of empathy as a complex emotiocognitive process (Ianotti, 1975a;
Feshbach & Feshbach, 1969; Frączek, 1977). Here we regard empathy as an exclusively emotional phenomenon.

Empathy is believed to be one of the factors most effective in inhibiting aggressive behavior. If the emotional expression of another person indicates his
malaise, then the content of the subject's experienced arousal would be also
negative. Aggression often results in the victim's distress. Empathizing with
the suffering victim means experiencing a state of negative arousal, which may
act as an aggression inhibitor.

An analysis of empirical data, however, indicates no simple relationship between
the two variables. The data have been derived from two sources: (a) research
into the relationship between a person's capacity for empathy and his or her
aggressiveness (both variables were considered there as dispositional traits)
and (b) experiments on the effect of empathogenic stimuli (i.e., indications
of physical suffering) on the dynamics of aggressive behavior.

Studies dealing with the relationship between empathy and aggressiveness yield
discrepant results. Some authors report a lack of correlation between these
variables (Ianotti, 1975a, 1975b), and others find developmental "transitions"
(Feshbach & Feshbach, 1969), that is, a positive correlation between the two
variables becomes transformed into a negative one, with subjects' age. No differences between persons differing in their capacity for empathizing were found
with respect to their aggression intensity (Mehrabian & Epstein, 1972).

Certain discrepancies can be also seen in results obtained in research into the
role of empathogenic cues in the regulation of aggressive behavior dynamics.
In a number of studies, physical suffering of the victim was found to diminish
aggression (Baron, 1971a, 1971b; Buss, 1966; Geen, 1970). Other authors, however, report an increase in aggression level, resulting from perceived victim's
suffering (Baron, 1971a, 1971b; Hartmann, 1969; Swartz & Berkowitz, 1976).

What may be the causes of equivocal results? Before proposing an answer to
this question, we shall suggest a possible mechanism underlying the influence
of empathy on aggression.

REACTIVITY AND CAPACITY FOR EMPATHY

We assume that empathy (regarded as a person's sensitivity to emotional states
of other people) is higher in those indicating higher reactivity level (as defined
by Strelau, 1974). According to the definition proposed by Strelau (1974),
reactivity is a relatively stable ratio (typical of a given person) of the
response intensity to the intensity of stimulus eliciting this response. In
the Strelau Temperament Inventory, the property of "strength of excitation" is
investigated, among other things. This concept is inversely related to that of
reactivity; that is, the stronger the nervous system, the lower the reactivity
level. Thus, here we use the term low reactivity. The concept of reactivity
and of the related phenomenon, that is, the demand for stimulation, are not
presented here, as they are discussed in detail by other authors in Volumes 1
and 2 of the present work (cf. A. Eliasz and Strelau).

Highly reactive people have an increased empathic sensitivity in that they are able to perceive relevant stimuli (i.e., the emotional expression of another person) that are too weak to be perceived by those with a low reactivity level. Moreover, highly reactive persons, as compared with low-reactive ones, can be supposed to have stronger orientation to social stimuli (Eliasz, A., 1980), which is due both to their relatively small demand for stimulation and, probably, to their relatively high motivation for having a more precise regulation of stimulation.

Research by A. Eliasz (1980) confirmed that highly reactive persons were more susceptible to social influences than were low-reactive ones. Moreover, it was found that in the former the considerable susceptibility to social influences was accompanied by a lack of behavioral adjustment to stimulation from the physical environment. The latter phenomenon suggests certain selectivity in responding to external stimulation and, more accurately, an orientation to people. On the other hand, in low-reactive people a relatively small susceptibility to social influences is associated with modification of behaviors appropriate to the conditions of the physical environment.

The larger sensitivity to social stimuli, observed in highly reactive people, may have specific consequences for their ability to empathize. From the thesis that empathy may be related to reactivity level, it follows that the former variable will affect the amount of stimulation received by the person. An empathic response to another person's state is connected with receiving a considerable amount of stimulation. Thus, a highly reactive person may either avoid opportunities for behaving empathically (when another threatens with stimulation overload) or seek such occasions when stimulation is insufficient (e.g., in monotonous situations). An analysis of this relationship shows the function that can be fulfilled by empathy in the process of regulation of stimulation.

A hypothesis can be constructed to the effect that highly reactive people are motivated to empathize when other persons' emotional expression is not too vivid, or, on the other hand, in the case of very strong empathogenic cues, when the subject feels he can control his partner's situation and thus can influence the emotional state of the other. If this is true, in highly reactive persons prosocial behaviors might appear as a consequence of empathy. Occurrence of empathy in this category of people may lead also to other responses, including defensive behaviors (such as anxiety and a tendency to self-reassurance, by means of avoidance and suppression of information about other people's suffering), and attacking the person toward whom the subject's empathic emotions are directed (it does not have to be a physical attack, but, e.g., depreciation of the victim; Reykowski, 1979).

A different type of responding is expected in low-reactive people. In their case empathy may serve to provide them with new stimulation. From the previous reasoning, certain conclusions follow, concerning control of aggression. As aggressive behavior evokes pain and suffering of the victim, empathic response should inhibit such behavior if the person seeks stimulation. It is under the latter conditions that aggression may become an attractive form of activity, the more so if it evokes strong emotions, and if observation of the victim's suffering is associated with empathy. It may be supposed that such a phenomenon will be particularly pronounced in people with an extremely low reactivity level. The supposition is supported by data obtained in studies on psychopaths (Quay, 1977). So-called "primary psychopaths" having a large need of stimulation were found to regard typically aversive stimuli as desirable. In their case, these stimuli (including empathy toward a person experiencing aversive states, e.g., toward the victim of one's own attack) could also serve as positive reinforcement.

So far our discussion deals with the mutual relationship between reactivity and empathy. What can be said about the relationship between reactivity and aggression?

EFFECT OF REACTIVITY ON AGGRESSION FORMATION

According to Reykowski (1977), reactivity can be directly related to the formation of certain types of aggressive behavior. A specific class of aggressive behavior (spontaneous aggression) is included, which is performed by a person for whom the very realization of such aggressive action gives satisfaction. For low-reactive people, this type of aggression may serve as a means of stimulation regulation, acquired by learning and aimed at attaining the optimal stimulation level. Development of spontaneous aggression is possible because the low-reactive person's demand for stimulation is large, and aggression may provide him or her with strong stimulation -- both because of the properties of aggression (i.e., intense, dynamic motions) and because of its consequences (i.e., the sight of injuries, blood, and suffering). Even breaking certain social norms, connected with aggressive behavior toward other people, may be highly stimulating for low-reactive people; such aggression on its own may be a desirable method of stimulation regulation for these people.

Other forms of aggression can be also distinguished, namely, impulsive and instrumental aggression (Frączek, 1979). Does the relationship between reactivity and spontaneous aggression apply to other types of aggression as well? The answer to this question is rather complex. It is conceivable that in a situation where aggression occurs in response to an attack, and thus is a form of self-defense (reactive aggression), a reverse regularity may arise, and thus type of aggression may be positively correlated with high reactivity level. On the other hand, when the aim of aggressive behavior is to attain certain goals (instrumental aggression -- aggression connected with task performance -- and, particularly, spontaneous aggression), then a positive relationship may hold with reactivity.

The following predictions may be made about the effect of reactivity on the relation between empathy and aggression.

The role of empathy in the regulation of aggression dynamics may vary, accordingly to the aggressor's reactivity level.

1. In low-reactive people, empathic experience in response to the victim's suffering may appear only due to much stronger cues of suffering than would occur in highly reactive people. Therefore, it can be said that in the low-reactive person, in contrast to the highly reactive person, there will be no empathic response to either weak or moderate emotional expression of the victim concerning his or her own attack. Thus, there will be no inhibition of his aggressive behavior toward the victim.

2. If an empathic response appears (e.g., as a consequence of focusing attention on the partner's state), then in low-reactive people empathic process may develop. Despite its aversive content, it may serve as a source of desirable stimulation, leading to an increase of the person's arousal level, and finally resulting in the optimal stimulation level attainment (the latter phenomenon seems to be very rare, occurring in persons with extremely strong need of stimulation). Intensification of aggression may be an immediate consequence for behavior here.

In short, in the case of low-reactive persons, factors enhancing empathic responses will lead to an intensification of attack directed at the victim, whereas

in highly reactive people, the same factors will result in a reduction of the
aggression intensity.

STUDIES ON THE RELATIONSHIP BETWEEN EMPATHY AND AGGRESSION

The hypothesis posed here has been formulated on the grounds of a theoretical
analysis concerning the role of factors affecting aggressive behavior control
(Reykowski,1977). Some data obtained by H. Eliasz (1979) in her research on
aggressive behavior regulation can be regarded as an empirical verification of
this hypothesis.

Method

In the author's experiment, 90 girls aged from 17 to 19 years, students of a
secondary school in Warsaw, were employed as subjects. The young women were
informed that the purpose of the experiment was to assess the role of punishment
in the process of learning. The experiment would have two phases. In the first
one, a girl would take the role of pupil; in the second one, the role of teacher.
These two phases would be different because of the type of task to be analyzed.

Three independent variables -- empathy, observation of the victim's suffering,
and aggressor frustration -- were manipulated. Eight separate experimental
situations were established, differing in respect of either the presence or
absence of one of the factors in question. Aggression was the dependent variable. Buss' machine (Buss, 1961) was used to measure aggression intensity.
A subject's physical aggression is manifested in the form of electric shocks
given to his partner, as a punishment for errors made in task performance. If
the subject presses a key on the apparatus, it releases an electric shock to
his partner (in reality the latter manipulation is simulated). Both the number
of the key pressed (i.e., the intensity of electric shock delivered) and the
duration of the shock are registered.

In half the cases a version of the "imagine-him condition" (Stotland, 1969) was
used to evoke empathy in the "aggressor" toward her partner. The subject was
asked to imagine the condition of her partner, including the latter's current
mental state (thoughts and feelings), as well as assessment of her actual situation and its perspectives. The girls were allowed a period of time to complete
this task. In our research they were asked, besides, to describe their own
feelings. The manipulatory procedure was introduced in the middle of the experiment, and on its completion the girls returned to their "proper task" of inflict-
ing punishment.

Delivery of electric shock was followed by signs of the victim's physical suffering (groans, shouts). These were reproduced from a tape recording, after each
girl's aggressive responses reached a certain intensity. Four different signals,
varying with respect to the victim's suffering, were used. Signals were transmitted by loudspeakers placed in the experimental room; duration of each signal
was about 1 s.

Before the experiment proper, a procedure aimed at frustrating our subjects was
employed. They had to perform a task required by their partner. The task consisted in answering the question: "What requirements should be fulfilled to
make marriage happy?" Answers given by the girls were arbitrarily assessed by
their partners: negative evaluations were given to those who were to be frus-
trated; and positive ones, to those who were to be protected from frustration.
The evaluations were descriptive and were made on a 5-point rating scale. When
the experiment was finished, the girls were thanked for their participation.
There was then a short conversation between the experimenter and each girl,

aimed at relaxing her. The experimenter adopted a positive role toward the girl.

After research was finished, all the girls were informed of the actual purpose of the experiment.

In the experiment, subjects' reactivity level was measured by means of the Strelau Temperament Inventory. The latter variable measurement was continuous; that is, groups were not differentiated according to the variable level obtained.

Results

The relationship between empathy and aggression was found in the research to be complex and dependent both on situational factors and on traits of the person displaying aggressive behavior.

To verify the hypothesis concerning the relationship between empathy and aggression dynamics, an analysis of variance was used. It indicated no significant changes either in the mean of intensity or mean of duration of aggressive behavior registered before and after empathy manipulation. Significant differences, however, were found in variance values concerning aggression intensity; namely, in groups subjected to empathy manipulation, the variance range was larger than that in nonempathized groups. The result led us to an assumption that in empathized groups the magnitude of variance was due to other factors; sources of this variation might consist in such properties of the group under study, which produced different effects of empathy manipulation on aggression dynamics in persons differing in reactivity level.

Pearson's correlation was used to determine the relationship between reactivity level and aggression dynamics as a result of empathy manipulation. The following four indexes were taken into account in the analysis: (a) the intensity and (b) duration of aggression, and differential indexes for (c) the intensity and (d) duration (obtained as a result of the difference between mean values of aggression indexes in stage II of the experiment, as compared with stage I).

Data illustrating the intensity of correlation between subject's reactivity level and their aggression intensity in stages I and II are shown in Table 1. The data presented here indicate that in three subgroups (E_4, E_5, E_7), out of the four submitted to empathy manipulation, there is a significant correlation between reactivity and aggression intensity: either in stage II of the experiment (E_4, E_7), or in employing the differential index of aggression intensity (E_5) (differences between aggression intensity of indexes before and after empathy manipulation were statistically insignificant). The following interpretation of this result seems possible: in neither of the empathized groups was reactivity correlated with aggression indexes before the procedure of empathization; in other words, no correlation between reactivity and aggression intensity appeared. The occurrence of a positive correlation after empathy manipulation indicates that the scores earlier dispersed are now ordered according to the principle: the lower the reactivity level, the stronger the aggression. This means that low-reactive girls who had manifested strong aggression before empathization maintained their aggression intensity after the procedure, whereas those low-reactive girls whose prior aggression indexes had been low, intensified their aggression. Thence, aggression intensity level in the low-reactive group became equalized, which is expressed by the significant correlation.

At the same time, no significant correlations between reactivity level and aggression indexes (in stages I and II, and in differential indexes) were found in the non-empathized subgroups (C, E_1, E_2, and E_3).

TABLE 1. Comparison of correlation coefficients between aggression index values and reactivity levels

Groups and stage		Index of correlation coefficients			
		Intensity	Time	Intensity $^\Delta$	Time $^\Delta$
Empathy manipulation					
E_4	Stage I	0.39	-0.03	0.25	-0.12
	Stage II	0.49*	-0.14		
E_5	Stage I	0.38	-0.74	0.75***	0.69
	Stage II	0.71**	-0.63		
E_6	Stage I	0.36	0.02	-0.06	-0.45
	Stage II	0.38	-0.33		
E_7	Stage I	0.48	-0.06	0.22	0.23
	Stage II	0.62*	-0.16		
No empathy manipulation					
C	Stage I	-0.38	0.35	0.10	0.08
	Stage II	-0.49	0.33		
E_1	Stage I	-0.02	0.24	0.20	0.38
	Stage II	0.21	0.37		
E_2	Stage I	0.19	-0.42	0.11	0.38
	Stage II	0.09	-0.29		
E_3	Stage I	-0.39	0.09	0.03	-0.18
	Stage II	-0.24	-0.05		

Note. Characteristics of groups:

E = empathy
F = frustration
E_1 = (E = 0, PP = 0, F = 1)
E_3 = (E = 0, PP = 1, F = 1)
E_5 = (E = 1, PP = 0, F = 1)
E_7 = (E = 1, PP = 1, F = 1)

PP = perception of pain
C = (E = 0, PP = 0, F = 0)
E_2 = (E = 0, PP = 1, F = 0)
E_4 = (E = 1, PP = 0, F = 0)
E_6 = (E = 1, PP = 1, F = 0)

* $p < .05$
** $p < .01$
*** $p < .006$

These data allow us to conclude that in low-reactive girls the manipulation aimed at arousal of empathy with the victim resulted in an intensification of aggression directed at the latter. Neither signs of the victim's physical suf- fering nor the aggressor's frustration were found to affect the nature of the relationship in question.

The regularity obtained can be interpreted in terms of the content and function of the psychological process evoked in low-reactive persons by the procedure of empathization. Perhaps in their case the latter manipulation resulted in activation of imaginative processes concerning aggression realization, its con- sequences, and the state of the victim, but perceived from the subject's view- point, and not from that of the victim, with whom the subject had been expected to identify herself. As noted earlier (cf. Reykowski, 1977), not only the very act of aggression, but also imagining of such an act, may be highly stimulating, which in the case of a permanent deficit of stimulation might result in aggres- sion intensification, by means of an enhanced general arousal level.

Support for this reasoning comes from data obtained from the girls' reports written after the empathy manipulation. These reports were categorized according to the following criteria: (a) whether they indicated the occurrence of an empathic process, (b) whether the description of the partner's experiences was made from the subject's viewpoint only (lack of empathy), and (c) whether they included only the description of the partner's behavior (data insufficient for a conclusion about empathy occurrence). Analysis of these data has shown that in almost 73% of the low-reactive girls no empathic response was observed, as they described their partner's experiences from their own viewpoint only. In the remaining 27% empathic response was observed. On the other hand, among highly reactive girls, only 24% of descriptions belonged to the category "the partner's feelings from my own viewpoint," whereas empathic response was found in almost 40%.

For reports classified into the C category, 36% of highly reactive girls indicated this type of response; whereas in low-reactive girls, there were none. It was im- possible to determine by means of the chi square test the statistical significance of differences in the frequency of responses of particular type, yielded by low- and highly reactive subjects, because the C category (data insufficient for con- clusions about empathy occurrence) probably included girls responding empathically, but either unable or not wishing to describe it. In short, the three distin- guished categories were not disjunctive.

These data seem to justify a conclusion that a person's reactivity level influ- ences the effectiveness of empathy manipulation. In accordance with our hypo- theses, nonempathic responses were registered in 73% of low-reactive girls and in only 24% of highly reactive ones. It should be assumed, then, that the analysis of the victim's situation (without empathizing with him) could serve as a stimulating factor, leading to an increase in the general arousal level and, in consequence, in aggression intensification. The reasoning seems to be correct, on condition that aggressive behaviors displayed during the experiment were either slightly or moderately stimulating and, therefore, that the occurrence of the response did not lead to their surpassing the optimal arousal level.

In the next step of analysis, an attempt was made to determine the function of empathogenic cues in the regulation of aggression dynamics, in persons differing in reactivity level. It was indicated by means of variance analysis that in the group of low-reactive girls perception of the victim's suffering affected aggres- sion intensity ($F = 3.71$, $p < 0.05$).

A comparison of the significance of differences between means of duration of electric shocks indicates that low-reactive girls who had perceived signs of the victim's pain responded with stronger aggression (M = 519 ms) than did those who had had no contact with the victim's suffering (M = 367 ms). On the other hand, in highly reactive girls, the stimulus in question had no effect on the intensity of aggression toward the victim.

CONCLUSIONS

The results suggest that for low-reactive people, observation of the partner's physical suffering is an aggression-stimulating cue. According to our predictions, in low-reactive persons the importance of this stimulus in regulation of aggression is due mostly to its "energetic" component, and not to its conditioned emotional meaning.

Contrary to predictions of the deterministic model of the relationship between psychological traits and behavior, it is not true that aggressiveness (as a personal disposition) is responsible for aggression, while experience of empathy leads to altruistic behaviors. Our research seems to indicate that aggression is liable to be regulated by mechanisms that should not be identified with aggressive "dispositions," namely, by the demand for stimulation, whereas empathy may yield various behaviors (evoking either a reduction or increase in aggression intensity). The actual effect of empathy on aggressive behavior depends both on situational variables (stimulation load, the presence of empathogenic factors), and on the traits of the person displaying aggressive behaviors (i.e., on his reactivity level). Thus, there is a whole system of relationships, and not a simple relation of the trait-behavior type.

This system of regulators of aggressive behavior may be even more complex, because reactivity (considered as an individual trait) is not unchangeable. Reactivity level may vary under the influence of the person's experience. This probably may result in changes in the dynamics of aggressive behavior and in varying effectiveness of aggression control, due to the individual's empathic experiences.

REFERENCES

Aronfreed, J. M. (1968). Conduct and conscience: The socialization of internalized control over behavior. New York: Academic Press.

Baron, R. A. (1971a). Magnitude of victim's pain cues and levels of prior anger arousal as determinants of adult aggressive behavior. Journal of Personality and Social Psychology, 17, 236-243.

Baron, R. A. (1971b). Aggression as a function of magnitude of victim's pain cues, level of prior anger arousal and aggressor-victim similarity. Journal of Personality and Social Psychology, 18, 48-54.

Buss, A. (1961). The psychology of aggression. New York: Wiley.

Buss, A. (1966). Instrumentality of aggression, feedback and frustration as determinants of physical aggression. Journal of Personality and Social Psychology, 13, 153-162.

Cattell, R. B. (1957). Personality and motivation structure and measurement. Yonkers-on-Hudson: World Book.

Dymond, R. (1949). A scale for measurement of empathic ability. Journal of Consulting Psychology, 13, 228-234.

Eliasz, A. (1980). Temperament and transituational stability of behavior in
the physical and social environment. Polish Psychological Bulletin, 11 (3),
143–154.

Eliasz, H. (1975). Znaczenie percepcji bólu doznawanego przez ofiare dla
regulacji agresywnego zachowania się (Significance of observation of the
victim's pain cues as regulator in aggressive behavior). In A. Frączek (Ed.),
Z zagadnień psychologii agresji (Problems in the psychology of aggression).
Warsaw: PIPS.

Eliasz, H. (1979). Empatia jako regulator dynamiki agresji wobec cierpiacej
ofiary (Empathy as a regulator of dynamics of aggression toward suffering
victim). Unpublished doctoral dissertation, University of Warsaw.

Eliasz, H. (1980). The effect of empathy, level of reactivity and anxiety on
interpersonal aggression intensity. Polish Psychological Bullegin, 11 (3),
169–178.

Eysenck, H. J. (1953). The scientific study of personality. New York: Wiley.

Feffer, M. (1959). The cognitive implications of role-taking behavior. Journal
of Personality, 27, 152–168.

Feshbach, S., & Feshbach, N. (1969). The relationship between empathy and
aggression in two age groups. Developmental Psychology, 1, 102–107.

Frączek, A. (1977). The role of emotional control and empathy in the regulation
of social-interaction. Paper presented at the meeting of the fourth conference
of the ISSBD, Pavia, Italy.

Frączek, A. (1979). Czynności agresywne jako przedmiot studiów eksperymentalnej
psychologii społecznej (Aggressive acts as a research subject of experimental
social psychology). In A. Fraczek (Ed.), Studia nad psychologicznymi mechanis-
mami czynności agresywnych (Studies in the psychological mechanisms of aggressive acts). Wrocław: Ossolineum.

Freud, S. (1937). A general selection from the works of Sigmund Freud. In
J. Rickman (Ed.), London: Hogarth Press.

Geen, R. G. (1970). Perceived suffering of the victim as an inhibitor of
attack-induced aggression. Journal of Personality and Social Psychology, 81,
209–216.

Guilford, R. P. (1959). Personality. New York: McGraw-Hill.

Hartmann, D. P. (1969). Influence of symbolically modeled aggression and pain
cues on aggressive behavior. Journal of Personality and Social Psychology,
31, 162–171.

Ianotti, R. (1975a). The effect of role taking experience on altruism, empathy
and aggression. Paper presented at the meeting of the conference of The
Society for Research in Child Development, Denver, CO.

Ianotti, R. (1975b). Many faces of empathy: Definition and evaluation of empathy
in children. Unpublished manuscript.

Mehrabian, A., & Epstein, E. (1972). A measure of emotional empathy. Journal of
Personality, 40, 525–544.

Mischel, W. (1968). Personality and assessment. New York: Wiley.

Quay, H. C. (1977). Psychopathic behavior: Reflections on its nature, origins and treatment. In I.C. Uzgiris and F. Weizman (Eds.), The structuring of experience. New York: Plenum Press.

Reykowski, J. (1975). Osobowość jako centralny system regulacji i integracji czynności człowieka (Personality as a central system of regulation and integration of human actions). In T. Tomaszewski (Ed.), Psychologia (Psychology). Warsaw: Państwowe Wydawnictwo Naukowe.

Reykowski, J. (1977). Spontaniczna agresja i spontaniczne czynniki ja hamujące (Aggression as a process intrinsically motivated and intrinsically inhibited). Przeglad Psychologiczny, 20, 203-228.

Reykowski, J. (1979). Motywacja, postawy prospołeczne i osobowość (Motivation, prosocial attitudes and personality). Warsaw: Państwowe Wydawnictwo Naukowe.

Reykowski, J., & Kochańska, G. (1980). Szkice z teorii osobowości (Essays on the theory of personality). Warsaw: Państwowe Wydawnictwo Naukowe.

Stotland, E. (1969). Exploratory investigations of empathy. In L. Berkowitz (Ed.), Advances in experimental social psychology, Vol. 4. New York: Academic Press.

Strelau, J. (1974). Temperament as an expression of energy level and temporal features of behavior. Polish Psychological Bulletin, 5 (3), 119-127.

Strelau, J. (1982). Temperament a osobowość: Związki i zalezności (Temperament and personality: Relationships and dependencies). In J. Strelau (Ed.), Regulacyjne funkcje temperamentu (The regulating functions of temperament). Wrocław: Ossolineum.

Swartz, Ch., & Berkowitz, L. (1976). Effects of a stimulus associated with a victim's pain on later aggression. Journal of Personality and Social Psychology, 14, 95-101.

Tomaszewski, T. (1975). Podstawowe formy organizacji i regulacji zachowania (The basic forms of organization and regulation of behavior). In T. Tomaszewski (Ed.), Psychologia (Psychology). Warsaw: Państwowe Wydawnictwo Naukowe.

Zawadzki, B. (1970). Wstep do teorii osobowości (Introduction to theory of personality). Warsaw: Państwowe Wydawnictwo Naukowe.

17

Hypertension and Response to Stress: Need for Stimulation?

Tatiana Klonowicz, Hanna Ignatowska-Świtalska, and Bożena Wocial

There is now evidence that environmental situations producing unpleasant
emotions of fear, annoyance, anger, and anxious expectations may all be connected with an acute rise in blood pressure. This phylogenetically old reaction
was meant to prepare the organism to cope with potentially dangerous situations.
It has been suggested (Brod, 1971) that "frequent mobilization of this reaction
may, by overtaxing some of the links in the chain of physiological events, cause
this reaction to become eventually disregulated, protracted, and fused" (p. 316).
This now useless defense mechanism produces long-lasting psychosomatic disturbances that are very difficult to live with and to treat.

The present study was designed to investigate the pattern of response to stress
as determined by hypertension. It is believed that disturbances in coping and
physiological adaptation are at least partly responsible for the vicious circle
leading to and sustaining psychosomatic symptoms. In line with Wolf (1971), who
sees a disease as a reaction to, rather than an effect of, noxious forces, it
has been hypothesized that there are both specific (level of performance under
stress) and nonspecific (general psychological and psychophysiological stress-
induced changes in human functioning) differences in response to stress between
healthy and hypertensive people.

METHOD

The subjects performed a simple mental task (adding up columns of four two-digit
figures) under continuous noise delivered through earphones (30 min). The noise
itself consisted of a specially prepared tape recording of superimposed sounds
of urban traffic, unintelligible bits of speech, and occasional bursts of noise
produced by industries. This mixture of sounds was selected as an analogue of
the complex noises present in the urban environment, which are believed to be
an increasingly important hazard to public health. The tape was played at
approximately 90 dB. The subjects were run individually.

Measures

Two measures of performance were taken into account: proficiency (total number
of columns added within 30 min) and number of errors. To collect data on work
dynamics, every 5 min a line was drawn on the test sheet indicating the amount
of work done in subsequent 5-min periods of work.

The aftereffects of stress were assessed by means of Thayer's Activation-
Deactivation Adjective Check List (AD ACL, short form) and biochemical tests
[assessment of noradrenaline (NA), adrenaline (A), and prostaglandin $F_{2\alpha}$ (PGF)
blood plasma levels].

The AD ACL is a 20-item, self-report test of transitory activation or arousal
states. The test yields four subscales measuring four activation dimensions:
General Activation, Deactivation-Sleep, High Activation, and General Deactivation
(Thayer, 1978a).

Noradrenaline and adrenaline were measured by the fluorimetric method, and plasma
concentration of prostaglandin $F_{2\alpha}$ was determined by specific radioimmunoassay.

The AD ACL and biochemical measures were taken before and immediately after the
30-min work period. For the biochemical measures, 30 ml of venous blood were
withdrawn through an indwelling catheter before (pretest) and after (posttest)
the working period. All subjects gave their informed consent to participate
in this study.

Subjects

Twenty male volunteers participated in the study: 10 patients with essential
hypertension (H, mean age: 26.8 years) and 10 controls without hypertension
(-H, hospitalized patients without psychosomatic disturbances; mean age: 32.9
years).

RESULTS

Level of Performance

An analysis testing the hypothesis of group differences in proficiency revealed
no significant differences between healthy and hypertensive volunteers. The
mean proficiency score was 102.2 in healthy and 103.1 in hypertensive group;
the scores for subsequent 5-min periods ranged in both groups from 16.3 to 17.6.

However, there are significant group differences in total number of errors as
well as in the dynamics of errors throughout the experiment (Figure 1).

Thus, hypertensive subjects exposed to continuous noise respond less accurately
than do healthy ones ($t = 3.284$, $p < .01$). The curve representing the error
score in healthy persons rises slowly, reflecting slightly increasing fatigue.
The error score in the hypertensive group is the highest at the beginning of
the experiment, and the curve is almost V-shaped, with its lowest point reached
at about the 20th minute of work.

Aftereffects of Stress

A comparison of AD ACL scores revealed significant group differences (Table 1).
Comparisons between scores were conducted using Student's t test.

Most relevant to the hypothesis is the evaluation of the change in High Activation
and General Deactivation levels. Here we have a significant difference between
pretest and posttest High Activation scores in healthy volunteers, the posttest
level being significantly higher than the initial (prework) level. At the same
time, there is a significant decrease on the General Deactivation dimension.
According to Thayer (1978b), the two scales could be regarded as opposite components of a general bipolar dimension; thus, the experimentally induced changes
reflect the arousing effect of noise as a stressor.

In the hypertensive group, a change along only one -- General Deactivation scale
-- is revealed; the posttest level is lower than the pretest, suggesting an
increase in arousal.

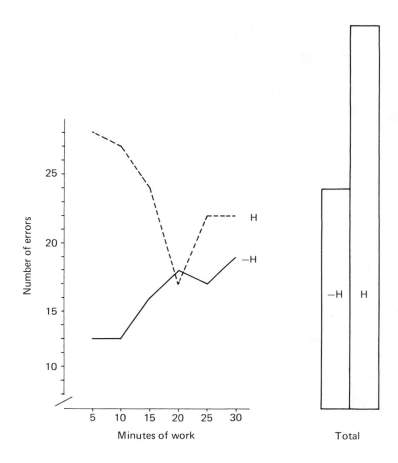

FIGURE 1. Accuracy of work (error scores) in two groups of volunteers (hypertensive, H, and nonhypertensive, -H).

An intergroup comparison of pretest scores reveals significant differences along all but one (Deactivation-Sleep) dimension. The hypertensive volunteers have a significantly higher initial High Activation Score (t = 2.603), whereas their scores on the General Activation and General Deactivation dimensions (respectively, t = 2.614 and t = 2.549) are significantly lower than those of healthy persons (p < .05). These three scores taken together reflect pronounced group differences in tension, anxiety, and discomfort at the beginning of the experiment. The biochemical data are presented in Table 2.

In both groups there is a significant increase of adrenaline and noradrenaline plasma levels. It is worth noting that the percent increase in noradrenaline excretion is more pronounced in healthy subjects ($\Delta\%$: -H = 46.03, H = 30.64, χ^2 = 3.089, .1 < p < .05). The data reveal significant group differences in $PGF_{2\alpha}$. There is a significant increase in $PGF_{2\alpha}$ in healthy subjects, whereas

TABLE 1. Activation-deactivation (AD ACL) scores in healthy (-H) and hypertensive (H) volunteers

Group and test	G Act	D Sl	H Act	G Deac
-H				
Pre	13.6	8.7	6.5	16.0
Post	12.8	9.5	8.4	14.0
t	n.s.	n.s.	2.969*	2.778*
H				
Pre	9.6	9.6	10.3	12.6
Post	8.9	10.7	10.2	9.5
t	n.s.	n.s.	n.s.	2.619*

Note.   G Act = General Activation; D Sl = Deactivation-Sleep; H Act = High
Activation; G Deac = General Deactivation.   The potential range of scores on
each dimension is from 5.0 to 20.0.

*p < .05

TABLE 2. Adrenaline (A), Noradrenaline (NA), and Prostaglandine F ($PGF_{2\alpha}$)
plasma levels in healthy (-H) and hypertensive (H) volunteers

Group and test	A (ng/ml)	NA (mg/ml)	$PGF_{2\alpha}$ (pg/ml)
-H			
Pre	.29	.63	7.3
Post	.42	.92	11.3
t	2.575**	3.054**	3.758*
H			
Pre	.25	.62	18.9
Post	.36	.81	20.9
t	3.236**	2.348**	n.s.

*p < .05
**p < .01

in the hypertensive group exposure to stress induces an almost negligible elevation of $PGF_{2\alpha}$. On the other hand, there is a significant difference in the
$PGF_{2\alpha}$ initial levels; the data presented in Table 2 show that the intergroup
difference in this respect is more than twofold.

DISCUSSION

Measures of performance corroborate Broadbent's (1963) statement that noise
leads to active but inaccurate behavior. The effect of noise is more pronounced
in the hypertensive group.

Increases in plasma level catecholamines are well documented. The intergroup
difference in noradrenaline secretion seems of interest because of the suggested
relationship between higher NA and better performance on mental tasks (Frankenhaeuser & Patkai, 1964). Higher noradrenaline increase in healthy subjects
parallels their better performance on our task.

The increase in plasma $PGF_{2\alpha}$ level following exposure to stress may reflect an
elevated brain or cerebral vessel prostaglandin synthesis. It has been shown
recently that PGs are a group of first mediators of cell response to stimulation
(Hanukoglu, 1977). This is supported by Hedge (1977), who reported that
indomethacin, a PG synthesis inhibitor, inhibits stress induced by the release
of adrenocorticotropic hormone (ACTH). The results of our healthy subjects
corroborate this hypothesis as well. Thus, the changes in blood plasma catecholamines, PGs, AD ACL scores, and performance level in healthy volunteers are
consistent with the data on noise effects (Cantrell, 1974).

The results of hypertensive persons seem less clear. Two sets of data deserve
special attention: the PGs plasma level and the AD ACL scores following exposure
to stress. In the light of the well-established prostaglandin deficiency in
hypertension, our data appear rather surprising. The same is true for the AD
ACL scores: one might expect sick, and therefore less resistant subjects to be
more affected by the stressor. In both cases significant differences between
healthy and hypertensive volunteers appear before stress, that is, at the moment
of pretest measurements. Therefore it is believed that the elevated initial
plasma $PGF_{2\alpha}$ level as well as the initial discomfort as measured by AD ACL
reflect the anticipation of stress (anticipatory arousal).

According to our data, psychosomatic and healthy people display different patterns of response to stress. Anticipation of stress (worrying) is by far more
pronounced in the hypertensive group. Irrespective of whether this preparedness
is adequate, it affects the adaptive mechanisms on both psychological and psychophysiological levels.

We can only speculate about the nature of the mechanism determining these reactions. The stressful effect of noise and many other environmental stimuli is
ascribed to their arousal properties. It seems, therefore, that the most plausible explanation of the phenomena observed is the lower need for stimulation in
hypertensive as compared with the healthy group. It has been shown that the
lower need for stimulation is associated with higher sensibility and arousibility.
This explains the earlier and easier triggering of anticipatory activity.

Some additional evidence supports this interpretation. Hypertension is accompanied by higher neuroticism: the mean score on the "neurotic triad" (Depression,
Hypochondria, and Hysteria, as measured by the Minnesota Multiphasic Personality
Inventory, MMPI) was significantly higher in hypertensive persons as compared
with the healthy (21.6 vs. 15.6, t = 1.634, p < .05). Neuroticism is known
to augment a person's perception and prediction of stimulation load, to increase

arousability, and, in consequence, to reduce the requirement for stimulation. And because the interaction of the internal level of stimulation with the activational properties of environmental stimulation exceeds the person's capacities, the level of performance suffers. This deterioration is more pronounced in subjects with lower need for stimulation, the hypertensive patients.

The proposed model for an indirect influence via neuroticism of hypertension does not exclude the direct linkage. It has been argued (Eliasz, 1974; Sales, Guydosh, & Iacomo, 1974) that individual differences in need for stimulation are determined in large measure by the physiological mechanism of stimulation processing. Individual differences in this respect are due to the augmenting/reducing properties of this mechanism. The discrepancy between individual capacities determined in this fashion and supplied stimulation is deleterious to health and is supposed to be a risk factor in psychosomatic diseases. The reverse may be true as well: the onset of psychosomatic disturbances may be a signal for the organization of defense mechanisms on both psychological and psychophysiological levels. The latter would be responsible for the changes in the physiological mechanism of stimulation processing and the former for the employment of further defense mechanisms.

REFERENCES

Broadbent, D. E. (1963). Differences and interactions between stressors. Quarterly Journal of Experimental Psychology, 15, 205-211.

Brod, J. (1971). The influence of higher nervous processes induced by psychosocial environment on the development of essential hypertension. In L. Levi (Ed.), Stress, society, and disease. London: Oxford University Press.

Cantrell, R. W. (1974). Prolonged exposure to intermittent noise. Laryngoscope, 84 (Suppl. 1).

Eliasz, A. Temperament a osobowość (Temperament and personality). Worcław: Ossolineum, 1974.

Frankenhaeuser, M., & Patkai, P. (1964). Catecholamine excretion and performance during stress. Perceptual and Motor Skills, 19, 13-14.

Hanukoglu, O. (1977). Prostaglandins as first mediators of stress. New England Journal of Medicine, 296, 1414.

Hedge, G. A. (1977). Roles for the prostaglandins in the regulation of anterior pituitary secretion. Life Sciences, 20, 17-33.

Sales, S. M., Guydosh, R. M., & Iacomo, W. (1974). Relationship between "strength of the nervous system" and the need for stimulation. Journal of Personality and Social Psychology, 29, 16-22.

Thayer, R. E. (1978a). Factor analytic and reliability studies on the Activation-Deactivation Adjective Check List. Psychological Reports, 42, 747-756.

Thayer, R. E. (1978b). Toward a psychological theory of multidimensional activation (arousal). Motivation and Emotion, 2, 1-34.

Wolf, S. (1971). Patterns of social adjustment and disease. In L. Levi (Ed.), Stress, society, and disease. London: Oxford University Press.

18

Activity and Reactivity: Theoretical Comments and an Experimental Approach

Wolfgang Schönpflug and Hermann Mündelein

In his influential textbook, Psychologia, Tomaszewski (excerpted in Tomaszewski, 1978) draws the fundamental distinction between activity and reactive behavior. Reactive behavior is described as stimulus bound and rather stereotyped; activity, on the other hand, is described as goal oriented and flexible. Whereas reactive behavior is determined by features of the present situation, activity is directed toward the future. Similar distinctions use such concepts as conscious and unconscious behavior, voluntary and involuntary action, and controlled and automated processes.

MEASURES OF REACTIVE BEHAVIOR

Complex and untrained motor patterns are examples of goal-oriented behavior, whereas highly trained performance and autonomic responses are frequently presented as examples of reactive behavior. Autonomic responses (e.g., the eyelid reflex, galvanic skin reactions, and heart accelerations) show fast and stable alterations with changes in stimulation. Thus, they appear as autonomous events, unrelated to the stream of ongoing activity. The impression of an autonomous, anecdotal event, however, may be misleading. Possibly, this impression arises only because the stimuli applied also enter the situation as unrelated, anecdotal events. If stimuli were integrated into the situation at hand, the reaction would not stand out from the ongoing behavior. Good illustrations of this point are presented in studies of eyelid behavior and heart rate changes. The eyelid closes if the conversation with a nonfamiliar partner touches on an intimate topic (Argyle & Dean, 1965). This can be interpreted as defensive behavior rather than as a pure eyelid reflex. In studies of mental work (Schulz & Schönpflug, 1982), heart rate follows task involvement, increasing with effort and decreasing with hesitation in accepting the task, or resignation in continuing ineffectual procedures. In this case, heart activity appears as an integral part of ongoing behavior.

If we study activity as defined by Tomaszewski, we must not fail to include measures of internal, physiological processes that commonly are regarded to be more reactive in nature. These processes may share the goal orientation of motor and mental behavior because they may have the function of tuning the organism (Gellhorn, 1943) to enable it to reach its goals. Every musician tunes his instrument before he performs. The person who strives for his goals

The study reported in the second part of this chapter was supported by a grant from Deutsche Forschungsgemeinschaft to W. Schönpflug.

uses himself as an instrument. So he has to tune himself to reach a state in which he can perform as he wants to perform. From this point of view, internal physiological processes are regarded as acts of self-regulation rather than as reactions to the environment.

SELF-REGULATORY BEHAVIOR

Of course, self-regulation -- regarded as a prerequisite of external regulation -- may vary considerably with individuals, thus leading to individual differences in speed, mobility, and energy level. Although the possibilities of acquisition of self-regulatory styles should not be underrated, Strelau's (1974) suggestion of biological, temperamental factors contributing to the individual variance is well supported. Temperamental traits in Strelau's sense may represent a general biological outfit, which, by tuning the organism, puts some formal constraints like speed, energy level, and endurance on a person's behavior.

The idea of a phase of goal-oriented behavior that is self-regulatory in nature has explicitly been considered in a recent experiment by Jürgen Otto (1982). In this experiment, subjects 14 to 18 years old were observed while they participated in a racing contest using model cars. One of the central problems in this study was the subjects' awareness of their arousal state, their concern for a relation between arousal and performance, and their techniques of modifying their arousal state. Their heart rate was continuously monitored by a telemetric device. Observers registered their overt behavior; in addition, questionnaires were applied to obtain subjective reports. The subjects were allowed a comparatively wide range of regulatory activities. They could rehearse and check the equipment on request. They were permitted to ask questions about the race and their partners. Strelau's (1972) inventory was also administered to the subjects; thus, we related interindividual differences in the variables observed to the dimensions of the theory of temperament as proposed by the Warsaw group.

The study of overt actions, including acts of external regulation, requires an analysis of the operations that make up the total action. For the purpose of identifying such operations, a taxonomy is needed. Although such a taxonomy cannot be presented in detail here, the following dimensions deserve further consideration:

1. Executive versus orienting operations: executive operations are likely to bring about changes or inhibit alterations, whereas orienting operations (e.g., observations and measurement procedures) lead to representations of situations and events.

2. Primary versus secondary operations: primary operations promote the action toward the goal state immediately (e.g., driving a car toward the center of the town), whereas secondary operations are rather instrumental for the execution of primary operations (e.g., filling the gas tank of the car).

3. Dispatching versus preventive operations: dispatching operations refer to problems at hand (e.g., filling a gas tank that has just become empty), whereas preventive operations are rather motivated by problems yet to arise (e.g., filling an extra can of gasoline for the eventuality that gas stations are closed later).

4. Operations directed toward the active person himself (i.e., immediately contributing toward self-regulation) versus operations directed toward the environment (thereby also contributing to external regulation).

The definition of these dimensions leans heavily on Tomaszewski's (1978) taxonomy of actions and on his concept of functional structure of activity. The structure of activity is defined by the set of operations represented during the course of an action, and it can be assumed to vary with individuals and situations. In a recent study performed by Mündelein and Schönpflug (1983), an attempt was made to assess complex activity structures, (a) in highly realistic settings; (b) with rather detailed and continuous records of behavior; and (c) extending the time of observation over some hours, comparing states of alertness with states of fatigue. A short account of this study will be given in the following section.

METHOD

A computer was essential for long-term, continuous, and detailed data recording; therefore, we attempted to simulate a realistic environment that is highly computer controlled. We found such an environment in an insurance company, where employees worked on applications for claims. After some field observations, the task situation was simulated in the laboratory. Subjects were seated in a room that looked almost like an office. They faced a monitor and could send messages by means of a keyboard. Monitor and keyboard were connected with a PDP 11/40 computer. Stored in the computer was a set of 80 cases, requesting claims for different types of damage. Subjects were free to display each of these cases on the screen, whenever and for as long as they wished. They were asked to make decisions on each application according to the standard insurance regulations. To reach their decision, they had lists of customers, contracts, and payments available, which could be displayed on the screen. Their main task and primary activity consisted of selecting applications, searching the file number of the applicant, comparing the conditions of the contract with the actual damage, and checking the validity of the contract in relation to due payment of premiums. This is what thousands of office workers actually do from Monday to Friday, and it formed their set of primary operations; this set could be broken down further into orienting and executive components.

There were also operations that could be interpreted as secondary or instrumental: Checking the list of problems to organize the progress of work, or checking the list of commands used for communication with the computer (e.g., STOP, GO). The latter list was typed on a sheet of paper and located within the desk. Whenever this list was picked up, a microswitch was operated. Preventive measures also could be taken. Obviously, the subjects could not continue during a computer breakdown. Therefore, prevention of a computer breakdown was introduced as an additional operation. Breakdowns were actually simulated, ostensibly due to overload caused by the number of simultaneous users. The experimenters pretended to give priority to their subjects. They gave the instruction: "By calling a routine SYSTEM you can receive information about the state of the system. If it is approaching overload you may declare PRIORITY. Then -- for a certain amount of time -- it will not be you whose terminal will be shut off." By regularly checking the system the subjects could obtain information about impending breakdowns, and could take steps to prevent them. If the subjects declared PAUSE, they could interrupt their work and go for a rest into an adjacent room.

Altogether, the situation allowed for a high degree of personal freedom. Nevertheless, a full record of the person's operations could be obtained, stored, and analyzed. The experimental task kept all subjects busy for at least 3 hr, and had to be terminated for technical reasons after 4 hr if the subject had not yet finished.

Seventy-two subjects were tested. They were mainly unemployed office workers, registered at a local labor office. Before the experiment, they were familiarized with the experimental situation; they then took two personality tests:

Spielberger's anxiety questionnaire, in the German version by Laux, Schaffner, and Glanzmann (1979), and Strelau's (1972) temperament scale in a German translation kindly made available by the Psychology Section of the Karl Marx University at Leipzig (Vorwerg, 1975).

Besides assessing the structures of activity in general, the intention of the study was to correlate questionnaire scores and activity records. However, it was not easy to derive clear-cut predictions from the literature. So far as correlations with reactivity scores are concerned, there were initially only two hypotheses, based on the description by Strelau (1975):

1. High-reactive subjects will perform more operations.

2. High-reactive subjects will engage in a higher proportion of secondary and preventive operations.

The hypotheses referring to anxiety measures are not listed here, because the correlations with anxiety scores are not presented in the data section. Some conclusions, however, may be drawn from the correlations between reactivity and anxiety scores (Table 1). A high correlation is found between Trait-anxiety and Excitation, as already reported by Strelau and Maciejczyk (1977).

RESULTS

The analysis of data reveals some differences between high- and low-reactive subjects. High-reactive persons use more preventive system checks ($p < .08$), have a higher proportion of secondary operations in their records ($p < .05$), have fewer errors in communicating with the computer ($p < .05$), and are somewhat superior in the number of correct decisions ($p < .05$). A finding that should be corroborated further relates to time spent on single tasks. Whereas high-reactive persons spend significantly more time on tasks followed by wrong decisions, they use less time on tasks completed without error (Table 2).

TABLE 1.   Correlations between measures of anxiety and reactivity.

	Trait Anxiety	Excitation	Inhibition	Mobility
State anxiety	.47	−.44	−.24	−.28
Trait anxiety	--	−.64	−.34	−.22
Excitation			.40	.52
Inhibition			--	.26
Mobility				--

Note. All coefficients are significant at the .05 level with $N = 72$; coefficients above .25 are significant at the .01 level.

TABLE 2.   Interaction between reactivity and the average time in seconds spent on tasks followed by correct or incorrect decisions.

Decision	Reactivity	
	low	high
Correct	86.7	80.8
Incorrect	90.4	113.9

NOTE.   Data from individuals with the highest scores (N = 24) and the lowest scores (N = 20) in reactivity (total sample: N = 72).

In general, the group of high-reactive persons, as categorized by application of Strelau's test, exhibits increased concern with actual and impending problems, is more successful in avoiding errors, and shows more endurance with tasks beyond his or her competence.   These conclusions fit well into Strelau's (1974) theory of reactivity and also correspond with his earlier findings (Strelau, 1975). What is disappointing, however, is the size of the correlations between questionnaire scores and behavioral measures; the highest value obtained in a large correlation matrix is .33.   This observation is to be contrasted to the high correlations obtained between different questionnaire scores (cf. Table 1), on the one hand, and between different behavioral scores, on the other.   Obviously, there is a high proportion of common variance between the behavioral measures (a) number of operations,   (b) number of decisions,   (c) number of correct decisions,   (d) number of secondary operations,   (e) number of system checks, and (f) number of priority declarations.   The reason why the variance of these behavioral measures and the variance of the questionnaire scores do not converge to a higher extent may lie in the different nature of the data.

Further interpretations may be justified after continued analysis of the collected data.   At least two additional points will be subject to further investigation:

1.   Stability of activity structures over the time of the experiment.

2.   Relation of overt operations to heart rate measures taken continuously by means of a telemetric device.

After the clarification of the second point, the discussion should also return to the theoretical issue raised in the first part of this chapter: the impact of organismic tuning or self-regulation for goal-directed activity.

REFERENCES

Argyle, M., & Dean, J. (1965). Eye-contact, distance, and affiliation. Sociometry, 28, 289-304.

Gellhorn, E. (1943). Autonomic regulation. New York: Interscience.

Laux, L., Schaffner, P., & Glanzmann, P. (1979). Manual für den Fragebogen zur Erfassung von State- und Trait-Angst (STAI-G). Weinheim: Beltz.

Mündelein, H., & Schönpflug, W. (1983). Regulation und Fehlregulation im Verhalten VIII. Über primäre (unmittelbar zielgerichtete) und sekundäre (auxiliäre und präventive) Anteile von Tätigkeiten. Psychologische Beiträge, 25, 71-84.

Otto, J. (1982). Regulation und Fehlregulation im Verhalten VI. Anforderung und Kapazität beim Warten und beim Ansführen von Tätigkeiten. Psychologische Beiträge, 24, 478-497.

Schulz, P., & Schönpflug, W. (1982). Regulatory activity during states of stress. In L. Laux and W. Krohne (Eds.), Achievement, stress and anxiety (pp. 51-73). Washington, DC: Hemisphere.

Strelau, J. (1972). A diagnosis of temperament by nonexperimental techniques. Polish Psychological Bulletin, 3, 97-105.

Strelau, J. (1974). Temperament as an expression of energy level and temporal features of behavior. Polish Psychological Bulletin, 5, 119-127.

Strelau, J. (1975). Reactivity and activity style in selected occupations. Polish Psychological Bulletin, 6, 199-206.

Strelau, J., & Maciejczyk, J. (1977). Reactivity and decision making in stress situations in pilots. In C. D. Spielberger and I. G. Sarason (Eds.), Stress and anxiety, Vol. 4, pp. 29-42. Washington, DC: Hemisphere.

Tomaszewski, T. (1978). Tätigkeit und Bewußtsein. Weinheim: Beltz.

Vorwerg, M. (1975). Einstellungspsychologie. Berlin: Duetscher Verlag der Wissenschaften.

19

Activity Structures as Related to Individual Differences in Temperament

Peter Schulz

THE CONCEPT OF REACTIVITY

Strelau (1974) has defined temperament as "a set of formal and relatively stable traits manifested in energy level and reaction time parameters" (p. 119). The major dimension of behavioral energy level is reactivity. Reactivity is said to influence the activity of a person in three ways:

1. In stressful (difficult, extreme) situations, the person's reactivity has a direct impact on performance, in particular if the situation is of long duration (Strelau, 1977).

2. Reactivity has some influence on individual style of action (Strelau, 1977, p. 2).

3. Reactivity determines individual preferences for various situations according to their stimulation properties (Eliasz, 1973).

The experimental study reported here attempts to validate these three assumptions.

METHOD

Sixty subjects worked on 64 tasks. The experimental tasks were constructed as an analogue to problems encountered in administrative work.

Tasks

The subjects faced a display screen and a keyboard. The display was divided into two fields. The field on the right-hand side was reserved for the problem (e.g., a calculation had to be checked, or a decision had to be reached about an application). The other field was used to display additional information needed to solve the problem (e.g., price lists, allowances, and statements of account). Subjects could call for such information by pressing different buttons of a keyboard (Figure 1).

By pressing the button AT (see Figure 1), the subjects asked for the text of the problem, which remained in the left field until the task was finished. Additional information could be ordered by pressing buttons 1 - 15. This

The research reported in this chapter was supported by a grant from the Government of the Federal Republic of Germany (Bundesinnenministerium/ Umweltbundesamt) to Dr. Wolfgang Schönpflug.

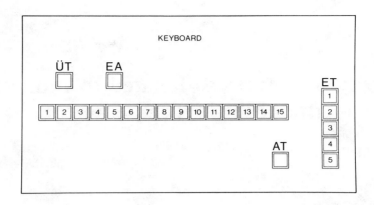

FIGURE 1.   The keyboard.

information appeared on the right side of the screen, one amount at a time.
The subjects were free to display the additional information as long and as
frequently as they wanted. Only one unit of information, however, could be
shown at a time. Because the subjects did not know in which way the 15 buttons
were associated with different bits of information, a directory was prepared
containing the list of information available and the number of each kind of
information on the keyboard. By pressing the button ÜT, the person could display this directory in the right field of the screen.

Only a small amount of the information available was relevant for the solution
of the tasks. This information had to be selected and processed. After finishing the task, the subjects could call for five possible alternative solutions
by means of the button EA. The solutions also appeared in the right field. By
pressing one of the buttons ET 1 to 5, the subjects made their decision in
favor of one of the five possible alternatives. Only one alternative was correct in all instances. After each decision, the display was cleared and the
subjects could either take a rest or call for the next task by pressing the
button AT.

Procedure and Design

The 64 tasks were divided into 6 series. Each series contained 10 or 12 tasks
of the same type. After working on one series the subjects answered 11 questions
concerning the attribution of failures (8), attentional lapses (1), changes of
achievement motivation (1), and satisfaction with performance (1). The questions
were displayed, and they were answered by pressing buttons on the keyboard.

After finishing the experiment, the subjects described their feelings and working strategies during the task. For this purpose a special inventory was constructed.

The behavioral data of the subjects during the experiment (information calls,
kind of decision), the answers to the questions in between the series, and the
time needed for each operation were recorded on-line by a laboratory computer
(PDP 11/40). The computer program was written by R. Klima.

Thirty subjects worked under a noise condition (traffic noise with a mean sound level of 68 dB), and 30 subjects worked in a quiet situation. According to their scores on the Strelau (1972) Temperament Inventory, the subjects were sub-divided into two further groups: high- and low-reactive persons.

RESULTS

The subjects had a mean reactivity score of 48.4. We obtained a correlation of $r = -.34$ between Reactivity and State Anxiety, which was measured by the State-Anxiety Inventory (Spielberger, Gorusch, & Lushene, 1970 ; German version Laux, Schaffner, & Glanzmann, 1979) immediately before the experiment began.

Performance

According to the concept of temperament, reactivity should have a direct impact on performance. To analyze the relation between performance and reactivity, an index combining the quality of the work and the time required was computed. This yielded an index of efficiency based on the ratio between correct responses and the time spent on tasks. High efficiency is expressed by a high value of the index. We call this index "performance efficiency." This index has already been used in stress research (Schulz & Schönpflug, 1980). As a result of our experiment, the overall performance efficiency was lower for high-reactive than for low-reactive persons. This holds true for all series of tasks except one (Figure 2).

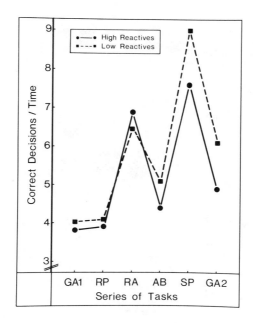

FIGURE 2. Efficiency of performance in six consecutive series of tasks for high- and low-reactive persons.

A more detailed analysis gave a more refined account of the differences between high- and low-reactive persons:

1. The difference in performance efficiency between the two groups increased with task difficulty. High-reactive persons were significantly less efficient in performance only on difficult tasks ($F = 5.68$, df $= 1,54$, $p < .01$).

2. The decrease of performance efficiency in high-reactive subjects performing on difficult tasks increased with time at work. The first and last series were constructed as parallel tasks. The difference score of efficiency (difference between series 1 and series 6) showed significantly higher values for high-reactive persons ($F = 8.51$, df $= 1,54$, $p < .01$).

The decrease in performance efficiency by the high-reactive persons was caused mainly by an increase of time required to work on the task. This extension of time was specifically due to the noise factor (Figure 3). An analysis of variance was computed over each block of tasks. The differences between the reactivity groups were significant for three blocks ($p < .05$) out of six, depending on the difficulty of the tasks.

The increase in time spent on a task in the high-reactive/noise group reflects the specificity of their operations, as further analysis indicates. High-reactive persons called more often for the directory and ordered more irrelevant information. Besides this, more time for difficult information-processing procedures was required, and the subjects hesitated before executing the next operation.

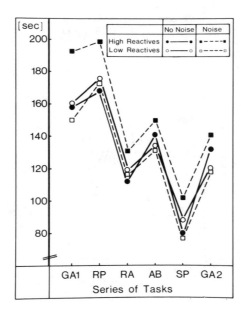

FIGURE 3. Time spent on one task in six consecutive series of tasks for high- and low-reactive persons working with and without traffic noise.

In summary: High-reactive persons working under the noise condition needed more time to search the relevant information, to plan ongoing actions, and to carry out difficult information-processing procedures. But they did not spend more time on easy information-processing procedures, and they were not compelled to compensate disturbances of information processing by ordering relevant information more frequently.

Activity Style

Following Strelau (1977), it can be assumed that reactivity has some influence on individual activity style. The measures of performance (Figures 2 and 3) did not indicate whether the extra time required by high-reactive persons under the noise condition was due to concentration deficiencies or to shifts in working strategy devised to compensate for noise effects. Thus it was of interest to discover if increased attentional lapses were repored by low- or high-reactive persons. Within the experimental session, six questions concerning those disturbances had to be answered after each series of tasks.

Figure 4 shows that low-reactive subjects reported stronger disruption of concentration during experimental work than did high-reactive persons, especially in the second part of the experiment. The differences between the groups were highly significant (p < .01) for five out of six series. Thus, it can be concluded that an increase in decision time by high-reactive persons was not due to concentration deficiencies but to a shift in activity style. The results

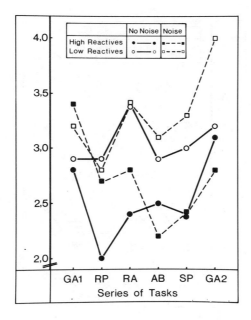

FIGURE 4. Reported attentional lapses on six consecutive series of tasks for high- and low-reactive persons as a function of noise.

indicate that high-reactive people prefer to vary their type of action to prevent disturbances from noise or difficult tasks.

There is further evidence of activity shifts in high-reactive persons when confronted with stressful conditions. Our inventory, which was answered immediately
after the experiment, contained questions concerning individual style of work.
The significant differences between high- and low-reactive persons should be
mentioned briefly:

1. High-reactive persons scored higher on the question: "I worked more care-
    fully and took enough time to solve the task when confronted with difficult
    tasks" (p < .01).

2. High-reactive persons scored higher on the question: "I took enough time
    to prepare for the following operation, especially before ordering further
    information" (p < .08).

Preferences for Various Situations

To test for individual differences in preference for various situations according
to their stimulating properties, we used the attribution behavior of high- and
low-reactive persons. We assumed that asking for factors responsible for failure
is a good method to analyze the avoided properties of a situation. Within our
experimental paradigm, subjects were asked after each series of tasks whether
unfavorable factors within the situation were responsible for their failures.

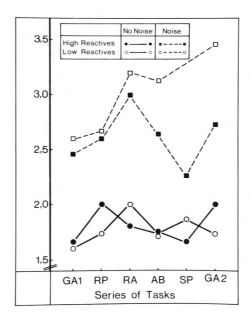

FIGURE 5. Subjects attributing failures to external conditions on six consecutive series of tasks for high- and low-reactive persons as a function of noise.

Figure 5 shows that low-reactive persons working under noise scored significantly higher (p < .05) when asked whether external factors determined failures. This holds true only for the second part of the experiment.

DISCUSSION

The results concerning the relationship between reactivity and performance are in line with the hypotheses stated by Strelau (1974, 1977). Performance degradation was found for high-reactive persons only when their activity was performed under stressful conditions. Besides other variables, duration of work, intensive noise stimulation, and difficult tasks are factors that make a situation stressful. As our results showed, the temporal structure of the activity was modified (Figure 3), and if the stressful conditions were augmented, the final outcome deteriorated. (High-reactive persons with low abilities tended to avoid difficult information processing and favored risky decisions instead).

The exclusive use of time parameters to estimate inefficiency in performance can lead to considerable contamination of factors. The results show that performance degradation can be indicated both by time prolongation as well as shortening of time. Both lead to performance degradation (Figure 2) if we define performance in terms of an index of efficiency. Thus changes of activity structures are intimately related to performance (Schulz & Schönpflug, 1982).

The increased time requirement of high-reactive persons performing under stressful conditions was due to shifts in working strategy. As demands increased, high-reactive persons spent more time preparing for the next operation. Thus the time prolongation can either reflect a certain style of work, due to longer preparatory activity, or to covert recovery periods that are needed because of fatigue. The latter interpretation is confirmed by a notion of Strelau (1975) that high-reactive persons confronted with prolonged activity "tend to organise their activity in an intermittent fashion," because they are more susceptible to fatigue.

The answers of high-reactive subjects concerning their individual work style are of considerable interest. According to Strelau, increasing time intervals in between operations serve as resting periods. According to the self-reports, however, they served to prepare for the operation that followed. If we take into account the fact that these shifts in strategy only occur when demands increase, the subject's own interpretation deserves more consideration than Strelau's initial suggestion implies.

Some additional remarks in a later paper (Strelau, 1977) are helpful because they draw attention to a different aspect: "Since a prolonged engagement in one and the same activity is likely to produce protective inhibition, these persons seek to vary the type of action in order to bring other nervous centers into play and give the previously engaged centers a chance to recover" (p. 17). Following this hypothesis, subjects can recover from one type of activity by executing another one. If this thesis can be accepted in general, the special hypothesis can be put forward that preparatory activities permit a recovery from executive activities.

Compensation of increasing demands by modifying working strategy may be classified as some kind of regulatory behavior. This behavior modification protects people from cognitions concerning the impact of unfavorable internal and external conditions of work. Thus high-reactive persons experience fewer disturbances of concentration (Figure 4). Low-reactive persons, on the other hand, try to reach solutions with minimal interruption; and, according to Strelau (1974, 1977), these persons do not try to recover until the work is finished. Thus we can predict: if low-reactive persons have to work under unfavorable conditions, interruptions of ongoing information processing probably occur. During these interruptions, low-reactive persons become more sensitive to the impact of internal and external stress factors on performance (Figure 4).

A further issue is the causal attribution of high-reactive people (Figure 5). There seems to be a contradiction between real performance degradation and corresponding attribution behavior. According to the objective data, higher scores of high-reactive persons on the questions were expected, whether aversive external conditions were responsible for failures during work. But the reverse was true. The differences were highly significant and well replicable.

This unexpected outcome can be explained by taking into consideration the fact that in real life high-reactive persons have, according to Strelau (1977) and Eliasz (1973), no preference for such stressful situations. In line with this assumption, we assume that the attribution data of high-reactive persons may reflect a certain attribution bias: because high-reactive persons try to avoid stressful situations in real life, they are not accustomed to attributing their failures to external conditions, as they did in our experiment.

REFERENCES

Eliasz, A. (1973). Temperament traits and reaction preferences depending on stimulation load. Polish Psychological Bulletin, 4, 103-113.

Laux, L., Schaffner, P., & Glanzmann, P (1979). Manual für den Fragebogen zur Erfassung von State- und Trait-Angst (STAI-G). Weinheim: Beltz.

Schulz, P., & Schönpflug, W. (1982). Regulatory activity during states of stress. In W. Krohne and L. Laux (Eds.), Achievement, stress, and anxiety, pp. 51-73. New York: Wiley/Hemisphere.

Spielberger, C. D., Gorusch, R. L., & Lushene, R. E. (1970). Manual for the state-trait anxiety inventory. Palo Alto, CA: Consulting Psychologists.

Strelau, J. (1972). A diagnosis of temperament by nonexperimental techniques. Polish Psychological Bulletin, 3, 97-105.

Strelau, J. (1974). Temperament as an expression of energy level and temporal features of behavior. Polish Psychological Bulletin, 5, 119-127.

Strelau, J. (1975). Reactivity and activity style in selected occupations. Polish Psychological Bulletin, 6, 199-207.

Strelau, J. (1977). Experimental investigations of the relation between reactivity as a temperament trait and human action. Unpublished manuscript, Warsaw.

Index

Abilities, 43
Activation, 46, 52
  -Deactivation Adjective Check List, 207–211
  level of, 97, 99, 103, 128, 131, 133
  and memory, 128–134
  theory and CNV, 87
Activity:
  and behavioral dynamics, 44
  cognitive control of, 150
  and cybernetics, 143
  formal-dynamic aspects of, 44
  functional structure of, 214, 215, 217
  goal-oriented, 213, 214, 217
  mental, 43–45
  motor, 43–45
  principal components analysis of, 45–46
  sign of, 155
  and speed, 45, 51–54
  structure of, 136, 139
  as temperamental trait, 43–45
  tempo of, 45
  temporal structure of, 136, 139–141
  types of, 51–54
  and working conditions, 120–121
Adrenaline, 207–211
Aggression, 185–192, 195–200, 202–203
  and external stimulation, 185–192
  and frustration, 185–187
  and imaginative processes, 202
  and personality, 185–192
  and psychopathy, 187–191
  and social interaction, 185
Antisocial personality disorder, 175
  (See also Psychopathy)
Anxiety, 107–109, 112–116
  in psychopathy, 179–182
  state-trait, 216–217
  and strength of nervous system, 95
Arousability, 211

Arousal, 107, 109, 115, 116, 136, 142, 163–171
  and activation, 27
  and evoked potentials (EPs), 91–96
  and CNV, 79, 87, 88
  and electroencephalograms (EEG), 26
  and learning, 91–96
  and psychopathy, 180
    optimal level of, 175–177
  in psychology experiments, 34–35
  varieties of, 34
Attributions, 224, 226

Canonical correlation analysis, 140, 145–149
Cardiac measures, 60
Cattell's Sixteen Personality Factors Test (16PF), 31
Change overload, 136, 138, 139, 141
Cognitive activity and problem solving, 143–150
Cognitive control, 163, 164, 169, 170
Competitive behavior, 214
Consciousness, 72
Contingent negative variation (CNV), 78
  and activation, 87
  and amphetamines, 87
  and arousal, 79, 87, 88
  and attention, 87
  and caffeine, 81, 84, 87
  and chlordiazepoxide, 81
  and excitation-inhibition balance, 81, 82, 87
  and excitatory conditions, 81, 82, 86–88
  and extraversion-introversion, 79–88
  and habitual action-preparedness, 79–82, 84, 85
  and inhibitory conditions, 81, 82, 86–88
  and intelligence, 79
  and mental efficiency, 80, 84, 85, 87

Contingent negative variation (CNV) (*Cont.*):
   and neuroticism, 79, 80, 84–86
   and nicotine, 78
   and nitrazepam, 87
   orienting and expectancy components, 86
   personality-X-condition effects: linear
      model for, 86, 87
      nonlinear model for, 81, 82, 84, 86,
         87
   in psychiatric patients, 78, 86
   and reaction time, 77–81, 85, 87
   and smoking, 88
   and white noise, 81

Defense mechanisms, 212
Demand characteristics, 36
Dichotic listening, 61, 69, 70
Differential psychophysiology, 44
Disconcordance response, 60, 64, 68
Drowsiness during experiments, 35
Drugs and CNV, 78, 81, 84, 87

Electrodermal activity, 60, 87–96
   and bioelectrical skin reactivity, 97–106,
      128
   resistance, 108–115
Electroencephalogram (EEG), 91–96
   and activity, 47–51
   alpha feedback, 32
   alpha index, 108, 110, 111, 114
   and extraversion-introversion, 25–38
   factor analysis of, 46–47
   factors, 31, 46, 47
   frequency bands, 31
   measures, 33
   and personality, 77, 86
      post hoc evaluation of research
         studies on, 29–31
   slow waves, 48–51
   spectral analysis, 46–47
   and stimulus complexity, 37
   synchronization, 47, 48
Empathy, 195–203
   and aggression, 195–202
   and self-report, 202
Error sources in experimentation, 32–34
   biases as, 34
   and experimenter sex, 34
   procedures as, 27–29
   subject strategies as, 27–29
Evaluation apprehension, 36
Evoked potentials (EPs), 60, 63, 65–67, 71,
   72, 91–96

$N_{100}(N_1)$ wave, 61, 62, 65, 66,
   68, 69, 71
N_{150} wave, 93–94
N_{200} (N_2) wave, 59, 61, 62–68, 69, 72
nonspecific vertex component, 68
P_{200} (P_2) wave, 68, 93–94
P_{300} (P_3) wave, 61, 62, 64, 65, 68,
   70, 72
   and sensation seeking, 77
   visual, and augmenting-reducing, 77
Evoked-response audiometry, 68
Excitation, 137, 216, 217
   -inhibition balance, 81, 82, 87
   processes, strength, and weakness of,
      128, 131, 133
   (*See also* Nervous system, properties of)
Extraversion-introversion, 98, 101–103,
   136, 163–171
   CNV, 79–88
Eysenck's drug postulate, 81
Eysenck Personality Inventory (EPI), 31,
   165, 170
   retest reliability of, 31–33
Eysenck's personality theory, 26–27

Factor analysis, 45

Habitual action-preparedness and CNV,
   79–82, 84, 85
Habituation, 60, 98
   generalization of, 64–65
Heart rate, 93–96, 108–110, 114, 115, 213,
   214, 217
Hippocampus, 69
Hypertension, 207–212
Hypoxia, 107, 108

Impulsivity, 33
Individual tempo, 45
   (*See also* Activity)
Information overload, 135, 136, 139
Information processing:
   and personality, 91–96
   state-limited and process-limited, 143
   top-down, bottom-up strategies, 163,
      164, 169, 170
   and verbal operations, 95
Inhibition, 137–141, 216–217
Intelligence:
   and CNV, 79, 80, 84, 85, 87
   and reasoning, 145–149
   and style of action, 143–149

Interpersonal overload, 136, 139, 141
Introversion (*See* Extraversion-introversion)

Law of strength, 129-131
  and reaction time, 131

Memory:
  consolidation of trace, 37
  echoic, 59
  and individual differences, 127-134
  long term, 59
  performance, 128, 129, 133
  processes of, 133
  short term recall, 37
Microstructure of experiment, 35
Minnesota Multiphasic Personality
      Inventory (MMPI), 211
Mismatch negativity, 62, 70
Mobility of nervous processes, 137-141,
      216-217
Multivariate analysis of variance, 140-141

Nervous system:
  properties of, 43, 44, 127, 133
  strength of, 91-96, 107, 135-138
    and memory, 127-134
    and problem solving, 145-149
  (*See also* Properties of nervous system)
Neuronal mismatch, 59-64, 68-72
Neuronal model, 59-61, 64, 68, 69, 71
Neuroticism-stability, 27, 102, 136
  and aggression, 185-187, 191
  and CNV, 79, 80, 84-86
  (*See also* Anxiety)
Noise, 163-171
  effects of, 222-223
  preferences, 164, 167, 169, 170
  and recall, 131-134
  and stress, 207-212
  and CNV, 81
Noradrenaline, 207-211

Operational costs, 119-126
Orienting reaction (OR), 59-61, 68, 69, 71,
      72
  and P_{200}, 95
Orienting theory, 59, 61, 62, 68

Perceived control, 169-170
Perception of pain in others, 196-201,
      202-203

Performance:
  efficiency of, 221, 222, 225
  plasticity index of, 125
  in simultaneous tasks, 135, 140, 141
  and stress, 207-212
  and type of instruction, 123-124
Person-computer interaction, 143-151, 215,
      217
Polychronicity, 135-138, 140, 141
Preparatory activity, 225
Preventative actions, 214-217
Principal components analysis (PCA), 100
  of electroencephalograms, 46-47
Processing negativity, 70
Properties of nervous system, 97, 98, 104
  (*See also* Nervous system, properties of)
Prostaglandin, 207-211
Proximal stimulus pattern, 59
Psychoactive drugs and CNV, 81, 84, 87,
      88
Psychomotor indexes, 48
Psychopathy, 175-182
  and aggression, 187-191
  and anxiety, 179-180
  assessment of, 175-176
  and coping with stress, 179-180
  and life stresses, 182
  and optimal level of arousal, 175-177
  and physiological arousal, 180
  self-report inventories for, 178
  and somatic symptoms, 180-182
  and SSS, 177-178
  and stimulation seeking, 175-179
  and stress, 179-182
  and violence, 179
Psychophysiological cost, 119-126
Psychophysiological traits, 97
Psychosocial context of experiments, 26,
      35-36
Psychosomatic disease, 207-211
Pursuit rotor, 137-138

Reaction time, 70
Reactivity, 107-112, 114, 116, 196-203,
      213-217, 219, 221, 222, 225
  and aggression, 198-199
  and empathy, 196-198
  and performance, 119-126
Refractoriness, 60
Regulation, theory of, 195
Regulatory functions, 97
Reticular system of brain stem, 27-
      28

Schizophrenic subjects, 38
Self-regulation, 102, 214
Sensation seeking, 38
Sensation Seeking Scales (SSS) and
        psychopathy, 117–178
    (*See also* Psychopathy)
Sensory adaptation, 60
Sensory deprivation, 107, 108, 115
Sensory drive, 153, 154, 156, 160
Sensory reinforcement, 153, 157, 158
Sleep deprivation, 102
Sleep N_2, 61
Slow wave complex, 69, 70
Smoking and CNV, 88
Sociability, 33
Social facilitation, 35–36
Social psychology of psychology
        experiment, 35–36
Spinal excitability, 72
State-Trait Anxiety Inventory, 208
Statistical errors, 36
Stimulation, 197, 198, 202, 203
    enhancement of, 153
    modality of, 158, 159, 160
    need for, 153–159, 211
    optimal, 153
    reduction of, 153
    seeking: and antisocial behavior, 178–179
    and psychopathy, 175–179
    and self report versus behavior, 178

self-exposure to, 153, 155, 157, 158
    sensory, 153, 158, 160
Stimulus-hunger hypothesis, 164–169
Stimulus significance, 60, 61, 69–70
Strelau Temperament Inventory (STI),
        108, 111, 112, 114, 121, 128
Stress:
    and anger, 207
    coping with, in psychopathy, 179–180
Style of action, 120, 159, 219, 223
    and temperament, 120–121
Subliminal stimulus change, 69
Systems approach, 127, 133

Temperament, 43, 51, 54, 163–171, 214, 219
    and intellectual traits, 143–150
    and problem solving strategies, 143–150
    traits of, 128
    and type of instruction, 122–123
Threat, 107, 108, 115
Transmarginal inhibition, 29

Variety seeking, 45
    (*See also* Sensation seeking)
Vascular measures, 60
Vigilance, 37, 163–171
Violence, 179

Yoked-control method, 165–166, 169